Mastering

English Language

D0309944

Macmillan Master Series

Accounting
Arabic
Astronomy
Australian History
Background to Business
Banking
Basic Management
Biology
British Politics
Business Communication
Business Law
Business Microcomputing
C Programming
Catering Science
Catering Theory
Chemistry
COBOL Programming
Commerce
Computer Programming
Computers
Economic and Social History
Economics
Electrical Engineering
Electronics
English as a Foreign Language
English Grammar
English Language
English Literature
Financial Accounting
French 1
French 2
German 1
German 2

Hairdressing
Human Biology
Italian 1
Italian 2
Japanese
Keyboarding
Marketing
Mathematics
Modern British History
Modern European History
Modern World History
Nutrition
Office Practice
Pascal Programming
Philosophy
Physics
Practical Writing
Principles of Accounts
Psychology
Restaurant Service
Science
Secretarial Procedures
Social Welfare
Sociology
Spanish 1
Spanish 2
Spreadsheets
Statistics
Statistics with your Microcomputer
Study Skills
Typewriting Skills
Word Processing

Mastering

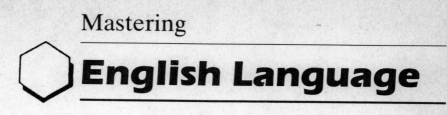

English Language

Second Edition

S. H. Burton and J. A. Humphries

HUGH BAIRD COLLEGE
LIBRARY

MACMILLAN

© S. H. Burton 1982
© S. H. Burton and J. A. Humphries 1992

All rights reserved. No reproduction, copy or transmission of
this publication may be made without written permission.

No paragraph of this publication may be reproduced, copied or
transmitted save with written permission or in accordance with
the provisions of the Copyright, Designs and Patents Act 1988,
or under the terms of any licence permitting limited copying
issued by the Copyright Licensing Agency, 90 Tottenham Court
Road, London W1P 9HE.

Any person who does any unauthorised act in relation to this
publication may be liable to criminal prosecution and civil
claims for damages.

Published by
THE MACMILLAN PRESS LTD
Houndmills, Basingstoke, Hampshire RG21 2XS
and London
Companies and representatives
throughout the world

ISBN 0–333–51506–4

A catalogue record for this book is available
from the British Library

Printed in China

First edition 1982
Reprinted 9 times
Second edition 1992
10 9 8 7 6 5 4 3 2 1
01 00 99 98 97 96 95 94 93 92

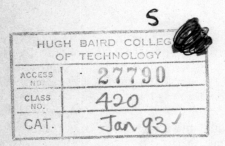

HUGH BAIRD COLLEGE
OF TECHNOLOGY

ACCESS NO.	27790
CLASS NO.	420
CAT.	Jan 93

⬡ Contents

⬡ Acknowledgements

The authors and publishers wish to thank the following for permission to use copyright material:

The Conservation Trust for an extract from a Conservation Society publication.

East Anglian Daily Times Company for various pictures.

The Economist for adapted material from *The Economist*, 11 January 1991.

Hodder & Stoughton Publishers for 'The Last Lesson' by Alphonse Daudet from *Forty Short Stories*, trans. J. C. Reid, 1965, Edward Arnold Publishers.

Ewan MacNaughton Associates for 'Oh, to be wet in England' by Cassandra Jardine, *The Daily Telegraph*, 6 August 1991. Copyright © 1991 The Daily Telegraph plc.

The Original London Walks for promotional material by David Tucker.

Oxford University Press for an entry from the *Concise Oxford Dictionary*, 8th edition, 1990.

The Spectator for material from the 13 July 1991 and 26 January 1991 issues of *The Spectator*.

Times Newspapers Ltd for an extract by Godfrey Smith in *The Sunday Times*, 27 January 1991. Copyright © 1991 Times Newspapers Ltd.

A. P. Watt Ltd on behalf of the Literary Executors of the Estate of H. G. Wells for an extract from *The History of Mr Polly* by H. G. Wells, 1910.

Every effort has been made to trace all the copyright-holders, but if any have been inadvertently overlooked the publishers will be pleased to make the necessary arrangement at the first opportunity.

1 Speaking and listening

1.1 Using language

Of all human activities, talking is one of the most popular. Just stop, look and listen to the number of conversations and verbal exchanges that take place. Concentrate on the sounds made and note how they range from the loud and demonstrative to the quiet and appealing.

The ability to converse demands intelligence, but it is a skill that does not require speakers and listeners to be particularly clever. It is practised by all sorts and conditions of men, women and children.

We learn the art of conversation in our early childhood years and do not have to work 'hard' at mastering the methods. How different it all is when we attempt to learn a foreign language later in life.

It is not necessary to have a large vocabulary in order to make ourselves understood. In the 1920s C. K. Ogden devised what he called 'Basic English' and used a vocabulary of about 800 words. Surveys of people's speaking habits reveal that many have a limited 'diet' of words. On the New York subway, for example, it was discovered that the average adult passenger used a vocabulary of under 1000 words.

Yet our minds are much richer than our vocabularies sometimes suggest. A study of canal-boat children whose education, though not intelligence, was limited showed that, although they used only about 500 words while talking with one another, their knowledge of the meanings of other words extended to almost 10,000. They certainly showed themselves able to listen effectively.

Only in comparatively recent times have the skills of speaking and listening been encouraged as well as tested. The saying that children should be seen, but not heard, sounds strange to generations who believe that assertiveness and social success depend on the facility to express oneself with confidence.

The areas in which language has to be used are many and complex. Consider the ways in which we are all dependent on words and their accepted meanings as they are conveyed by the human voice and interpreted by the brain. Here are just a few: survival; information; shopping; business; learning; travelling; company; relationships; singing; games.

1.2   Speakers and listeners

Oral communication is a complicated process. However, there are certain habits that human beings quickly develop in order to make the exchange of spoken words a relatively simple matter.

The main feature of a conversation is the way in which the talkers allow one another to 'have their say'. By the series of signals, given by the tone of voice, a hand gesture, or a facial expression, the speaker, who has taken the active position, invites one of the listeners, who has until then volunteered to be in the passive position, to take the active role and make a corresponding series of verbal responses.

Most conversations are conducted on this 'active–passive' basis in which the roles are frequently exchanged. There are occasions when two or more people want to speak at the same time or, more commonly do not wish to listen. This is an 'active–active' encounter.

When two people are bored with each other's company or when one is more interested in hearing about the other than in relating his or her own experiences, then this is a 'passive–passive' situation.

For the purpose of this book there are three basic situations presented:

1 The speaker is talking *to* an audience. We call this 'individual' talk.
2 The speaker is *taking part* in a conversation or discussion *with* another person. We call this 'paired talk'.
3 The speaker is *taking part* in a discussion *with* several people. We call this 'group talk'.

In each of these situations, the speaker's success in obtaining the hoped-for response depends partly on being a good speaker, partly on having good listeners and certainly on being a good conversationalist.

● *For effective oral communication its participants must be able to speak and listen well and have a ready tongue, ear and eye.*

1.3   Speaking – being apt

Most days you speak to and with many different people about various things, for various purposes and in various situations.

Some of what you say can be thought out beforehand. For example, you can prepare a talk and you can get ready to take part in discussing a subject that has been announced in advance. Much of your speaking has to be done spontaneously – 'off the cuff'. Both kinds of speaking, prepared and spontaneous, can be learnt. With experience and practice, you can become an effective speaker in the various situations of your working and social life. Knowing how to get a spoken 'message' across is not a mysterious 'gift'. It is an acquired skill.

To understand how your speaking can be improved by a thoughtful practice, ask yourself these questions:

- Who is listening to me?   (Audience)
- Why am I speaking?   (Purpose)
- What do I want/need to say?   (Topics)
- How can I say it effectively? (Style)

Of course you would not be speaking fluently were you to pause to assess these questions as you were speaking. Yet the ideas should be in the back of your mind before you begin to speak and while you are conversing. Remember: The first letters of Audience–Purpose–Topics–Style spell 'APTS' and that is the main part of APTNESS – which has a dictionary definition of 'a natural ability'. There's no greater boost to your confidence than to feel that what you are doing has a natural, spontaneous source of inspiration.

1.4   Audience

Beware of your listeners and be aware of them! How do they 'relate' to you? Ask yourself the following questions:

- Are they people of my own age?
- Do I know them well?
- Do they share my interests?
- Are they friends or are they 'in authority' in some way?

Getting your message across is a matter of choosing *appropriate* language and speaking in an *appropriate* manner. That is why it is important to have a sense of audience.

Your awareness of your listeners and of your relationship with them helps you to choose suitable words and to converse in a suitable style. What works well with one listener or a group of listeners will not necessarily work with another. Speakers who are sensitive to the nature of their audience are always more likely to obtain the response for which they hope.

If you think back now to the conversations that you have had in the past day or two, you will realise that success depends very much on 'striking the right note' – and the right note for one listener may be quite the wrong note for another.

--- **Activity 1.1** ----------------

Take one example. Imagine that the details of a job you would like are known by a friend, your mother, a teacher and your prospective employer. Work out *how* you would ask each of them for details of the features of the job that interests you, e.g. the specifications of the work – hours demanded – prospects – pay.

- Your listeners are much more likely to pay attention and to respond in the way you want them to if they recognise that you have taken the trouble to 'tune in' to them.

1.5   Purpose

You do not – or you should not – speak because you enjoy the sound of your own voice. You speak for a purpose. It may be to give information or instructions, to make a request, to create a friendly atmosphere, to persuade someone to agree with your point of view, to share your enthusiasms and interests with other people . . . and these are just a few of the purposes you may have when speaking. There are many other possibilities.

Whatever your particular purpose for speaking may be, keep it clearly in mind. Keep in mind, too, the nature of the situation in which you are speaking – friendly chat, serious discussion, an interview, giving a formal talk, and so on.

Your sense of purpose and your awareness of 'the speech situation' (which, of course, includes your sense of audience) helps you to get the response you want from your listeners by:

- keeping to the point;
- choosing suitable words;
- speaking in an apt way.

Put your tone of voice to the test in Activity 1.2 by showing how you alter your way of expression according to the intention that you have in mind.

— Activity 1.2 —————————————————————

Here is a piece of factual information:

> Trains leave Victoria Station, London, for Gatwick Airport every 15 minutes – on the hour and every quarter-of-an-hour – from 05.30 until 22.00. In addition, there is a train at least once an hour throughout the rest of the night until 05.00 in the morning.

1.6   Topics

There is no quicker way of losing your listeners' attention than by wandering off the topic. When you do that they 'switch off' and go 'glassy eyed'. Again, it is your awareness of your audience and your sense of purpose that must be your guide. Remember: *A*udience – *P*urpose – *T*opics make your conversation 'APT'.

1.7   Style

Effective speech may be described as 'the right words spoken in an appropriate manner'. The quality to aim for may be summed up by the key – 'RATE':

*R*elevant control of subject matter;
*A*ppropriate language to audience – from formal to informal, from the
carefully considered to the casual according to the listeners and to the
occasion;
*T*one of voice and manner of delivery;
*E*xpressive vocabulary to give accuracy and interest.

All these qualities are of little consequence unless the speaker is capable of *clarity* of speech and *pleasantness* of delivery. If you mumble, your listeners cannot hear you. If your pronunciation and intonation are faulty, they are put off. If you speak too rapidly, they will find it hard to understand you. If you speak too slowly, they get impatient. If you do not vary your pace, they are bored by the monotonous delivery.

1.8   Listening – paying attention

As pointed out earlier, speaking and listening are twinned. The 'active' speaker becomes the 'passive' listener. Yet to be effective, the listener must be prepared to take a positive role.

Paying attention matters. Though it is the speaker's duty to try to win and hold interest, the listener has to make an effort too. Cooperation is vital to ensure that conversation takes place. The difficulty of the listener's task depends on the speaker's skills. The better the latter, the easier the former.

We all sometimes hear without listening – and sometimes it does not matter very much. Many radio programmes and much background music are little more than what has been called 'audible wallpaper'. It is to be heard, but not noticed. However, when the person speaking matters to us, or the subject is important (or both), we have to concentrate, pay attention and *listen* to what we are hearing.

1.9   Listening – taking it in

Undoubtedly you have often been advised to make notes when listening to talks and lectures. Although it is a good exercise that encourages alertness and concentration, you cannot record everything. It is best to jot down just the key points.

You cannot write notes while you are taking part in conversations and discussions, but you *can* get into the habit of making mental notes. It is a matter of 'latching on' to the really important things said. Then you can reply to them in a meaningful way. Good listening leads to good speaking. Your own contributions to the talking are more likely to be confident, fluent *and* to the point, if you listen properly.

Listeners sometimes have only a hazy impression of what has been said – quite often because they are so keen to give expression to their own ideas and opinions. It is difficult 'taking in' what another person is saying when you are intent on 'giving out' your own viewpoint. In fact, conversation is a matter of 'give and take' . . . but not simultaneously!

Activity 1.3

Here is a transcript of part of a conversation in which neither of the two speakers was really listening to the other. It is an 'active–active' encounter referred to earlier. Just 'listen' to the speakers:

Kate The fox is such a beautiful wild animal, I can't understand people wanting to hunt it – it's cruel – utterly unnecessary cruelty – no point in it at all . . .

Brian It's very skilful, you know, working for a pack of hounds. I mean – following the scent for miles across country . . .

Kate It makes me angry – it doesn't harm anyone – just lives there in the wild, yet it's hunted down for pleasure . . .

Brian Fox hunting's gone on for years – hounds and horses are part of the scene – in the country, people would miss them – everyone, most people, that is, join in – the excitement is what it's all about – makes it all worthwhile, I think.

Whether you share Kate's or Brian's opinions is not, at the moment, important. It is obvious that neither of them is taking in (or taking up) the points that the other is trying to make. Their conversation is not getting anywhere and they might just as well be talking to themselves. Sparks may fly in an 'active–active' conversation, but they tend to generate more heat than light.

1.10   Listening – stated meaning and implied meaning

As you already know from everyday experience, the meaning of what people say is not always to be found *solely* in the statements they make. The way in which they make their statements (the tone of voice, for example, and the choice of language) sometimes conveys as much as – perhaps even more than – the statements themselves.

For instance, take the verbal expression, 'uh-huh'. Can you understand what it means from just its appearance in print? Certainly not – for it has to be interpreted in context. Imagine a situation in which someone enquires whether he can use a footpath that appears to go through private property. Here's the question – 'Is this a public right-of-way?' The person answering the question may reply with a negative gesture – 'uh-huh!', with a positive response – 'uh-huh', or with an uncertain look – 'uh-huh?'.

If you meet someone you have not seen for a long time and he/she says, 'I am pleased to see you again', it is not only the stated meaning you notice. You also notice the tone of voice – warm or cold or neutral. You notice the emphasised words:

I *am* pleased to see you again
I am *pleased* to see you again
I am pleased to see *you* again
I am pleased to see you *again*

You notice whether the words are accompanied by a smile, a frown or a frosty look.

These are very simple examples of the part that statements and implications play in conveying meaning. It is just as important to be aware of what is implied as it is to pay attention to what is stated.

These examples also illustrate the importance of the 'non-verbal signals' that accompany speech – facial expressions, gestures, stance and general bearing. Whether you are speaking or listening, you must remember that 'non-verbal communications' play a large part in face-to-face talk. When you are speaking, try to ensure that your facial expressions, tone of voice, gestures and the way you stand or sit reinforce your message. Try to look interested in what you are saying! Notice any 'feedback' that is coming from your audience. Do they look as if you have their attention or are they restless and bored? Do they seem to be agreeing with you or are you antagonising them?

Similarly, when you are listening, *look* as if you are interested. Show the speaker that you are attending, that you are *taking part* in the 'oral exchange' by following what is being said and getting ready to contribute when it is your turn to speak. The knack of being able to give undivided attention to the person who is addressing you is not only a courtesy, but a much appreciated and relatively rare human attribute. The cultivation of this art will bring unexpected rewards – for there are many people with excellent hearing, but comparatively few with effective listening skills.

1.11 Putting thoughts into words and testing them

We often use the expression – 'It's easier said than done' – meaning that it is simpler to devise what to say than to complete the intended action. What is surprising is that the words themselves actually come so easily! Most of us are quite competent in using them. However, it is our level of skill that we must aim to raise.

The following exercises are intended to give you the opportunity of putting your abilities to the test. First, though, a set of objectives is needed. In order to complete a fine piece of work you have to convince yourself that you have scored well in each of the following areas. Commit to memory the various targets needed and use the mnemonic 'CIROFF' to help you:

Clarity   – the content of information and vocal delivery must be clear;
Interest   – the audience should respond positively;
Relevance – the topics in question have to be considered;
Order   – a sensible sequence of connecting ideas is necessary;

Fluency   – minimal hesitation and a moderate speed are admirable;
Finish   – ideally the ending should be strong and memorable.

Before you start to prepare a topic, compose a speech, judge a talk or assess a discussion, write down these six key objectives. Use them as your 'beacons' and devise a scoring system that incorporates them.

Perhaps each objective could carry 10 marks and so 60 is 'perfection'. Maybe you could score as in cricket with 6 being the maximum number of 'runs'. Remember that 36 has been scored off one over of six deliveries only once in first-class cricket!

Activities 1.4

1 Record a short talk from the radio or television using a cassette or video recorder. Make sure that the subject interests you. Try to select an item of about five to ten minutes duration. An 'Any Questions' type of programme is ideal. Give marks on the CIROFF scale. (*C*larity – *I*nterest – *R*elevance – *O*rder – *F*luency – *F*inish).

2 Prepare a short talk yourself. Choose a particular interest of yours, details of a place that you have visited, or give your views on a public issue of the moment. As you prepare it remember the six key objectives. Record it, be brave enough to play it back and then award yourself an appropriate score based upon the six important features.

3 Choose a television programme that has some controversial appeal to at least four or five of you. Watch the programme and discuss it the following day, making sure that the tape-recorder is running. When you assess the quality of the discussion, award the marks for the overall quality of the group effort, but, at first, do it individually and discreetly. Then reveal the marks and see whether you agreed.

4 Use as a starting-point the discussion noted previously between Brian and Kate. When you have finished, you should note that an improvement has taken place as the ideas have become yours rather than theirs!

5 Five people should each prepare a topic that lasts for about three minutes. After the first participant has delivered his or her ideas, the others should discuss it until a chairperson intervenes and asks the second person to introduce his/her subject. The discussion that takes place at the end should be primarily concerned with the 'non-verbal communications' that occurred. Refer to eye movement, facial expressions, gestures, posture and overall attentiveness.

6 From a discreet distance watch people conversing. Try to assess how effective they are even though you may not be able to hear their words. If you are abroad on holiday, notice how conversa-

tions take place in other languages and in different environments. Try to assess how effective they are even though you may not be able to understand their words. People certainly have a knack of being able to express themselves spontaneously.

2 Writing and reading: an introduction

2.1 In daily use

School and college work necessarily involves a lot of writing and reading, but it is not only for purposes connected with your studies that you need to be proficient in those two skills. You depend on them every day in carrying out the practical transactions and social exchanges of 'ordinary' living. A moment's thought will remind you of how often you write and read to get things done (form-filling, making competition entries, for example) to maintain personal relationships (answering letters from relatives and friends, for example) to relax (reading newspapers and skimming through magazines, for example). Practice in using these skills to deal with 'real life' situations is as important as practice in using them for academic purposes.

2.2 In English examinations

The fact that writing and reading are called for in a great variety of situations and for many different purposes is reflected in the wide range of assignments and questions set in English language examinations. A thorough course of preparation must, therefore, include a correspondingly wide range of practice. That is why many different kinds of writing and reading exercises are provided in this book, each chapter of which is concerned with one or another of the various ways in which you will be tested.

Your English syllabus covers several 'work areas': practical, directed, discursive and creative writing; summary; understanding and response. (These are in addition to the oral skills described and practised in Chapter 1.) The work areas just named may include distinct, though related, kinds of writing and reading. For example, practical writing includes letters and memoranda. Creative writing includes narration and description. Examination papers testing understanding and response include passages of factual writing and passages of imaginative writing.

There is no need to give a complete list of the various kinds of writing and reading you are required to do in your English examination. They are all described and practised, chapter by chapter, in the rest of this book.

2.3 The basic skills

Every piece of writing and reading you have to do – of whatever particular kind – is first and foremost a test of your *literacy* (your ability to use the basic skills without which you can neither write nor read competently). You may be writing a story or extracting factual information from a newspaper article, or making a report, or compiling an instruction sheet, or studying a text on which comprehension questions are set – whatever the nature of the task, its successful performance depends on your possession of those fundamental skills. That is why the chapters dealing with the different kinds of writing are preceded by a series of short chapters in which the basic skills of written language are quickly revised and practised. Similarly, the practice passages testing understanding and response are preceded by brief hints on how to improve your reading skills.

2.4 Summing up

The 'guidelines' followed by examiners in assessing candidates' use of English when writing and reading (*and* when speaking and listening) indicate very clearly the qualities and skills needed for success.

Candidates are required to show that they can use language *accurately*, *appropriately* and *effectively* for different purposes and in a variety of situations.

Some years ago the Shell Oil Company devised a memory device for its executives that can easily be applied to the requirements for anyone wishing to improve their skills in writing and reading. Executives were asked to remember the four letters '*H–A–I–R*'. The order in which they were asked to recall them was slightly different, in that:

1 '*A*' stood for *A*ccuracy;
2 '*I*' for *I*magination;
3 '*R*' for *R*esponsiveness;
4 '*H*' for *H*elicopter.

Apply these in the following way:

Accuracy is needed whenever words are created;
Imagination is required in all communication skills;
Responsiveness is demanded in any literary activity;
Helicopter suggests that ability we have to 'hover' with our mind's eye, to 'oversee' what we are doing and to manage the tasks that we can pick up and put down at will.

③ **Planned writing (1): structure**

3.1   Contents

Think about *what* you need or want to write before you start. This advice may seem obvious, but it is all too easy to rush into a piece of writing without having a clear idea of what you are going to say. There are several considerations to bear in mind – your subject; your purpose; your readers; the form of writing that you are using (letter, report, story and so on).

Obviously, these circumstances vary from one 'writing situation' to another. To be effective, the contents must be *relevant* and *appropriate* to the particular situation.

A vital feature of success in structuring ideas effectively concerns the *generation* of ideas. The subject that confronts you has to be thought about and ideas created in your mind before they can be translated into words on paper. Harnessing the power of your brain and applying its energy to the topic in question is sometimes called 'brain-storming'. Here are some approaches to help you.

Activity 3.1

Take a single sheet of paper. Make a box in each of the four corners and let them act as 'signposts' bearing the headings:

Subject; *Purpose*; *Form*; *Readers*

Under each of the headings write notes along the following lines to indicate the direction that you wish to take:

1 Subject   identify the main topic and, perhaps, major points of your intended piece of work.
2 Purpose   to explain, explore or entertain? Indicate which category.
3 Form   letter, report, story, essay, speech or diary entry, etc.?
4 Readers   extent and age of intended audience. Are the readers known to you or are they, as yet, anonymous?

Write the main theme of your letter, report, story, essay or speech, etc. in the middle of a fresh sheet of paper. Then jot down any and every idea that occurs to you in the next few minutes. Do not worry where they are placed in the paper. Some ideas will follow in sequence, some will be random and some will start a new train of thought. Where ideas seem irrelevant, do not worry for they may be

---

of use later on. Where there is an obvious link between a run of ideas, fan them out across the page on a series of lines drawn to resemble the branching growth of a tree, from trunks to branches and from the branches to several twigs. It is important to keep going and not to allow ideas to dry up. If you stop you will create a blockage in the flow of ideas feeding out from your brain. Use various devices to keep ideas flowing. For example:

- Reverse thinking – new for old; fast for slow; negative for positive;
- Imagine that you are in a time-machine, retreating and advancing;
- Picture yourself as a part of the scene;
- Take imaginary slow-motion shots as though a camera;
- Look at the problems from other points of view;
- See the subject in terms of chaos, failure . . . or even solution;
- Play the part of a god, devil, a practical joker or a saint.

After you have collected as many ideas as possible, you may want to start to organise them. There are three steps in order to do this.

1 *Highlight the titles*   See if you have any words that would summarise a group of ideas. Underline them, highlight them with a marker or box them around so that they stand out visually on the page.
2 *Count the concepts*   Give a priority to your various titled concepts. Number them in an order that appeals to you.
3 *Encase the ideas*   Use a coloured marker to gather together all the various ideas that fit under the various titles you have selected and ring them into a series of 'balloons'.

In order to show how 'brain-storming' can be developed, an example will be worked out. First the page-outline will be produced (Figure 3.1), then the notes that reflect the ideas as they occur (Figure 3.2) and then the paragraphs with their various topics (Figure 3.3).

Subject Career Choices Prospects and Dangers	STAGE 1	**Purposes** Explore – Advise and Comment

On Choosing a Career

Form Article for Magazine		**Readers** 15–20 year-olds

Figure 3.1 Brain-storming: (stage 1) the page outline

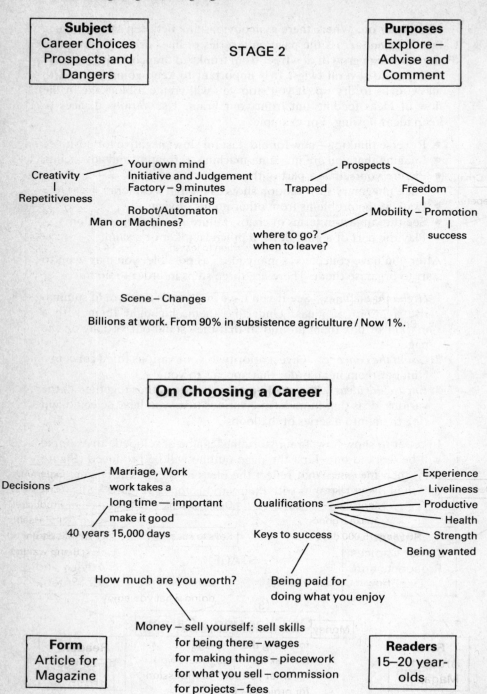

Subject
Career Choices
Prospects and
Dangers

STAGE 2

Purposes
Explore –
Advise and
Comment

Creativity
|
Repetitiveness

Your own mind
Initiative and Judgement
Factory – 9 minutes
training
Robot/Automaton
Man or Machines?

Prospects

Trapped

Freedom
|
Mobility – Promotion
|
success

where to go?
when to leave?

Scene – Changes

Billions at work. From 90% in subsistence agriculture / Now 1%.

On Choosing a Career

Decisions

Marriage, Work
work takes a
long time — important
make it good
40 years 15,000 days

Qualifications

Experience
Liveliness
Productive
Health
Strength
Being wanted

Keys to success

How much are you worth?

Being paid for
doing what you enjoy

Money – sell yourself: sell skills
for being there – wages
for making things – piecework
for what you sell – commission
for projects – fees

Form
Article for
Magazine

Readers
15–20 year-
olds

Figure 3.2 Brain-storming: (stage 2) ideas as they occur

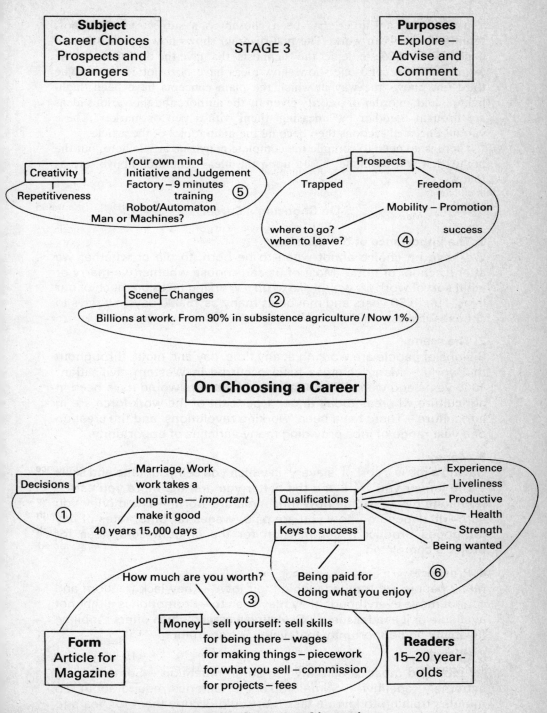

Figure 3.3 Brain-storming: (stage 3) paragraphing topics

'On Choosing a Career' has been chosen as a subject to show how 'brain-storming' can work. The first diagram shows how a plain sheet of paper can be made to depict the 'signposts' that give the directions for the exercise. The second one shows how ideas have been jotted down. The third one shows the way in which the main concepts have been 'high-lighted' and an order of priority given by the author, and the various ideas are brought together by 'encasing' them with a pen or marker. These various enclosed sections then become the main topics of the article.

There is no need to compile the complete magazine article here, but the points that will be made, based upon the ideas generated above, are as follows:

On Choosing a Career

1 The importance of the decision
We have no choice about when to be born, to die or whether we attend school or not! – Most of us can choose whether we marry or what sort of work we would like to do – Working takes up much of our lives – up to 50 years and maybe as many as 15,000 days – It pays to choose wisely.

2 The scene
Billions of people are working at any time, day and night, throughout the world – Many changes have occurred in Western civilisation: 1000 years ago well over 90 per cent of workers would have been in agriculture whereas today under 1 per cent of the work-force are in agriculture – There have been 'working revolutions' and the creation of a vast range of jobs providing many varieties of opportunity.

3 Money
Having a job is a sort of 'slavery' in which you sell your time and skills – The longer you work and the better you are, the more you earn – Someone has to decide how much you are worth – The money you earn will depend on how you are paid: wages for time; rates of pay for goods produced; commission for the amount sold; fees for projects completed.

4 Prospects
Many people are trapped within their jobs – They lack freedom and cannot move even though they may wish to – Promotion is either not available or it evades them – Selecting a career which offers mobility, flexibility and opportunity to develop is important.

5 Creativity
All jobs and most careers involve some repetition – Some work is extremely repetitive – Some workers in factories require about ten minutes training to learn a task that could occupy them for years to come – The leading question involves personal development – Does

your work require you to show initiative, judgement and versatility or are you required to be a robot? – Well-paid, well-dressed maybe, but an automaton, nevertheless.

6 The key to success

'Work out what you like doing most . . . and get someone to pay you for doing it!' – In the end you have to have a number of attributes – health, strength, liveliness, the urge to work and the desire to complete the task that is set; at least one of the two achievements from the past – qualifications or experience; and one very necessary person – someone who wants you to work for them and be paid by them.

___ Activity 3.2 ___

Try a 'brain-storming' exercise yourself. A good starting exercise is to consider the time that you spend or have spent at school. By the day you leave (or left) you will probably have completed at least ten years of schooling. Each year consisted of a minimum of 200 days attendance and each day involved about five hours of teaching. That is 10,000 hours of instruction, tuition or just presence in the class-room. That is a long time and it should provide you with many memories.

3.2 Beginning, middle and end

You have seen while 'brain-storming' that it is important to establish an *order* in which you are going to present material. This ability to set out the content in a clear and sensible sequence is one of the basic skills on which all effective writing depends.

It is important to take an overall view of the material that you are intending to use. Try to place the information in the relevant sections: Introduction (beginning); Body (middle); Conclusion (end).

___ Activity 3.3 ___

Look at the following six sentences that have been placed in random order, but which can be sorted out to form a full paragraph with a definite beginning, middle and end. Build the paragraph to show that you appreciate its construction.

(a) In the days when some horizons, especially in mountainous areas, had not been reached by humans, the map-makers had difficulties.

(b) The great travellers of the past and present have been explorers, sometimes in the geographical sense, yet always in the expansion of their mental horizons.

(c) These may have indicated ignorance, but often they promoted curiosity and resolve.

(d) Travel supposedly broadens the mind.

(e) Far from repelling would-be travellers from the unknown, they actually attracted the explorer who wanted to broaden his view and extend man's knowledge.

(f) They had to leave blank spaces on their maps.

In a way you have devised a mental journey for your readers and encouraged them to take a definite route through what could have been a maze or jungle of ideas. Consider the writer to be a guide . . . and therefore your achievement will be to help your reader to reach a satisfactory and informed conclusion.

3.3   Coherence

The framework just described helps you to present your material *coherently*. You should have sorted out the contents so that the items cohere or 'stick-together'. Do not allow your readers to be misled by allowing material to appear 'out-of-place'.

3.4   Sequence and connections

It is the logical sequence that matters. Connections should be made within a considered structure. In this way there are no 'loose ends'. Careful planning means that the attention of readers should be directed without fuss. Sometimes it may be useful to give a signal that a turning-point in the argument or a vital new addition to a description is about to be made. Linking expressions such as 'however', 'even so', 'on the other hand', 'yet' or 'in addition' can indicate the beginning of a new stage in the development of your material while, at the same time, emphasising its continuity.

3.5   For analysis and discussion

Here is a paragraph taken from the diary of the late J. R. Ackerley. He had obviously been annoyed by part of a news programme during a visit to the cinema.

The Movietone News this week had a Christmas feature. A large number of flustered turkeys were driven towards the camera, and the commentator remarked that the Christmas rush was on, or words to that effect. Next they were seen crowded about their feeding trough, making their gobbling turkey fuss, and the commentator observed, with dry humour (again I do not remember his exact words), that it was no use their holding a protest meeting, for they were 'for it' in the morning.

Similar facetious jokes followed them wherever they went, hurrying and trampling about in their silly way. For to make them look as silly as possible was no doubt part of the joke and easy to achieve. Turkeys, like hens, like all animals, are beautiful in themselves, and have even a kind of dignity when they are leading their own lives, but the fowls, in particular, look foolish when they are being frightened.

(J. R. Ackerley, My Sister and Myself)

Activities 3.4

Attempt the following exercises in order to test the passage with the ideas suggested in the last four sections of the book.

1 Imagine that J. R. Ackerley used the 'brain-storming' method described in the earlier section. Recreate the notes that he could have devised in order to produce this paragraph.
2 Indicate those of his ideas that should be considered as part of the Introduction, those within the Body of the writing and those that are definitely within his Conclusion.
3 Write a similar paragraph of your own that looks at a human activity which can be made to appear strange and foolish-looking when viewed in a certain way. Examples: traffic jams; activities on a crowded beach; certain sporting events; examinations in schools; children's interests in food and its consumption.

Now look at the following passage which was the beginning of a talk given by Professor Gwyn Jones and then reprinted. Try to assess how well the features mentioned in sections 3.2 and 3.3 have been observed. Coherence, sequence, connections and continuity were advised. Here it would be useful to look at a map of the North Atlantic, but the main thing is to consider the ways in which the passages of time, place and generations are shown as well as the forces that drove men on these journeys.

In the ninth century, Swedish and Norwegian sailors discovered among remote and empty seas the remote and empty island known ever since as Iceland. Before the tenth century was out, the sailors from Norway and Iceland discovered, among even remoter and emptier seas, the remoter and emptier island known ever since as Greenland – and a pretty large island it is too. Finally, round about the year 1000, the sons and grandsons and great-great grandsons of these same sailors, from havens in Norway, Iceland and Greenland, lashed by tempest, nudged by fog, herded by wind and wave south and west of all known marks and bearings, came at last to the furthest reaches of the ocean and landed, battered but resolute, on the eastern shores of lands we now know as Canada and the United States of America.

(Gwyn Jones, Westwards to Iceland)

— **Activity 3.5** —————————————————————————

1 Show how the author makes certain ideas cohere or 'stick together' by repeating key words.
2 Jot down the sequences of people and places involved in these explorations and show when the various journeys occurred.

4 Planned writing (2): paragraphing

4.1 One topic at a time

Your first aim should be to generate sufficient ideas to make the content of your writing worthwhile. Your second should be to present it in an orderly way. The three-part structure (Introduction–Body–Conclusion) recommended in Chapter 3 helps you to do that.

In any of these three parts – and especially when you are dealing with the main substance (the body) of your subject matter you may need to include more than one topic. Each separate topic should be dealt with in a separate paragraph.

- *A paragraph is a distinct section of a passage of writing. It is concerned with one topic – and only one.*

Help your readers to understand quickly and clearly what each paragraph is about. Do not confuse them by including any material that is not strictly relevant to the topic with which the paragraph is concerned.

4.2 The topic sentence and paragraph unity

Build each paragraph on a 'topic sentence' – so called because it announces the topic being dealt with in that paragraph.

- *The topic sentence tells your readers what the paragraph is about. All the other sentences in that paragraph should be seen to have a direct bearing on the subject matter indicated by the topic sentence. That is what is meant by 'paragraph unity'.*

In Section 3.2 when the basic structure of a well-made piece of writing was described, you were recommended to think of it in terms of taking your readers on a mental journey. The same concept can be applied to the construction of a well-made paragraph. Think of the topic sentence as a 'signpost'. It tells your readers where the paragraph is going. Then having indicated the 'route' you are taking, stick to it. Do not wander off into 'byways'. Each paragraph corresponds to one particular stage of the 'journey'. When you have completed it, start on the next stage, in a *new* paragraph.

4.3   The position of the topic sentence

As it acts as a 'signpost', it is best to place the topic sentence at the beginning of the paragraph. All the other sentences in the paragraph should then follow on in a sensible sequence.

This method of working will produce a well-made paragraph:

1 Think hard about the particular point you intend to make in the paragraph. This will be your subject for the complete paragraph. You way wish to apply a little 'brain-storming' here and write a few notes to ensure that your ideas are in place before you start.
2 Work out a topic sentence in which you express the essence of that point.
3 Check that everything you include in the rest of the paragraph is closely related to the point made in the topic sentence. You will need to expand and develop that point – but do not get away from it.
4 Use all your material signposted by the topic sentence. Complete it before you move on to the next topic – in the *next* paragraph.

4.4   Two well-made paragraphs to study

These two paragraphs, *A* and *B*, are examples of thoughtful and disciplined expression. The particular aspect of subject matter being dealt with is clearly stated in a topic sentence at the beginning. All the other sentences are clearly seen to bear on that point, explaining and developing it. No irrelevant matters are included.

A

This is a bleak time to eke a living out of the North Sea, whether you are a fish or a fisherman. British fishermen's incomes have fallen by 6 per cent in real terms since 1980, which would not seem too bad if fish were not getting scarcer. The stocks of adult North Sea cod have halved since 1982 and those of haddock have fallen by two-thirds. Pollution may be partly to blame; so may the mysterious and spontaneous variations common among fish populations. But most scientists think that the fish shortage has a single cause – over-fishing. Another shortage will result – of fishermen's income.

(Adapted from *The Economist*)

--- Activity 4.1 --

Put paragraph *A* to the 'topic test'. Take the points made in the opening sentence – Bleak time for (1) fish; (2) fishermen. List under the two groups that are suffering the problems that are affecting them as outlined in the rest of the paragraph.

B

The difficulties of watching an animal of nocturnal and secretive habits are great. Even now much of the badger's life remains a mystery. How can we tell what happens in the labyrinth of dark tunnels that constitute his home, known to us as the badger's set? We know that he makes only rare appearances by day; that he retires to his set at dawn, and emerges at dusk. Since badgers are very much awake by night, we presume that most of their time underground is spent in sleep. We know that they have large retiring chambers into which they take cartloads of bedding comprised of the most handy material, dry grass, bracken, leaves, herbage of different kinds; anything that is within convenient distance of the set and will make a comfortable bed.

(Eileen A. Soper, *When Badgers Wake*)

Activity 4.2

The main topics of paragraph *B* are to be found in the first sentence. They are: difficulties; nocturnal habits; secretive habits. List beneath each of these topics the points made by the writer in the rest of the paragraph.

4.5   Keep the paragraph tight and keep moving ahead

In a well-made paragraph each sentence adds something to the point being dealt with in that paragraph and announced in the topic sentence. It may provide further information. It may expand an explanation or develop an argument. Whatever its particular contribution, it keeps the paragraph moving ahead to complete one stage of the piece of writing of which it is a distinct part.

● *If you lose sight of the paragraph topic you will stray 'off course', wandering into 'by-ways' or 'dead ends'.*

That fault, and it is a common one, is illustrated by the paragraph printed below. The topic sentence at the beginning states clearly what the paragraph is about, but the writer then introduces irrelevant information. The forward movement of the paragraph is checked and attention is distracted from the main point.

To help you to see where the unity of the paragraph is broken, the sentences dealing with the irrelevant points have been printed in italics. It is because they deal with matters that have nothing to do with the topic covered in this paragraph that they get in the way. The paragraph is loosely made and its forward movement is checked.

The consultant engineer's report explained the cause of the intermittent failure of the water supply to the two houses situated at the top of the

North Hill. *Both these houses, which stand in extensive grounds, were built in the pleasant early Victorian style of architecture much in evidence in mid-Devon.* The small-bore main connecting them to the private reservoir had recently been extended to serve a farmhouse situated lower down the hill. *This was a substantial modern building erected on the site of the old Manor Farm.* For most of the year, the farm's own well provided it with an adequate supply, but in dry spells water was drawn from the mains to fill a large reserve tank. *From there it was circulated to the farmhouse and its outbuildings by an electric pump.* When the farm tank was filling it exerted a considerable pull on the water supply from the small reservoir to which all three properties were connected by the common main. This caused a temporary by-passing of the right-angled junctions through which the two houses at the top of the hill drew their water. Consequently, the pressure in their pipes dropped and their supply was cut off until the farm tank was full.

4.6   Some basic paragraph patterns

These standard paragraph patterns provide useful guidelines when you are considering how best to develop a paragraph out of a topic sentence.

(a) Illustrations and examples

In Mrs Tompkin's kitchen on washday chaos reigned. Pulled out from under the draining-board, where it lurked for six days of the week, the washing-machine gurgled in its ration from the hot-water tap. Round it, a lake – fed by a leaky hose connection – rippled in the draught from the kitchen door. Half in and half out of the lake lay a jumble of dirty clothes, topped by a melancholy cat. At the kitchen table two rowdy children stuffed bread and jam into each other's hair. And Mrs Tompkins, maddened by the noise, darted wildly from table to sink, from sink to clothes, expanding vast quantities of energy to very little effect.

(b) Enumeration

The paragraph is developed by listing items or ideas referred to in the topic sentence.

When Sir Christopher Hogg became chairman of Courtaulds, he took the axe to it. I watched the numbers appear on the (ticker) tape; £100 million write-offs, seven major plants shut, the final dividend cut down to zero. I asked him that day why he had dealt so drastically with the dividend. He said that the seriousness of the situation spoke for itself, and when thousands of Courtaulds people had been put out of

work, the shareholders could not expect to carry on as if nothing had
happened.

(The Spectator)

(c) Cause and effect

The paragraph is developed by looking at the causes and effects referred to
in the topic sentence.

> The problem of over-population must be tackled with the utmost
> determination. For the undeveloped countries this is a matter of life and
> death, and all usable help in communications and technology should be
> offered by the developed countries. At the same time, the developed
> countries should publicly accept the aim of stabilising their own
> populations, both as an example and because their citizens will, for some
> considerable time, go on consuming and polluting far more than those in
> the rest of the world.
>
> (The Conservation Society)

> All the millions of words written on losing weight could be condensed to
> just two: Eat Less. So ruled Dr Desmond Morris in his best seller, *The
> Naked Ape*, and truer words were never written. Yet homo sapiens does
> not like his truths quite so stark, and so a multi-million pound industry
> has mushroomed to teach us a thousand different ways to diet. All fall, it
> seems to me, on just one count. They have no power to fool the tum
> (stomach). Send down radishes and raw carrots till kingdom come; the
> tum is not deceived. It knows it is being short-changed and will tell you
> so.
>
> (Godfrey Smith in *The Sunday Times*)

(d) Comparisons and/or Contrasts

The paragraph develops the comparison and/or contrast stated in the topic
sentence. A paragraph may, of course, concentrate on either comparison
or contrast. The structure is the same in either case.

> Human nature is full of contradictions; look at the way most people love
> to get letters and hate to write them. There are, it is true, people who are
> indecently fond of writing letters, such as lovers and the people who sign
> themselves 'One of many' or 'A reader', and write to the papers
> attacking some article in yesterday's issue; but these are on the whole
> oddities, like the folk who adore listening to lectures, or those who will
> keep on chasing a buzz and rattle from station to station on their radio all
> night, or those who like to move house often. Most people dislike
> moving, dislike letting other people talk, and in particular dislike
> answering letters. As regards the last it is safe to assume that an ordinary

man only writes a letter when he wants to get an answer to it, a motive
that regularly disappears if he receives a letter himself. The dislike of
writing letters probably arises from general human laziness; but the
craving to receive letters has, seemingly, deeper and more mysterious
roots.

(Karel Capek, *Intimate things*)

(e) Definition

The paragraph gives a full explanation of a term or terms used in the topic
sentence.

> It is important to remember that the word 'tragedy' as a term of literary
> criticism or identification is – or should be – used more precisely than its
> everyday applications. Newspaper headlines label as 'tragedy' every
> plane, train or car crash that involves loss of life. In literature an event of
> that kind, though shocking, is not necessarily tragic. Tragedy in its
> literary sense is concerned with the downfall, defeat or death of an
> individual or of a group of people whose overthrow, by reason of
> character or position, carries with it a significance for humanity as a
> whole. The audience (reader or watcher) is emotionally engaged in the
> fate of the tragic personages and feels their story to be meaningful for all
> people. *Macbeth* is not the tragedy of Duncan: it is the tragedy of
> Duncan's murderer.

That paragraph was neatly 'rounded off' with an apt illustration to
support the definition of tragedy.

4.7   Putting topics to the test

Now try to devise paragraphs for yourself. Remember that the topic
sentence gives you the lead for the beginning; your ideas should explain,
expand and illustrate in order to form the substance of the middle; your
ending should, ideally, make reference to something in the first part that
enables you to 'round off' the theme.

Activities 4.3

Here are five topic sentences that could introduce paragraphs along
the same lines as the examples given above:

(a) Illustration and example: Wars are no longer confined to
distant battlefields, but are often
witnessed live on our television
screens and are, consequently,
brought home to us.

(b) Enumeration: There are many ways of boring the
young.

(c) Cause and effect:	When people eat, drink, smoke, work or sleep too much, they cause problems for themselves and trouble for others.
(d) Comparison and contrast:	In many ways the state of being very young resembles the condition of being very old.
(e) Definition:	What constitutes a 'good' holiday? The pursuit of enjoyment can be hard work!

A well-constructed topic paragraph has been likened to the creation of a bonfire. Think of the ways in which a bonfire is prepared and lit and then develops a fiery life of its own. See whether you can appreciate the connections with a paragraph.

First, the material is gathered together from various sources. It is carefully piled to ensure that everything will eventually burn. This is the equivalent of the 'brain-storming' technique of bringing ideas together. The intention is that they should ignite a response in the observer or reader. The striking of the match and the initial flare of the flame should attract attention with their sound and light. This is the function of the topic sentence – to cause readers to hear something arresting and to have initial light cast upon the subject. Then as the fire burns there are sequences of clouds of smoke and waves of flame. These are the equivalents of individual sentences, with their visible signs of material being displayed coupled with the enlightenment that the reader should receive. As the bonfire smoulders it gives off a glow, a series of crackles and an occasional shower of sparks. Here is the paragraph's last sentence, which should have a particularly abrasive or penetrating quality.

⬡5 Plain sense (1): well-made sentences

5.1 Making sense

Words flow through our minds all the time. When we are talking and listening our main attention is to make sense of them. When we are writing, our primary purpose is to put them into a sensible and meaningful order. In the last two sentences the words, 'sense' and 'sensible', have been used. It is natural that they should be – for the word 'sentence' itself is derived from the Latin word *sententia* and the French word *sentire* which mean 'to sense' or 'to feel'. Whenever we are using sentences we are employing our mental powers that have a 'feel for the words'. It is, perhaps, one of the reasons why people gesticulate and, in particular, use their hands when speaking – for they are almost literally feeling for words.

As ideas flow through our minds we have to control them. As we express ourselves in writing, we have to order these ideas in such a way that our readers can understand us without difficulty. Clarity of expression is our major aim. Effective speed in response to others is vital for good communications. This section is about helping you to make sense.

Your first aim is to express your meaning clearly. How far you succeed in doing that depends very largely on your ability to write well-made sentences. Deal with your subject-matter item by item in a series of clear-cut sentences and it will make plain sense to your reader.

Obviously, you cannot follow that advice unless you know what a sentence is! There are many ways of defining a sentence, but this definition provides the best starting-point for your immediate purposes:

- *A sentence is a group of words that makes* complete *sense on its own.*

Because that statement tells you what a sentence does, it gives you a test that you can apply to your own writing. When you have written a group of words that makes complete sense on its own you have written a sentence. If a group of words does not make complete sense on its own, it is not a sentence.

Express your meaning item by item – one thing at a time – sentence by sentence. Be sure to obey this basic rule.

- *Begin the first word of a sentence with a capital letter and put a full stop after the last word.*

The capital letter and the full stop act as signals, marking each sentence off from the others. The capital letter with which the first word begins tells your readers that you are beginning a sentence. The full stop after the last word tells them that you have completed it. When your readers see those signals they expect the group of words that is enclosed between them to make complete sense. If it does not, you have put the capital letter and the full stop in the wrong places.

The definition with which we started can now be expanded to take in the points just made:

- *A sentence is a* distinct *and* self-contained *unit of meaning. Its contents make plain sense without needing help from words outside its own boundaries.*

5.2   Incomplete sense: sentence fragments

Although it is essential to begin the first word of a sentence with a capital letter and to put a full stop after the last word, the use of those two 'sentence markers' is not in itself sufficient to guarantee that the words that come between them give the complete meaning. When a writer does that, the words between the capital letter and the full stop make a 'sentence fragment', *not* a sentence.

These three short extracts from students' work illustrate the mistake. Each contains one sentence fragment: a group of words marked off as if it were a sentence when the meaning is, in fact, incomplete.

1 The new managing director insisted on seeing weekly returns from all the firm's branches. *To keep sales figures under close scrutiny.*

2 *Failure to achieve a decisive victory before the snow began.* The disastrous retreat of the French army was the inevitable consequence of being ill-equipped to ensure the severity of the Russian winter.

3 A few curious onlookers were kept back by one officer, while the other tried to pacify the man on the balcony. *Waiting for the arrival of the fire-fighters with ladders.*

As you see, in each extract there is one group of words that pretends to be a sentence when it is not. When you read these pieces of writing you probably wondered how the writers could have made such an obvious mistake. But they did! So be on your guard. Sentence fragments clutter up your writing and make it hard for your readers to take in what you are trying to say. Well-made sentences make plain sense.

5.3   Jumbled sense: run-together sentences

An equally common mistake occurs when a full stop is used too late. When that happens, one sentence runs on into the next one. The two units of meaning are then jumbled together and the plain sense that each would make on its own is lost.

Here are some examples of 'run-together' sentences:

1 I was given an interchangeable-lens camera for Christmas a zoom lens is what I want now and I shall buy one when I can afford it.

2 Difficult routes were not attempted in the first few days later on, when basic techniques had been learnt, the best of the beginners were being taken up the less dangerous crags.

3 Excellent examples of local crafts are displayed in the regional capital, in the outlying villages prices are lower and that is where sensible visitors do their bargain hunting.

In each of those three pieces of writing the same mistake is made. One complete and distinct unit of meaning (one sentence) is carelessly allowed to run into the next. Each would make plain sense on its own. Run together the sense of one becomes jumbled up with the sense of the other. Reshape each passage into two well-made sentences and the writer's meaning comes through quickly and clearly, like this:

1 Full stop after *Christmas*. Begin a new sentence with *A zoom lens* . . .
2 Full stop after *days*. Begin a new sentence with *Later on* . . .
3 Full stop after *capital*. Begin a new sentence with *In the* . . .

5.4   Order and sense

Obviously, a sentence cannot convey its intended meaning unless it contains the right words; but more than that is required. The right words must be set down in the right order. Detailed advice about choosing the right words is provided in Chapter 8. Here, we are concerned with word order.

At an early stage we all learn that words set down haphazardly cannot make sense. For example, anyone would recognise at once that 'dog cat chased the the' is not a meaningful arrangement of words. Set down like that, they are gibberish. Yet those same words can be arranged in an order that makes a perfectly intelligible statement: 'The dog chased the cat.' (or, of course, 'The cat chased the dog.')

Nobody who knows anything about how the English language works would displace the order of words so drastically as to write nonsense (such as 'dog cat chased the the'). Carelessness about word order, however, is a common cause of muddled sense and misunderstood writing.

The facts you need to know about word order and sentence structure follow. Study them carefully. They will help you to write sentences that say what you intend them to say – clearly and quickly.

5.5 The simple sentence

Words have their meanings and dictionaries can help us to clarify them. Meanings have to be communicated and to do this we use sentences, which detail, expand and explain our ideas. It is a complicated process, but in conversation most people have an ability 'to put things across' quite effectively. The sentence is used as the basic unit in our speech patterns in order to help us regulate the flow of words. The way we breathe does not allow us to go on and on without a pause. These pauses or divisions which are so necessary in conversation are, of course, used when we write. They enable the .reader to see that the writer is in control of his material, marshalling his ideas and managing to hold attention.

Knowing how a sentence is constructed gives power and confidence to' the writer. It enables him to perform effectively and master the skills of communication.

The basic unit that needs to be understood is that of the simple sentence. It consists, at its simplest, of a subject and a finite verb. Look at the following examples in which the subject has been put in italics.

Day breaks.

The sun will set.

Values change.

Tom ran.

These sentences make sense in themselves. Only two skills are needed – one is to be able to pick out the word or words that indicate the person, creature, thing or quality about which the writer has something to say. In other words, you have to find the subject. The other is to be able to recognise the finite verb – the word or words that express the action. In these cases they are, of course – *breaks* – *will set* – *change* – *ran*.

A problem that can occur is that sometimes people confuse the finite verb with the so-called infinite parts of the verb. 'Finite' means 'to have. an end or limit'. 'Infinite' means 'without end or limit'. In the examples given above you can see that the 'breaks' is confined in this sentence to what happens to the 'day' and that 'will set' is limited in this case to what 'the sun' will do. 'Change' is applicable here only to 'values' and 'ran' refers directly to the actions of 'Tom'. If you were looking at matters in a much wider way – in fact at topics that appear to be 'without end or limit' such as 'breaking' – 'setting' – 'to change' – 'to run' – then you would be using the infinite parts which are not limited by a subject. The main feature to remember is that the simple sentence must have a subject and a finite verb.

Activity 5.1

Although simple sentences are not necessarily short, here are five examples of very brief sentences. Pick out the subjects and the finite verbs.

Snow will fall.

Everyone was singing.

The travellers arrived.

The parcel has been delivered.

Sheep graze.

The difficulty of being able to spot the two essentials of the simple sentence – the subject and the finite verb – occurs when further information is added and they appear to be 'lost' within a longer range of words. Take the sentences just given in 'Activity 5.1'. They can be made longer, have additions to the subject and more information about the verb, but remain essentially simple sentences.

Heavy snow will fall during the winter months.
Nearly everyone in the party was singing loudly on the coach.
The tired air-travellers thankfully arrived safely two days later.
The important parcel has been delivered by special courier.
Most sheep of the mountain variety graze for much of the time.

It is useful to be able to use simple sentences in order to create a good effect. They can be direct, dramatic and make a point clearly. However, too many of them can lead to a jerkiness of style and cause irritation to the reader. Take the following example:

Christmas is supposed to be a time of good-will. High expectations occur. Children want presents. Relatives visit one another. Families need feeding. Consumption is high. Drink flows. Money disappears. The weather keeps people indoors. The elderly tell many stories about the past. The increased incidence of divorce proceedings does not reflect goodwill.

Here are a number of ideas that are linked. It is reasonably clear that the author feels a misgiving about the festive season. The observations have a certain logical connection. However, the presence of eleven consecutive simple sentences does hinder the flow of the passage. There is jerkiness and, probably, irritation caused here, but there are ways of avoiding these tendencies and they are explained in the next sections.

5.6   Double (or compound) and multiple sentences

The flow of ideas and the smoothing of sentence patterns can be improved by combining two or more simple sentences into double (compound) or multiple sentences.

Simple sentences: I had no change. The ticket machine accepted only £1 coins. I went across to a parked car.

Double sentence: I had no change and the ticket machine accepted only £1 coins.

Multiple sentence: I had no change and the ticket machine accepted only £1 coins, but I went across to a parked car.

A *double* sentence has this structure: simple sentence + simple sentence

A *multiple* sentence has this structure: simple sentence + simple sentence.

Double and multiple sentences are built up of simple sentences linked together by *coordinating conjunctions*. These are: *and, but, for, neither . . . nor.*

Another way of linking two simple sentences is to use a *semi-colon*. It marks a distinct pause between two closely-linked statements in the same double or compound sentence.

Some people call their midday meal dinner; others refer to it as lunch.

A red sky at night is the shepherd's delight; a red sky in the morning is the shepherd's warning.

5.7   The complex sentence

All the sentences that we have discussed so far have been simple sentences (in the grammatical sense of that term), for double and multiple sentences are in fact a series of linked simple sentences.

Here is a different kind of sentence:

I paid the boy who delivered the newspapers.

That is not a simple sentence, for it contains more than one finite verb. There are two finite verbs in the sentence: *paid* and *delivered*. Nor is it a double sentence. In a double sentence each separate part (clause) can stand alone and make sense:

I had no change (*and*) the ticket machine accepted only £1 coins.

But although 'I paid the boy' can stand alone and make complete sense, 'who delivered the newspapers' cannot.

So, although there are two finite verbs, one part of the sentence is different in status from the other. Each part is a *clause* – a group of words containing a finite verb and forming part of a sentence. Yet one of the clauses is an independent utterance and the other is not.

Main clause: I paid the boy

Dependent (or subordinate) clause: who delivered the newspapers

A *main clause* is a group of words containing a finite verb, forming part of a sentence and making the main statement.

A *dependent or subordinate clause* is a group of words containing a finite verb, forming part of a sentence, and *dependent* upon (*subordinate* to) the main statement.

__ Test 5.1 __

(Answers in Answers section at end of book.)
Divide the following sentences into main clause and subordinate (or dependent) clause.

1 He was driving the car that I nearly bought.
2 This generator provides the electricity that supplies the village.
3 Just as I reached the station the train pulled away.
4 Before the film ended the audience began to leave.
5 The whistle blew as he scored the winning goal.
6 I hope you understand main and subordinate clauses.
7 What I said at the meeting was reported in the papers the next day.
8 The answer to your question is that the economy of the country needs more investment.

A *complex* sentence contains a main clause and one or more dependent or subordinate clauses.

A dependent or subordinate clause does the work of an adjective, an adverb or a noun.

Adjectival clause: This is the time *when the ghost walks*.

Adverbial clause: Although he did not feel well, he ran quickly.

Noun clause: I knew *that she was going to leave me*.

As you can discover from any grammar book, there are several different kinds of adverb clauses (nine, as a matter of fact!) and there are five different ways in which a clause can do the work of a noun.

Examination requirements do not justify spending time on learning the detailed analysis needed to identify each separate kind of clause. The important thing for you to recognise is that each word (and each group of words) that you use in a sentence plays a part in the structure of that sentence as a whole.

The information about clauses given in this section will help you to develop your understanding of the 'architecture' of English sentences. In

Sections 5.8 and 5.9 you will find help in planning the structure of your own sentences and using a variety of sentence patterns.

5.8   Sentence patterns: variety and control

The writer's need is to find the right kind of sentence pattern to fit the job in hand and to avoid monotony. As with his choice of vocabulary, his use of sentence patterns should be guided by his sense of purpose and his sense of audience. A variety of patterns helps to hold attention and the control of sentence lengths gives a mastery of pace. The overriding aims of an author should be to put his meaning across clearly and hold his reader's interest.

(a) Simple sentences

Simple sentences fit the writer's purpose when he is describing rapid action or making an uncomplicated statement. As an introduction, or a conclusion, or at a climactic point in an argument, the brevity and plainness of such a pattern may be invaluable. But a prolonged series of simple sentences is jerky and monotonous. It sounds childish. It is inadequate to express thoughts of any complexity, especially where there are interconnected ideas and gradations of emphasis and/or importance. So it is best to reserve the simple, and often short, sentence for arresting attention when a dramatic flourish serves the need of the writer. If a number of short sentences are used consecutively, the effect is to quicken the pace. This can help in a piece of story-telling. It can, however, allow ideas to run away and become lost.

(b) Double and multiple sentences

The combination of separate simple sentences into double and multiple sentences lessens the monotony, but the repetition of coordinating conjuctions soon tires the reader and draws his attention to the fact that the writer has a very limited range of sentence patterns at his command.

(c) Adjective and adverb modifiers

The inadequate resources of (a) and (b) above, can be supplemented by using accurately placed 'modifiers'. These, either as single words or phrases, economise on words and tighten up constructions. The loose sprawling *undirected* sequence of double and multiple sentences in series is transformed into tighter, more disciplined writing. Compare passage 1 with passage 2, below:

(1) Exmoor was the scene of an experiment. The experiment was a remarkable one. It took place in the nineteenth century. John Knight ploughed up many acres. He was a vigorous and inventive man. The land

he ploughed was moorland. Up to that time it was barren. He also limed it. He used ox-ploughs. John Knight was followed by his son. He continued his father's work. He used steam-ploughs. He got better results with these than with his ox-teams.

(2) Exmoor was the scene of a remarkable experiment in the nineteenth century. John Knight, a vigorous and inventive man, ploughed up and limed many acres of barren moorland. John Knight's son continued his father's work. The steam-ploughs used by him were more efficient than his father's ox-teams.

Activities 5.2

Do study the ways in which passage 2 has been 'improved' by the use of modifying words and phrases. Copy it word for word and, as you perform the task, notice that it contains three simple sentences and one double sentence. Remember that the writer's purpose was narrative – he was describing a sequence of events – and these uncomplicated constructions were suited to his needs. He wrote a taut passage by condensing and by slotting in modifiers.

Try a similar exercise yourself by taking the following series of simple sentences and converting them into the type of passage that you have just copied. There is no need to follow the same pattern slavishly, but look for the 'short cuts' that create the improved flow of ideas.

Britain has seen many changes. There have been periods of rapid growth. The economy developed strongly in the 1950 and 1960s. Governments used some of their resources to expand higher education. It was considered beneficial for more students to study more subjects. Students were encouraged to study in distant universities and colleges. They had to live away from home. Governments were keen to encourage an intelligent, flexible and *mobile* work-force. These measures helped.

(d) Complex structures

When the writer needs to express ideas of any complexity, a more complex sentence pattern is essential. This is especially so when we must convey a main idea that is subject to qualification and/or extension. Whenever ideas are probed and matters thought out, it is necessary to detail, illustrate and pin-point certain features. The reader has to be led from a position of, perhaps, complete ignorance of a subject to a frame of mind where he accepts a conclusion put forward. It is a complex business and demands a complex sentence pattern. However, do not confuse the word 'complex' with the word 'difficult'. The former refers to the subtle ways in which a sentence is constructed; the latter is a feature to be avoided.

The writer of the following discursive passage was arguing a point of view and advancing reasons to sustain his ideas. Only complex sentence patterns could serve those purposes.

I have already referred to scientific research, which is an integral part of the activities of our universities. However important may be the contributions made by full-time research institutes or from industry, the university must remain the centre of research activity in the country. There, after all, is the future research worker fashioned from undergraduate material. There is the fully-fledged research worker most likely to retain a breadth of outlook as the result of regular teaching activities, often on subjects unrelated to his own research, and also through intercourse with those engaged in other disciplines. There, above all, he has the fullest opportunity to inspire others with his own vision. And if he does not do this, however brilliant he may be, he has only partially fulfilled his purpose.

Whatever lowers the standards of the universities as a whole, therefore, lowers the standards of scientific research, with all that this means for the country's future. All of us are most concerned at the ever-mounting costs of the National Health Service, but it is largely by raising health standards by the fruits of research that it is likely to be kept within bounds and made more efficient. The conquest of tuberculosis alone is estimated to have saved the country £60 million a year in treatment costs and in the productive capacity of young lives. Economies that affect our standard of medical research are, therefore, short-sighted, if only from a financial point of view.

Activities 5.3

In the preceding passage the occasional employment of simple sentences with conclusive effect is of particular interest. Can you spot them?

Try to pick out the main clauses of each sentence. Then make a careful note of how the author begins each sentence. Three consecutive sentences begin with the word 'There', perhaps in order to stress the sequence of what he considers to be convincing ideas.

Finally, undertake a judgement of your own. The two requirements stressed in this section are 'variety' and 'control'. To what extent do you consider that the author has been successful in varying his approach and controlling his ideas? The actual topic that he has presented may not excite you. Yet he has maintained your level of interest? Remember that this decision about *interest levels* is the one that other people will be making about your style of writing.

5.9 Order and proximity

In the next chapter we shall be looking at the work done by words in the sentence and considering the so-called parts of speech. However, it is useful to look first at the clusters of words and the order in which we use them within sentences. This helps to develop a sharper eye for patterns and structures which are so necessary for maintaining interest levels and for developing those personal and accurate styles of expression.

(i) The meaning of a sentence depends upon the *order* in which the words are arranged. For example, in the two sentences *The batsman struck the ball/The ball struck the batsman* we know by the order (and by the order alone) that 'batsman' is the *subject* in the first sentence and the *object* in the second. The word itself does not change, but we know from its position in the sentence (*in relation to* the position of the other words in the sentence) whether it is functioning as the subject or as the object. We know this because we know how the English language works. Our understanding depends upon the word order. It follows that, as writers, we must use words in their proper order if we are to make ourselves understood. Order is the first law of English.

(ii) Words often do their work in sentences, not as individual words, but as *clusters of words*. This is especially true of verbs. In the sentence '*The wanted man was about to board a plane at Heathrow when he was arrested*' – the first verb is 'was about to board'.

(iii) We get a clearer insight into sentence construction when we regard a sentence as being a structure built up from clusters of words than when we look at it as if it were made up of individual words added to each other. In the sentence just quoted, for example, the word-clusters are: *The wanted man//was about to board//a plane//at Heathrow//when he was arrested*.

Here is a diagrammatic view of the same sentence:

$$\text{The wanted man} \longrightarrow \text{was about to board} \longrightarrow \begin{cases} \text{at Heathrow} \\ \text{a plane} \\ \text{when he was arrested} \end{cases}$$

Those two ways of dividing up the sentence are useful because (a) they show clearly each word-cluster from which the sentence is built, and (b) they show clearly the relationship that each cluster has with the others.

We can describe *at Heathrow* as an adverbial phrase of place modifying the verb *was about to board*. We can describe *when he was arrested* as an adverbial clause of time modifying the same verb.

But for practical writing purposes the important thing is to develop a sense of 'what goes with what'.

(iv) *The rule of proximity* states that those parts of a sentence that 'go with each other' to establish order *must be positioned as near to each other as possible*. If you break the rule of proximity you will write absurdities such as: 'Grandfather clocks are much sought after by collectors with brass faces and wrought-iron hands.' Observing the rule of proximity saves you from muddled sentences, ambiguity, verbosity, downright rubbish and, of course, embarrassment.

At a well-attended church service a minister of religion wanted to contrast the pessimism expressed in the particular Old Testament reading that he had given with the optimism found in the New Testament reading that he was about to give. Alas, he forgot that an attractive soloist had just given a beautiful rendering of a well-known piece of music, which had acted as an interlude between the two readings. His words that were intended to preface his second reading by commenting on the first were: 'Now after all that moaning and groaning!' This drew a spontaneous roar of laughter from the congregation and smiles of wry amusement from the soloist, who was not accustomed to being commented on in this way. The discomfited minister had neglected the rule of proximity.

Test 5.2

Answers in the Answers Section at the end of the book.

Use the mark // to divide these sentences into their basic word clusters.

Example: The borough's newly appointed chief executive officer// was threatening to resign//within a month of his appointment.

1 Very few people are able to buy everying they want for their houses during the first year of their married life.
2 The result of the poll ought to have been declared by the presiding officer soon after midnight.
3 A red-faced customs official, apologising profusely for the mistake, returned the travellers' passports to them after a long delay at the airport.

Fall into the following 'proximity-traps' by completing sentences in order to create a series of humorous or misleading statements:

1 The girl asked the policeman wearing . . .
2 The boy spoke to the elderly man skating . . .
3 Wanted: a piano stool for a lady with . . .

⬡ 6 Plain sense (2): correct usage

6.1 What is grammar?

The grammar of a language is a description of the way in which that language behaves. French grammar is a description of how the French language behaves. Russian grammar is a description of how the Russian language behaves. English grammar is a description of how the English language behaves – and so on.

Grammar is not a collection of hard-and-fast rules. It is more flexible (and therefore, more useful) than that. Grammar gives an account of the way in which a language is used by those who use it well. A living language changes; and grammar takes note of changing linguistic practices.

Of course, it is possible to communicate in speech and in writing without a knowledge of grammar. We learn to use our language by listening, speaking, reading and writing. The more practice we have in listening and in reading, the better we learn to speak and to write, provided that we listen and read attentively and apply the lessons of *good* models to our own use of language.

A knowledge of grammar is a handy tool and an understanding of it speeds up our language learning. It encourages efficiency, widens the range of linguistic resources, helps us to choose and use the forms of language best suited to each particular situation. It assists us in communicating with a great variety of people in the varied circumstances that confront us every day.

6.2 The work that words do in sentences: the parts of speech

(a) The same word can do different jobs

It is important to get this straight at once. A word is a particular part of speech *according to the work that it is doing*. For example:

    1 We are expecting a guest tomorrow.
    2 Is the guest room ready?

In sentence 1 *guest* is doing the work of a noun. In sentence 2 *guest* is doing the work of an adjective. The same word can do different jobs.

(b) The eight parts of speech

1 *Noun:* a word used to *name* something – e.g. table; Kate; honesty; team.
2 *Pronoun:* a word used to stand *for* (stand in place of) a noun – e.g. you; it; we; him; themselves.
3 *Adjective:* a word used to 'qualify' (describe) a noun – e.g. *new* table; *attractive* Kate; *firm* honesty: *beaten* team.
4 *Verb:* a word (or cluster of words) used to denote actions, states or happenings – e.g. He *entered* politics. He *became* a candidate. He *was elected* with a large majority.
5 *Adverb:* a word used to 'modify' (tell us more about) verbs, adjectives, other adverbs – e.g. He entered politics *reluctantly*. He soon became a *truly* popular candidate. He was elected *almost* immediately with a large majority.
6 *Preposition:* a word used to express a relationship or to show the position between one thing and another – e.g. The letter *from* the tax inspector puzzled me. This is an excellent river to fish *in*. They were selling lettuces *at* 20p each.
7 *Conjunction:* a word used to connect one part of a sentence to another – e.g. I am fond of reading *but* I haven't been to the library lately. The customer paid by cheque *because* he hadn't enough cash. The lifeboat was launched *although* the sea was rough.
8 *Interjection:* a word (or words) 'thrown in', often to express a mood, and having no grammatical connection with or function in the rest of the sentence – e.g. *Well*, it was obvious to us all that he was tired. *Hello!* what's this? *Oh dear*, it's raining again.

It will help you to remember the eight parts of speech if you group them like this:

Group 1	*Group 2*	*Group 3*	*Odd man out*
nouns	verbs	prepositions	interjections
pronouns	adverbs	conjunctions	
adjectives			

Group 1 consists of words that name things, and words that describe the things that are named.

Group 2 consists of words that denote actions, states, and conditions of being, and words that describe (or modify) those actions, states and conditions of being.

Group 3 consists of connective words that link words (or groups of words) to other words (or groups of words).

Thus, to identify a word as a part of speech is to describe the work that it is doing in a sentence.

(c) Nouns

There are four kinds of nouns:

1 *Common nouns* name a member of or an item in a whole class of persons or things – e.g. man; farmer; dog; letter; figure.
  A common noun is the name common to all members of or items in the class named by the noun.
2 *Proper nouns* name an individual, a particular person, thing or place – e.g. *Robert* is a hard-working man. Like his father before him, he is a farmer. Several generations of his family have farmed in *Staffordshire*. Proper nouns always have capital letters.
3 *Abstract nouns* name qualities or states of mind or of feeling – e.g. His *diligence* was rewarded by *wealth*, which his *benevolence* employed for the *welfare* of the community.
  Abstract nouns name non-physical things.
4 *Collective nouns* name groups or collections of persons or things – e.g. There are eleven players in a cricket *team*.
  Collective nouns name a number of items that are regarded as a *whole*: crew; group; fleet, etc.

Note: Some writers list a fifth class of noun – the concrete (or material) noun – e.g. water; rubber; nylon.
In practice, however, these may be regarded as common nouns.

(d) Pronouns

There are five kinds of pronouns:

1 *Personal pronouns* stand for people – e.g. Let *me* have the ticket if *you* can't go.
  Personal pronouns may be nominative, accusative, possessive or reflexive – e.g. I (nominative) will let him (accusative) have the credit that is his (possessive) and claim none for myself (reflexive).
2 *Demonstrative pronouns* point to or at people or objects – e.g. I like *that*, but I suppose it's a lot dearer than *those*.
3 *Relative pronouns* relate to a previously used noun or noun equivalent (their 'antecedent') – e.g. The book *that* I am reading is due back at the library tomorrow.
  In that sentence *book* is the antecedent of *that*.
4 *Interrogative pronouns* introduce questions – e.g. *What* is that noise?
5 *Pronouns of number and quantity* – e.g. *All* are cheap, but *many* are of poor quality. Sorry, we've only a *few* left, but you can have *three* each.

Note: The idiomatic use of the pronoun *it* in an indefinite sense – e.g. It is fine, so the match should start on time. Is it far to London?

(e) Adjectives

Many words function both as pronouns and as adjectives. You can distinguish between them by remembering that a pronoun stands *alone* in place of a noun, whereas an adjective is used with a noun – e.g. Is that *his*? (pronoun); Yes, that's *his* pen (adjective).

There are several classes of adjectives:

1 *Descriptive adjectives* describe the qualities of persons, things, etc. – e.g. a *tall* man; a *black* dress; *quick* intelligence.
2 *Possessive adjectives* indicate possession – e.g. Is *your* house for sale? Yes, and I'd like to bid for *yours* (pronoun) if I get a good price for *mine* (pronoun). See note above on the distinction between adjectives and pronouns.
3 *Demonstrative adjectives*, like demonstrative pronouns, 'point out' – e.g. I cannot think why I like *that* film.
4 *Relative adjectives* introduce relative clauses – e.g. I'll give *what* time I can to it, but I'm very busy.
5 *Interrogative adjectives* introduce questions (direct or indirect) – e.g. *Which* way did he go? I asked him *what* decision he had reached.
6 *Adjectives of number or quantity* tell us how many or how much – e.g. *Few* voters showed *much* enthusiasm, and *ten* minutes sufficed to complete the ballot.
7 *The articles – the*, *a*, or *an* – that announce the coming of a noun.

(f) Verbs

The verb is the most important word in the sentence. In fact, *without a finite verb there cannot be a sentence*. These are the chief terms and definitions that you need at this stage.

Transitive, intransitive, auxiliary

Verbs used transitively   When the verb is transitive the action is performed to or on an *object* (in the grammatical sense of that term) – e.g. The electrician replaced the fuse.

Verbs used intransitively   When the verb is intransitive there is no object. The action refers/relates solely to the subject – e.g. The electrician whistled.

Notes on transitive and intransitive   The word 'transitive' means 'passing across or through'. When a verb is used transitively the action passes across *from* the subject *to* the object *through* the verb – e.g. The angry man kicked the door.
Many verbs can be used either transitively or intransitively – e.g. Solar Slipper is running at Epsom next week (intransitive). British Rail is running twenty extra trains in the West Region (transitive).

Verbs used as auxiliaries   An auxiliary verb 'helps' another verb to form one of its voices, tenses or moods (see below) – e.g. I *was* entranced by my first visit to the ballet.

The auxiliary verbs are: *be*; *have*; *do*; *may*; *shall*; *will*. They all help to express tense, voice and mood – e.g. I *shall* travel tomorrow. The car *was* driven by my father. *Has* she telephoned yet?

Person and number

1 There are three persons: *first* (I, we,); *second* (thou, you); *third* (he, she, it, they).
2 There are two numbers: *singular* (I, thou, he, she, it); *plural* (we, you, they).

Voice

There are two voices: *active* and *passive*. The voice is the form of the verb that knows whether the person or thing denoted by the subject acts or is acted upon – e.g. The electrician replaced the fuse (active). The fuse was replaced by the electrician (passive).

In the first sentence the subject (the electrician) performs the action. In the second sentence the subject (the fuse) has the action done to it. When the passive voice is used it denotes that the subject undergoes or 'suffers' the action (*passive* means 'suffering').

Tense

'Tense' means *time*. The tense of the verb denotes the time of the action. There are three tenses: *past*; *present*; *future* – e.g. I wrote (past); I write (present); I shall write (future). Tense also shows whether the action or state of being denoted by the verb is (or was, or will be) complete (*perfect*), or whether the action is (or was, or will be) incomplete (continuous or *imperfect*): e.g. I was writing (past continuous, or past imperfect). I had written (past perfect).

Mood

Verbs have three moods: the *indicative*; the *imperative*; the *subjunctive*.

The *indicative* is the mood used to make statements or to ask questions – e.g. He caught his train. Did he catch his train?

The *imperative* is the mood used in commands, requests and entreaties. It expresses the desire of the speaker and the verb is always in the second person because the implied subject is 'you' – e.g. Hand him the keys. Please close the door. Consider the penalties of failure.

The *subjunctive*, though still in frequent use in many languages (e.g. French) is little used in modern English. It is, however, correct in utterances where supposition and/or condition must be implied – e.g. If I were you I'd take their offer (*not* If I was you . . .).

As the following examples show, the subjunctive – rare though it is – plays an important part in expressing meaning: 1. If Johnson were fit, he'd be in

the team. 2. If Johnson is fit he'll be in the team.
In 1, where the subjunctive is used, the implication is that Johnson is not
fit. In 2, where the indicative is used, the question of his fitness is left open.

The infinitive
This is the form of the verb containing the word 'to'. For example: to walk;
to think; to write. The verb also has a past infinitive: to have walked; to
have thought; to have written. The infinitive is not finite! That sounds (and
is) obvious, but it worth saying. As soon as a verb has a *subject* it becomes
finite, and it becomes finite because – with a subject – it is 'limited' by
having person, number and tense. The infinitive has no subject, so it has
neither person, number, nor tense – e.g. *infinitive* – to write; *finite form* –
He is writing (third person singular, present continuous or imperfect).

The present participle
This is the *-ing* form of the verb; to wait/waiting. It functions as an
adjective – e.g. The *waiting* mob grew rowdy.
It is also used with the verb *to be* to form the continuous (or imperfect)
tenses of verbs – e.g. I *am* waiting.

The past participle
This takes many different forms: beat/beaten; talk/talked; ring/rung;
bind/bound; break/broken, etc. We learn these quite naturally as we learn
the language. Young children often make mistakes with past participles.
For example, they hear 'sing/sung', so it is quite understandable that they
use 'bring/brung'. Candidates for the English-language examination are
not expected to make similar mistakes! The past participle acts as an
adjective – e.g. The ice on the frozen stream is *cracked*.
It also combines with auxiliary verbs to form perfect tenses and the passive
voice – e.g. He *has spoken* to the governors. His words *were spoken*
quietly.

The gerund
Like the present participle, it is an *-ing* form of the verb, but it functions as
a noun, not as an adjective – e.g. *Fishing* is a popular pastime. The sick
man's laboured *breathing* disturbed the other patients.

(g) Adverbs

An adverb modifies (adds to the meaning of) a verb, an adjective, or
another adverb.
Modifying an adjective – e.g. Fuel for jets is *very* expensive.
Modifying another adverb – They pay *really* well on the right routes.

An adverb can also be used to modify groups of words – phrases or clauses
– within a sentence – e.g.

1. We felt that we were nearly over the worst.
2. The government is regarded as a failure chiefly because it had promised so much.

In (1) *nearly* modifies the phrase 'over the worst'.
In (2) *chiefly* modifies the clause 'because it had promised so much'.

There are three kinds of adverbs: *simple*; *interrogative*; *relative*.

1 *Simple adverbs* tell us *when*, *where*, *how*, *how much*, or *how often*. They express matters connected with:

> *Time* – They arrived *early*.
> *Place* – When the red light shows, stop *here*.
> *Manner* – He works *slowly*.
> *Quantity, Extent or Degree* – We've *nearly* finished.
> I'm *very* tired.
> You've done *enough*.
>
> *Number* – Ring *twice*.

2 *Interrogative adverbs* are used in asking questions – e.g. *When* is your interview to take place? *Why* are you so worried about it?

3 *Relative adverbs* connect two clauses. They *relate* to an 'antecedent' (a word or group of words in another clause) – e.g. We have visited the house *where* Shakespeare was born. I think early summer is the time *when* the countryside is at its best.

(h) Prepositions

Preposition means 'placed before'. A preposition is used with a following noun or pronoun to show relationship between persons or things or actions – e.g. They must have entered *through* the window. Tell me *about* it. The mayor sent a letter *to* him and me.

A very important point is raised by that last example. A preposition 'governs' the noun or pronoun that follows it. That noun or pronoun must, therefore, be in the *accusative* (or objective) *case*. Be careful when a personal pronoun follows (is governed by) a preposition. Mistakes with case are common. The following examples are of *correct* usage: I sent a message *to him*. He sent a message *to me*. Don't broadcast this information, please – it's just *between you and me* for the present.

When the noun or noun equivalent is omitted, a word that was doing the work of a preposition does the work of an adverb: Meet me *inside* the public bar (preposition). Meet me *inside* (adverb).

(i) Conjunctions

Conjunctions are essentially 'structural' words. They link a word to another word, a phrase to another phrase, a clause to another clause – e.g. Gin *and* tonic, please (word to word). Are you going by car *or* by rail?

(phrase to phrase). He left a lot of money, *but* his heirs soon spent it (clause to clause).

Each of those examples contained a *coordinating conjunction*. The words, phrases and clauses linked by each conjunction were of equal importance, doing the same work as each other in their respective sentences.

Subordinating conjunctions link subordinate clauses to main clauses (see Section 5.7) – e.g. He was sacked *because* he was pilfering from the stores. I shan't buy it, *although* I like it. The successful general never attacks *until* he has an ample reserve.

(j) Interjections

Well, we needn't spend any more time on them! (Turn back to earlier part of this section.)

Test 6.1

There is much material to absorb in this section so far. Do remember that you already use much of the language quite correctly and without struggling to think of the 'grammatical tags' that have been identified here. The point of being able to give names to the parts of speech is to improve knowledge about communicating and to enhance your skills of writing by developing increased confidence. Even if you feel unable to perceive all the parts given in the next exercises, credit yourself with considerable analytical powers for having seen that words perform different functions in a sentence.

Take a sheet of paper and list the eight parts of speech in a column on the left-hand side. If you need to remind yourself of the function of each, put the 'shorthand definition' alongside.

Noun	Name
Pronoun	In place of name
Adjective	Added to the name
Verb	Action
Adverb	Added to the verb
Preposition	Position indicated
Conjunction	Junction between words
Interjection	Thrown in!

Study the following sentences and place the words in their appropriate places in the column. Answers in the Answers Section at the end of the book.

1 A person who analyses sentences has a strong mind.
2 The man who closely analysed every sentence he read showed strange behaviour.
3 In most newspapers there are sentences that are good examples.

4 Oh! you should occasionally stop, look and listen to the words around you.

Use your daily newspaper for practice. Look at the headlines and try to work out the function of each word. Remember that these headlines are often written in a form of 'shorthand' in that they do not always contain finite verbs. If that is so, they are not strictly sentences. However, they use language in a clever, incisive way and are worth looking at.

After you have tried to analyse, say, five headlines, look at the opening sentences of the stories that they introduce. These should contain finite verbs and be 'correct'. Put the words into the appropriate spaces on your grid to show that you recognise their functions in the sentence.

It is worth noting that the usual requirement for journalists is to bring the main facts and features into their first few sentences. The material conveyed in the latter part of their news items is often incidental and can be left out without loss of vital information. This is to make life straightforward for the sub-editors who have to cut stories to fit the page.

6.3   Agreement of subject and verb

The rule is that the verb must agree with its subject in person and in number only. That is why it is *correct* to write:
'Candidates are reminded that examination results, especially in English and Mathematics, are of interest to prospective employers.'
It is *incorrect* to write:
'Candidates are reminded that the result of their examinations, especially in English and Mathematics, are of interest to prospective employers.

The key words to note here are 'results' in the first example and 'result' in the second. The former required the plural 'are' and the latter really needed the singular 'is'.

There are three main causes of error in subject/verb agreement:

(a) Mistaking a singular subject for a plural – and vice versa.
(b) Failing to identify the true subject and making the verb agree with an *apparent* subject instead.
(c) Treating the subject as singular in one place and as plural in another.

(a) Singulars mistaken for plurals

These are all *singulars*: *anyone*; *anybody*; *each*; *every*; *everybody*; *everyone*:

> *Correct:*   All my journeys on that line *have* been uncomfortable.
> *Correct:*   Each of my journeys on that line *has* been uncomfortable.

Correct: Every man on that job *was* working as hard as *he* could.

Either and *neither* are *singulars*:

Correct: Either of these coats *fits* me, but I prefer the grey one.
Correct: Neither of his theories *holds* water.

Either . . . or/neither . . . nor when used in pairs can give trouble. When the two subjects are of the same number there is no problem:

Correct: Either Miss Jones or Miss Smith *is* going to accompany the guest.
Correct: I believe that neither the politicians nor the electors *are* very clear about the issue.

When the two subjects are of different number the rule is that the verb agrees with the *nearer* of the two:

Correct: Neither the pupils nor their teacher *understands* the new timetable.

Kind; *sort*; *type* are *singulars*. If you want to use them as plurals, you must add an *s*:

Correct: I find that the kind of book *pleases* older readers.
Correct: That type of question *is* being discontinued.
Correct: Those sorts of sweets *are* not selling well.

A pair of is *singular*:

Correct: A pair of pliers *was* found in his locker.
Correct: Insulated pliers *are* essential for electricians.
Correct: A sharp pair of scissors *is* needed for that job.
Correct: Those scissors *were* stolen from my shop.

Some multiple subjects are singular. When the sense of the sentence makes one of the elements in a multiple subject appear subordinate, then the subject is singular:

Correct: The chief inspector of accidents *and* his assistant *are* starting the investigation.
Correct: The chief inspector of accidents *with an* assistant *is* starting the investigation.

Together with and as *well as* cause a similar problem:

Correct: The genuine article, together with a skilful copy, *was* on show.
Correct: The protestor, as well as his wife, *was* subjected to abuse.

(b) Finding the true subject

The problem of 'attraction' crops up frequently. Plurals standing between the true subject and its verb 'attracts' us into making the verb plural when its true subject is singular:

Correct: A crate of bottles standing on the pavement *was* over-turned.
Correct: A collection of his paintings *is* on show at the town hall.
Correct: That herd of cows *contains* some prizewinners.

In those examples the true subjects were all collective noun subjects. Greater difficulty arises when a non-collective singular noun subject is separated from its verb by plurals:

Correct: The *wording* of examination questions presupposes that candidates understand grammatical terms and *is*, in con-sequence, misunderstood by ill-prepared candidates.

(c) Collective nouns

These can be singulars *or* plurals according to the sense of the sentence.
  If you are thinking of the group named by the collective noun as a *whole* – as one thing – treat it as a singular:

Correct: The team has been unchanged for half the season and *its* chances of winning the cup are excellent.
Correct: The government *has* decided that the compensation act must be amended.

If you are thinking of the separate individual items that make up the group named by the collective noun, treat it as a plural.

Correct: Occasional coughs, shuffling feet, one or two whispers showed that the audience *were* restless.
Correct: The plane touched down at 3 o'clock, and within a few minutes the team *were* through customs and, after a tour that had lasted six weeks, *were* heading for *their* homes.

  That last example illustrates the need for consistency. The singularity or plurality of the collective-noun subject affects subsequent pronouns and possessive adjectives as well as the verb. All the parts of speech must be handled in the same way. Too often you will hear or read news items in which consistency is flouted.

Incorrect: The government has decided to give priority to their policy for reducing inflation. (If *has* is correct it should be followed by *its*.)
Incorrect: The jury have been unable to agree on its verdict. (If *have* is correct – and it is because the members of the jury had

at least two different points of view – it should be followed by *their*.)

6.4 Problems of case

(a) Do not be afraid of 'me'!

The rule is quite clear and must not be broken: when the personal pronouns (first person singular and plural) are in the nominative case (when they are the subject) *I* and *we* are correct. In all other cases *me* and *us* are correct.

> *Correct:* Do you think that they are likely to give *you* and *me* an invitation?
> *Correct:* It has always been a problem for *us* idealists.
> *Correct:* The property was divided between my brother and *me*.
> *Correct:* The lawyer himself called in with the news and told my dad and *me*.

The last example, above, indicates the proper use of a reflexive pronoun.

The reflexive pronouns (*myself*; *yourself*; *himself*; *herself*; *itself*; *ourselves*; *yourselves*; *themselves*) are used to refer back to a noun or a pronoun that has already been used in the sentence.

> *Correct:* If you want something done properly, do it yourself.
> *Correct:* I was surprised that they fetched the shopping themselves. They usually get Mrs Jones to pick it up for them.
> *Incorrect:* The members of the club presented my wife and myself with a silver teapot.

The writer of that sentence is afraid of *me*. He dodged it by substituting *myself*. I wonder whether he would have written: 'The members of the club presented myself with a silver teapot'?

(b) Relatives cause trouble

It is *grammatical* relatives that we are discussing! They often prove to be a trap, yet the grammatical rule is clear.

The relative pronoun takes its person and number from its antecedent and it 'passes them on' to the verb of which it is the subject:

> *Correct:* Some good critics believe her to be one of the finest novelists that *have* emerged in the last five years.

relative pronoun: that; *antecedent*: novelists; *verb*: have emerged.

> *Correct:* In my judgement he is the best goalkeeper that *has* played for this club since England won the World Cup.

relative pronoun: that; *antecedent*: goalkeeper; *verb*: has played

> *Correct:*   The officer at Sandhurst was one of the many *who* retired from the service last year.
>
> *Correct:*   She was by far the best of the singers *whom* we auditioned yesterday.
>
> *Correct:*   Put Johnson down on the list of subscribers to *whom* we send the newsletter.
>
> *Correct:*   It is ironical, but I am quite sure that it was Peters, *whom* we sacked, *who* did such a splendid job for our rivals, Dart & Co.
>
> *Correct:*   He is the candidate *who*, I think, will win the election.
>
> *Correct:*   He is the candidate *whom* I think the best of a bad bunch.

6.5   'That which confuses'

The use of the relative pronouns can cause confusion. Remember:

Standing for persons:	who; whom; whose
Standing for things:	which
Standing for persons or things:	that

Though that can stand for either person or things, we use *who* or *whom* when the antecedent carries a strong personal flavour.

Compare: 'I am sure it was the man that I saw in the street' with 'I am sure it was Bill whom I saw in the street' (and remember that we *never* use 'which' to stand for a person.)

There is an important distinction between *that* and *which*. Use *that* to introduce a defining clause and *which* to introduce a non-defining clause.

Compare: 'The road *that* links Stafford with Newport is the A518.' with 'The A518, *which* carries a lot of traffic, links Stafford with Newport.'

They are both correct, but the first contains a defining clause and the second a non-defining clause.

What is a defining clause?

A defining clause is one that answers questions such as '*Which one?*' It gives us specific information about (it defines) its antecedents: 'The road *that* links Stafford with Newport . . .' (Which road? The road that links Stafford with Newport.)

What is a non-defining clause?

It is a clause that provides a description of – but does not precisely identify – its antecedent.

N.B. The non-defining clause is *always* marked off from the rest of the sentence with commas.

There is a difference in meaning between these two sentences:

> Students, who are entitled to free seats, should apply immediately.
> Students who are entitled to free seats should apply immediately.

In the first sentence the relative clause is non-defining, and it is marked off with commas. The sentence tells us that all students are entitled to free seats and that they should apply immediately. In the second sentence the relative clause is defining, and it is not marked off with commas. The sentence tells us that *some* students are entitled to free seats and that those who are should apply immediately.

All that sounds more complicated than it is.

Remember: use commas to mark off non-defining clauses; and use *which* to introduce them (when they relate to things).

Remember: do not use commas to mark off defining clauses; and use *that* to introduce them (when they relate to things).

A quick way to test the construction is: 'Commas comment; no commas define.'

Activity 6.1

Work out the differences in meaning between the following pairs and try to imagine the situations where they could cause trouble!

> My wife, who is French, has lived in England for ten years.
> My wife who is French has lived in England for ten years.

(Which sentence implies bigamy or even polygamy?)

> Women who have dull jobs appreciate their holidays.
> Women, who have dull jobs, appreciate their holidays.

(Which sentence maintains that all women have a very difficult time?)

> The car park that is full causes traffic congestion.
> The car park, which is full, causes traffic congestion.

(Which sentence indicates that traffic congestion is caused by having only one car park?)

> The meals, which were enjoyed, were worth paying for.
> The meals that were enjoyed were worth paying for.

(Which sentence shows that everyone at the table had a good time?)

Other pronoun problems

Watch out for 'Ambiguous reference'

Every pronoun must have a clear and readily identified antecedent. It may be possible to sort out the meaning of the following statement; but the writer makes it hard for his reader by using pronouns ambiguously.

> The chancellor's press secretary said that he would refuse to make a statement until the new measure was formally published, but that he was confident that it would surprise financial circles when it appeared.

Be warned that 'No reference' can cause problems
It is always dangerous to make *it, this* or *that* refer to a preceding phrase, clause or sentence. In the following example *This* (at the beginning of the second sentence) defeats the reader's attempts to assign to it any precise antecedent in the preceding sentence.

> Speaking in his constituency last night, the Home Secretary was eager to defend the government's recording in liberalising the criminal laws, reminding his audience that he had set up a Royal Commission, that its report was expected soon, and that he would give urgent consideration to it, to the evidence submitted to it, and to the majority view as expressed in the vote. This must inevitably influence his judgement of the complicated issue and, as he claimed, history's judgement of his record.

'Wrong reference' is a frequent error
Be aware that in official correspondence and regulations, the following can pass unnoticed:

> *A* suitable candidate for this post will have good grades in English and in Mathematics as well as reasonable grades in at least two other subjects at GCSE. *They* will also have good shorthand and typing speeds.

6.6   Putting phrases in the right places

We use language so naturally that we rarely stop to think about the ways in which we build words into larger linguistic structures – into phrases, clauses, sentences and paragraphs. While everything is going smoothly we neither wish nor feel the need to question what we are doing.

However, we all come across problems from time to time and find ourselves sadly reflecting: 'I knew what I wanted to say, but I couldn't find the words' or 'I know I didn't make myself clear' or 'I didn't make the best use of the material I had' or 'I hope the examiner reads it in the way I meant it.'

The two best ways to overcome these structural problems are:

1 To take thought before writing and to outline your sequence of ideas. This plan then gives an almost 'architectural' basis to your writing in that firm sentence structures and well-made paragraphs become ingrained.
2 To make sure that the phrases are in the right place and that they are 'cemented' by effective punctuation.

This chapter will finish with the advice that the comparison between building and writing is close and that phrases are like the sections of brick that have to be firmly in the right place to ensure strength.

A phrase is a group of words that makes sense, but not complete sense on its own. It is not an independent utterance. It has to become part of (to be 'built into') a larger word structure.

A sentence is a group of words that makes complete sense on its own. It is an independent utterance.

Grammarians argue about the definition of a sentence, but for our present (and very practical) purposes the definition just given is satisfactory. It works.

The following three groups of words are *phrases*:

1 at half-past eight;
2 at him;
3 on each front page.

The following three groups of words are *sentences*:

1 The newspapers arrived at half-past eight.
2 The headlines shouted at him.
3 His photograph was on each front page.

___ Activities 6.2 _____

Build each of the following phrases into a sentence:

1 over the bridge	4 at the end of the film
2 with considerable excitement	5 after the election
3 by the last day of the month	6 following the announcement

When you read through your sentences, you will probably feel confident that you have achieved a sense and good order. The ideas promoted should be complete in themselves and contained between the cementing forces of the capital letter at the beginning of the sentence and the full stop at the end.

It is necessary to avoid fragmentation that creates irritation and weakness. It occurs when the full stop is used too soon and cuts off a piece of a sentence.

Look at the following examples of *sentence fragments* and check to see whether you could have avoided anything similar:

1 Each week the principal meets the student committee. Chiefly to discuss routine matters.
2 The pupil's progress was remarkable. Considering his previous carelessness and evident boredom.
3 The young policeman kept back the onlookers. While his more experienced colleagues attended to the injured man.

Sentence fragments are caused by using a full stop too soon.

Run-together or fused sentences are caused by using a full stop too late.

Look closely at the ways in which there is a need for the full stop to be used more decisively in each of the following sentences:

1 My father bought me a train set when I was six later on he added accessories.
2 I must mow the lawn today there may not be another chance for weeks the weather is so bad.
3 Perhaps the best way of interpreting what politicians say is to believe nothing that is certainly my uncle's way.

Perhaps this is a good place to end the chapter, before we 'run-on' to the next topic, which is punctuation. Various ideas have been promoted here about seeing words, phrases, sentences and paragraphs in terms of architecture, structures, bricks and mortar. If these analogies are useful and help you to see your written work in terms of creating strong bonds between you and your readers, then it is to the good. The 'linking' ideas in the next section will be connected with signalling. Punctuation marks are the signals that we give one another when we write. They are the outward and visible signs of the ways in which we marshal our words.

7 Plain sense (3): accurate punctuation

All systems of human communication need guides. Sometimes these are in the form of teachers, sometimes they are printed manuals, sometimes word-of-mouth instructions and sometimes they are special codes which have taken years to devise.

The most obvious are the various sorts of body language through which the people signal to one another by eye, facial, hand or finger-gestures. Another is the complex system of road signs, indicators to traffic and hand signals used by motorists. These are embodied in the various Highway Codes. Then there are the gestures used for special needs – such as deaf-and-dumb signs; morse codes; referee and umpiring signals; ritualistic movements in religious practices.

The 'traffic' of written words has to be controlled and managed. That is what this book is about. Part of the business of control is to be able to indicate how the words should be divided and how the ideas that they convey should flow. We have to be able to halt words, slow their pace by pauses, allow people's remarks and speeches to be introduced and concluded, engineer interruptions, give emphatic gestures and suggest queries and mysteries.

All these features are possible through a series of dots, strokes and harmless-looking squiggles known as 'punctuation marks'. They are, in fact, a highly sophisticated communications-system that is universally applied to the English language and which can be learnt with rapidity. Trends in punctuation use vary according to grammatical fashions. The tendency today is towards lighter punctuation than was the practice only a few years ago: a trend that does nothing to lessen the writer's obligation to observe the accepted conventions.

This chapter lists the applications of all the punctuation marks that you must use at some time or another. It also offers advice on those cases in which there is choice.

7.1 The full stop

The full stop . is used:

1 To mark the end of a sentence, unless the sentence is a question or an exclamation.
2 To mark shortened forms of words. Its use as an abbreviation marker

varies, for some writers use the full stop to mark every shortened form. The following advice represents sound practice.

  (i) Use a full stop to mark the shortened form of a word *unless* the shortened form ends with the same letter as the full word.

    Examples: Oct. – October; Dr – Doctor; Mr – Mister. Strictly speaking, Oct. is an abbreviation, but Dr is a contraction – the middle of the word has been left out: D(octo)r.

  (ii) Abbreviations in very common use do not need full stops.

    Examples: BBC, EEC, RAF.

 (iii) Acronyms (names formed from the initial letters of the separate words making up the name) never have full stops.

    Examples: NATO, UNESCO.

3 Omissions are marked by three full stops. These are called ellipsis marks.

  Example: 'The inquiry must look into the honesty of . . . all parties.'

7.2   The comma

The comma , is used:

1 to separate words, phrases or clauses used in a series.
Examples: She bought flour, tea, milk, bread, and butter. She moved quickly through the barrier, around the shelves, past the check-out, and out of the shop. She walked down the road, found the bus stop, caught the first bus, and was back home in a few minutes.

    Many writers do not use a comma before 'and' in a series. They would write: 'She bought flour, tea, milk, bread and butter. The argument in favour of a comma before 'and' is that it reflects the sense more accurately.

Compare:

    She bought flour, tea, milk, bread, and butter

with

    Her breakfast consisted of coffee, cereal, bread and butter.

The example shows that the writer must think about his use of punctuation.

    You will not be *wrong* if you use, or do not use, a comma before the *and* at the end of a series. Try to make your punctuation reflect the shade of meaning that you are conveying.

2 to mark off introductory words from the main body of the sentence.
Example: In spite of this, progress has been rapid.

  (i) In that example the reader would have wondered how to read the sentence if there had not been a comma after *this*. In such a case, a comma is necessary.

Further examples: However, punctuation is lighter nowadays.

Because of that, delay was inevitable.

(ii) When there is no initial doubt as to how the sentence should be read, the comma after the introductory word(s) may be omitted.

Examples: In spite of this progress our profits are still too low.

In such a case there is no need for a comma.

3   to mark off words in apposition.

Examples: Napoleon, the Emperor of the French, threatened invasion.

Our Managing Director, Mr Michael Smith, is retiring soon.

4   to mark off a person or persons addressed.

Examples: In my view, gentlemen, we must economise.

I ask you, chairman, for your ruling.

5   to mark off a parenthesis.

Examples: Our latest model, mains- or battery-operated, is selling rapidly.

The strategy, drawn up long ago, worked very well at first.

6   to mark off a participial phrase.

Examples: Turning over the pages, he realised what a masterpiece it was.

Referring to our earlier correspondence, I find that your position has changed.

7   to mark off a non-defining relative clause (revise section 6.5). This is one of the most important uses of the comma. It is an outstanding example of the way in which the use of punctuation changes the sense of a sentence.

(i)   A non-defining relative clause must be marked off from the rest of the sentence by a comma (or a pair of commas).

Examples:

Commas, which are optional, are frequently used punctuation marks.

Rail concessions are available to senior citizens, who are usually well aware of their entitlement.

His final play, which was produced on television on the day of his death, set the seal of his greatness.

If the comma – or commas – were removed from these sentences, the meaning would be destroyed.

(ii)   A defining clause must *not* be marked off from the rest of the sentence by a comma. (It is advisable to introduce a defining relative clause with *that* rather than with *which* when the relative refers to a thing – see Section 6.5.)

Examples:

Commas that must never be omitted are those indicating a parenthesis.

Food products that were designed for microwave cooking did not become common until after 1985.

The report concentrates on the circumstances of early schooling that are the most detrimental to the adolescent.

Activity 7.1

Continue your study of commas in defining and in non-defining clauses by sorting out the differences in meaning between the sentences that follow:

1 The anthropologist made an exhaustive study of the islanders who were cannibals.
2 The anthropologist made an exhaustive study of the islanders, who were cannibals.
3 People under the age of twenty-six who are entitled to low fares should obtain their tickets from the special booking-office.
4 People under the age of twenty-six, who are entitled to low fares, should obtain their tickets from the special booking office.

7.3   The semi-colon

The semi-colon ; is used:

1 to separate items in a list when the items themselves contain commas.
   Example: Extras obtainable for this model include: car phone, with, or without amplifier; stereo system, with two or four speakers; electrically-operated windows, separate control or master-switch; tinted-glass; stainless-steel exhaust.
2 to separate clauses having a strong connection with each other that could be broken if they were divided into separate sentences.
   Examples: In an out-of-the-way place like this, old customs linger on; I have myself witnessed maypole dancing and Halloween rites.
   The immigrants had been led to believe that houses were easy to come by; however, six months of fruitless searching convinced them that this was not the case.
   Though, not doubt, tempted to make political capital out of the issue, the Leader of the Opposition was fair in his comments; but, to everybody's surprise, the Prime Minister's supporters showed little eagerness to support their leader.

7.4   The colon

The colon : is used:
1 as an introducer.
   Examples: You will find that his actual words were: 'I do not wish to attend every meeting.'
   In the study the following lots will be sold: bookcases, manuscripts, typewriter, desk.

2 It is *occasionally* used to divide main clauses, but only when there is a dramatic and sharp contrast between the statements.
Example: Man proposes: God disposes.

You will probably come across this use of the colon in your reading. For your purposes at this stage it is better kept as an introducer.

7.5 The question-mark

The question-mark ? is used:
after every *direct* question; and that *includes* commands and requests worded in the form of a question.
Examples: Are you going to the match tomorrow?
Will you send me a copy of next season's fixtures?

Do not use a question-mark after questions in reported (indirect) speech.
Correct: They asked why our quotation was late.

7.6 The exclamation mark

The exclamation mark ! is used:
 after interjections and exclamations.
Do not overdo its use. Emphasis is better achieved by careful word-choice and sentence-patterns than by peppering your writing with exclamation marks.

7.7 The apostrophe

The apostrophe ' is used:

1 to signal possession.
Examples: a man's cap; children's toys; ladies' dresses.

 (i) To singular noun add *'s* – James/James's pen.
 (ii) To plural noun *not* ending in s add *'s* – women/women's rights.
(iii) To a plural noun ending in s add only the apostrophe – boys/boys' shoes.

Notes
 (i) Singluar personal nouns ending in s sometimes cause trouble. Stick to this rule: when a singular personal noun ends in s make it possessive by adding *'s* – Keats/Keats's poems; Dickens/Dickens's novels; James/ James's car.
 (ii) Multiple noun possessives. Add the apostrophe to the last noun – Barnum and Bailey/Barnum and Bailey's Circus.
(iii) Compound noun possessives. Add the apostrophe to the last word – mother-in-law/mother-in-law's house.

(iv) NEVER use an apostrophe with possessive adjectives and possessive pronouns. They are already possessive. *For example:* Is that their car? Yes, it is theirs.
 (v) FINALLY remember that *it's* means 'it is'. You must not use an apostrophe with the possessive pronoun or the possessive adjective.
    Correct: The cat returned to its home.

2 to mark contractions.
  Examples: hasn't; didn't; two o'clock; the Summer of '90.

7.8   Inverted commas

Inverted commas ' ' and quotation marks " " are used:
to indicate the actual words spoken or written. Some authorities maintain that inverted commas are used to convey words that have been spoken and the quotation marks show words that have been written. However, it is common practice for either the single or double varieties to be used depending on the 'house style' of the publisher, company or writer. Just remember to be consistent.

Examples: He said, 'Let me have your answer by tomorrow.'
              Shakespeare wrote: 'There is a tide in the affairs of men'.
Notes

1 A comma or a colon is placed after the 'saying' verb and before the quoted words.
2 Remember to close the inverted commas or quotation marks when the direct speech or quoted material ends.
3 When there is quoted material within the direct speech it must be indicated.
   Example: 'My favourite remark,' she said, 'is Edmund Burke's observation, "Nobody made a greater mistake than he who did nothing because he could only do a little."'
4 The title of a book, poem or play should not be regarded as a quotation. It can be indicated by being underlined. This helps to differentiate between the title and, say, its leading character.
   Example: Shakespeare's *Julius Caesar* is primarily about Brutus and his relationship with both the living and the ghostly Julius Caesar.

___ **Activity 7.2** ___

Study the following and see whether you can spot why inverted commas and quotation marks have been used.

  (i) The witness said, 'I cannot be certain, but I think it was just after midnight.'
 (ii) The boy announced, 'My school motto, *"Mens bona regnum possidet"* means "A good mind possesses a kingdom."'

(iii) 'It does surprise me,' said the manager, 'that you can be so positive about this matter.'

(iv) 'Can you be sure that my cue is, "Have you seen him?"' asked the actor. (One question mark does the work of two.)

(v) 'I certainly enjoyed Jane Austen's *Emma*,' remarked the student, 'but I can't say that I particularly liked Emma herself!'

7.9 Round brackets

Round brackets ( ) are used:
   to mark off a strong parenthesis.

A pair of round brackets is used for this purpose when the writer feels that a stronger mark than a pair of commas is needed.
Example: Caesar's ambition (so skilfully denied by Mark Antony) was feared by Brutus.

7.10 Square brackets

Square brackets [ ] are used:
   to indicate that the words enclosed within quoted matter are not part of the original material.
Example: The critical passage is: 'I do not deny that it [the treasure] played some part in my plans.'

7.11 The dash

The dash – is used:

1 in pairs, as an alternative to the parenthetical use of round brackets.
2 to separate a 'summing up statement' from the items that have preceded it.
Example: The layout, the circuit, the components, the materials – all add up to an entirely new concept for such a transmitter.

7.12 The hyphen

The hypen - is used:

   to link together the elements of compound words such as: mother-in-law.

Many words that begin as hyphenated words lose the hyphen as they are absorbed into common use.
Examples: lookout, seaplane, weekend.

However, the hyphen plays a vital part in some words. Study the following:

> Have you re-covered/recovered your umbrella.
> I hear that all the players have re-signed/resigned.

7.13 Summing up

The intention of this chapter has been to show you the wide range of signs that are available to help you guide your words through particularly congested areas. These are, of course, the various areas, measured only in a relatively few square inches, available to you on notepaper, in examination scripts, in exercise-books, or on computer screens – in fact, wherever you wish to make your words create a lasting impact. The words not only have to convey the meanings intended, they have to be kept apart from one another. If they are not, muddles occur, meanings are lost, confusion reigns. The effective use of punctuation marks is a sign of good order.

This short 'crash course' that appeared in *The Spectator* should help us all to avoid 'crashes' of the linguistic variety. Take note . . . take care.

The argument about how much grammar should be taught in schools will rage on until there is no more grammar left to teach, or grammarians to teach it. Even educational minimalists, however, can scarcely object to a short crash course on the use of English, sent to me by a correspondent. It is the work of two Americans, Helen Ferril of the *Rocky Mountain News* and Ernest Tucker of a now-defunct Chicago newspaper:

1 Don't use no double negative.
2 Make each pronoun agree with their antecedent.
3 Join clauses good, like a conjuction should.
4 About them sentence fragments.
5 When dangling, watch your participles.
6 Verbs has to agree with their subjects.
7 Just between you and I, case is important too.
8 Don't write run-on sentences they are too hard to read.
9 Don't use commas, which aren't necessary.
10 Try to not ever split infinitives.
11 It's important to use your apostrophe's correctly.
12 Proof-read your writing to see if you any words out.
13 Correct spelling is esential.

⑧ Finding the right words

8.1 Vocabulary

(a) Definition

The Shorter Oxford English Dictionary supplies several definitions of the word 'vocabulary'. The one that we have chosen to use here fits the sense in which the word will be used in this section: 'The range of language of a particular person . . .'

(b) The advantages of a large vocabulary

Your vocabulary is the range of words that you can use. The larger it is, the better will be your performance in all aspects of English-language work. A large vocabulary helps you to express your ideas precisely, vividly and without repeating yourself in composition. You cannot do well in comprehension without a large vocabulary, for the passages and questions involve a range of words much wider than that of daily conversation. When summarising, the need to condense makes it essential that you have an ample stock of words from which to make an apt selection.

All other aspects of learning benefit from an extensive vocabulary. A good command of words adds greatly to your capacity to deal successfully with situations in business and leisure. A liking for words will also give you a great deal of pleasure and improve your conversational skills. In short, a good personal stock of words coupled with the ability to use them effectively gives confidence and commands respect.

8.2 Different vocabularies

(a) The wealth of words

The English language is rich in its enormous range of words, having been for centuries an 'importer' of words from other languages; words which it then anglicised and used as if they were 'native'. This flexibility in being able to incorporate and use foreign material is, perhaps, one of the reasons why so many people are attracted to the language.

Another source of wealth of words was the fusion that took place (over a long period) between the Anglo-Saxon (or 'Old English') language of the

English – itself already enriched by Celtic and Latin words – and the Norman-French language of the conquerers of 1066. This fusion resulted in profound changes in vocabulary and, of course, in grammar.

We have not the space to do more than mention the fascinating story of our English tongue, but we do recommend you to learn about it. A knowledge of its history helps you to use the English language with greater confidence and fluency. Five excellent (and quite short) books on the subject are: Otto Jesperson, *Growth and Structure of the English Language*: Henry Bradley, *The Making of English*; Simeon Potter, *Our Language*; Anthony Burgess, *Language Made Plain* and Bill Bryson, *Mother Tongue*.

Centuries of word formation and importation and language blending have resulted in a larger stock of words than is possessed by any other language. The Oxford English Dictionary lists about half a million words.

Not even highly educated people have more than a small fraction of this huge total of words at their command. Outstanding linguists may have a vocabulary of, perhaps, 25,000 or 30,000 words. An 'average educated' vocabulary is estimated at 12,000 to 15,000 words. You can get by in everyday English – used merely for the commonplace activities of life – with about 2500 words.

These numbers are approximate and they are not put forward as 'targets'. Your job – for the reasons stated earlier – is steadily to build up your stock of usable words.

(b) Listening and speaking; reading and writing

We all have four different vocabularies, used in the four separate communication activities – listening and speaking, reading and writing.

Of the words that we hear, we understand some that we are not confident enough to use in our own speech.

Of the words that we read, we understand some that we are not confident enough to use in our own writing.

Our listening vocabulary is larger than our speaking vocabulary. Our reading vocabulary is larger than our writing vocabulary.

Another way of putting it is this: we all have a passive vocabulary and an active vocabulary. By taking an interest in words (noticing them and thinking about their meaning and their use) we can enlarge both. The ideal is constantly to narrow the gap between our active vocabulary and an ever-growing passive vocabulary.

(c) Specialised and general

The chapter began with a definition of the word 'vocabulary'. The quotation from the dictionary was left incomplete. In full, the definition reads: 'The range of language of a particular person, class, profession.'

The English language has a vocabulary of half a million words. An individual has a vocabulary drawn from a total number of words theoretically available to him from that huge store and then applied to the situations in which he finds himself in the various activities of his life. That is his vocabulary – his general vocabulary.

The English class-system has seen as many changes as the language. It has been able to accommodate the demands of society. One interesting aspect is that surveys have revealed that people consider the standard of education to be a more important factor in determining an individual's status than the amount of money or quantity of possessions that he owns. An inquisitive mind is apparently rated more highly than an acquisitive tendency. This is a part of a particularly English cultural phenomenon and does not necessarily apply to American attitudes.

The individual may also have a specialised vocabulary, arising from particular circumstances of his life and work. An electrician, a nuclear physicist, a joiner, a doctor, a plumber, an airline pilot . . . all these, and many more, have to have specialised vocabularies in order to be able to do their jobs.

Lawyers, journalists, politicians, actors, printers, publishers . . . all have specialised vocabularies. So do cricketers, pupils at a particular school, football fans, pop-music addicts, Cockney, Yorkshire men and women, people who live in Devon and Cornwall, or Lancashire, or Somerset, etc.

When the specialised vocabulary arises from geographical circumstance we call it a dialect vocabulary, but it is a specialised vocabulary, just as an occupational or leisure-interest vocabulary is a specialised vocabulary.

Sometimes expressions belonging to a special vocabulary enter the general vocabulary of the language. For example, 'getting into the charts' is now used generally to describe the achievement of popularity. It has nothing to do with navigation; it originated in the vocabulary of the pop-music world.

No doubt you can think of many other examples of words that were once specialised but are now in the general vocabulary. (Have a look at Brewer's *Dictionary of Phrase and Fable* and Eric Partridge's *Dictionary of Cliché*. Both books are usually available in libraries.

With such exceptions, however, the words of specialised vocabulary, useful as they are, should be used only in the specialised context in which they have a precise meaning. The use of items from a specialised vocabulary in an inappropriate context is a fault (see section 8.6).

8.3 Building a vocabulary

Earlier, you were encouraged to take an interest in words. It hardly needs saying that you cannot build your vocabulary unless you become interested in words. You would not expect to become proficient in playing a musical instrument or a game in which you had no interest. You cannot expect to enlarge your vocabulary unless you take a lively interest in the words that you hear and read and in the words that you must speak and write.

'Taking an interest in' words means doing something about them. A genuine interest leads to activity.

First you must notice words. You must 'prick your ears up' when you hear a word that you have not heard before or – just as important – when you hear a word used in a way that you have not heard it used before. You must 'open your eyes' when you read a word that you have not seen written before – or again – used in a way that you have not seen it used before.

We do not need reminding just how much we are surrounded by words in our everyday lives. Radio and television services are broadcast day and night and sets are often left on; newspapers and magazines are constantly within reach; teletext appears in the living-room and fax-machines in the workplace; advertisements are devised to affect us consciously and subconsciously whenever we have a spare moment. The communications media use many techniques and words feature strongly. The impact of words, their ability to arouse and the appeal of the wittiness that they can convey are used by communicators to try to make us stop, look and listen. Yet we have to train ourselves to pick up what is valuable and to disregard what is irrelevant to us.

Then, having trained yourself to notice words that matter, you have 'follow-up' work to do. Most importantly, you must get into the habit of using your dictionary.

(a) Dictionaries

There are three kinds of dictionaries:
 (i) 'Desk' dictionaries. One volume, 'short' dictionaries, admirably suited to your present needs.
 (ii) 'Library' dictionaries. Multi-volume works of reference, providing exhaustive information about words – their meanings, their derivations (etymologies), their use in the past and their use nowadays. The most famous is the Oxford English Dictionary – the world-renowned OED.
(iii) 'Specialist' dictionaries. Devoted to the vocabulary of various specialised subjects. There are dictionaries of science, history, psychology, economics, geography, sports and pastimes, slang, clichés, proverbs, quotations, etc.

In this book we shall concentrate on desk dictionaries, since that is the kind that you must learn how to use.

(b) How to use your dictionary

Even though a desk dictionary contains fewer words than a library dictionary, it still contains a lot. There are 1428 pages in the body of the eighth edition of the Concise Oxford Dictionary, taking the reader from **aardvark** to **zymurgy**, plus 26 pages in the appendix.

Because the lexicographer (dictionary-maker or compiler) is cramming a great deal of information into one book he has to use abbreviations and a fairly complicated and rigidly observed system of 'code signals', such as different type-faces and brackets of various kinds.

To put your dictionary to good use you must familiarise yourself with the lexicographer's abbreviations, his symbols and his pronounciation signs. Not all dictionaries use identical 'codes' so you must get to know those that are used in yours.

Here is the Concise Oxford's entry for the word we are now discussing:

di.ctionary, n. Book dealing, usu. in alphabetical order, with the words of a language or of some special subject, author, &c., wordbook, lexicon (*French–English* &c., *d.*, of French &c. words with English &c. explanation; *d. of architecture* or *the Bible, Shakespeare d.*, &c.); *walking* or *living d.*, well-informed person; (*d. English, style*, &c., over-correct, pedantic. [f. med. L *dictionarium* (prec., —ARY[1])]

The lexicographer has tried to supply in that entry all the information about the word 'dictionary' that you are likely to need. He has also shown you some of the ways – those in most common use – in which you can employ it.

The list of abbreviations and other 'code signals' at the beginning of the *Concise Oxford Dictionary of Current English* (to give the book its full title) explains all the information given in the entry. If you know the code you can 'translate' the entry.

1 The word is pronounced with the stress on the first syllable ('di.c-tionary').
2 It is a noun ('n').
3 Its definition follows, and we learn from it that the words in a dictionary are usually ('usu.') arranged in alphabetical order. We also learn that a dictionary is either general ('the words of a language') or specialised ('of some special subject, author, &c.').
4 A dictionary is a 'wordbook' or 'lexicon'.
5 Examples of wordbooks or lexicons given: French–English Dictionary, containing French words with English explanations; and the '&c.' tells us that there are similar dictionaries of other languages; for example, a German–Spanish Dictionary would contain German words with Spanish explanations.
6 Examples of specialist dictionaries are: a dictionary of architecture, a dictionary of the Bible, a Shakespeare dictionary, etc.
7 We also learn that the word can be used figuratively (see Section 8.5). We can refer to somebody as a 'walking dictionary' or a 'living dictionary', meaning that he is well-informed. We can refer to somebody's use of English as 'dictionary English' or to his writing as

'dictionary style', meaning that his way of talking or writing is over-correct or pedantic.

8 Finally, we learn that the word is derived from a medieval Latin word – *dictionarium*. For further information about its derivation we are referred to the preceding word in the dictionary (prec.,'). That word is *diction* which, the dictionary tells us, came into English from the word *dictio*, which was itself derived from *dicere*, meaning 'say'.

You will not always need to squeeze every drop of information out of an entry; but you will *always* need:

1 to learn the pronunciation and spelling of the word;
2 to study the definitions;
3 to select from the definitions the particular sense (and usage) applicable to the context in which the word is being used or to the context in which you want to use the word.

You will find the answer to each of these in your dictionary.

The words in a dictionary are arranged in *strict* alphabetical order. So, *dictate* precedes *dictator*, which precedes *dictatorial*, which precedes *diction*. Write out the following words in the order in which they would appear in a dictionary.

equator	equatorial	equilateral
equate	equalise	equip
equal	equality	equine
equally	equinox	equilibrium

___ **Test 8.1** _____

(Answer in Answers Section at the end of the book.)
On each page of the dictionary that we are using two words are printed in bold type at the head. For example, on page 639 'largely' and 'last' appear at the top. Examine your own dictionary. Now explain what the two words tell you about the contents of page 639 in our dictionary.

(c) Notes on meaning

You are familiar with the instruction in comprehension questions to explain the meaning of a word *in the sense in which it is used* in the passage. And, earlier in this chapter, we saw that 'dictionary' and 'vocabulary' have more than one meaning. It is vital to remember that most words do.

● Multiple meanings are common. The particular meaning of a word depends upon the context in which it is being used.

So, when you are using your dictionary you must be very careful to select the meaning appropriate to the context in which you have found the word that you are looking up. You must be equally careful to ascertain that the word you are looking up can have the meaning that you wish it to convey in the context in which you are intending to use it.

We shall return to the subject of meaning and context, but here is an example to show how complicated a 'simple' word can be.

In our dictionary we find the word 'flock' can be used either as a noun or as a verb. As a noun it can be used to signify: a lock, tuft, of wool, cotton, etc.; material used for quilting and stuffing made from waste wool or torn-up cloth; powdered wool or cloth for paper-making; a light, loose particle precipitated during chemical or cooking processes; a large number of people; a number of animals of one kind, especially birds, feeding or travelling together; a number of domestic animals, usually sheep, goats, or geese kept together; the Christian body; a congregation, especially in relation to its pastor; a family of children; a number of pupils. As a verb it can describe the action of forming flocks, as in chemistry or cookery; the action of going about together in great numbers; the action of preparing wool, cotton material, etc., to make flock.

Your dictionary cannot tell you which of a word's potential meanings you need. It gives you as many meanings as it has space for, and it suggests some of the commonest ways in which the word is used. It is up to you to select the meaning and usage appropriate to your purposes.

(d) Notes on pronunciation

The best way of learning the 'code' supplied in your dictionary is to apply it to each word as you look it up. If you work out the pronunciation by referring from the word to the code you will soon know how the code works. It is a lengthy and usually pointless process to start by trying to learn the code by heart.

Nor should you suppose that the lexicographer lays down the law. He records the way (or ways) in which words are usually pronounced.

So, if you look up *pedagogy* your dictionary will tell you that the stress (or 'accent', as it is also called) falls on the first syllable; that the three vowels are short; that the first *g* is hard; the second *g* is either hard *or* soft ('gi, -ji); and that the *y* is pronounced like a short *i*.

Whatever particular symbols the 'pronunciation code' in your dictionary employs it directs your attention to:

1 the pronunciation of the vowels;
2 the pronunciation of the consonants;
3 the pronunciation of consonant pairs (such as rough/bough);
4 special difficulties of pronunciation (such as archangel *-k-*, but archbishop; orchard *-tsh-*, but orchestra *-k-*);
5 the position of the stress or accent.

(e) Notes on spelling

What your dictionary does is to record the accepted spelling; and it may draw your attention to accepted alternative spellings. Sometimes, you will find in the preface that a whole series of alternative spellings has been dealt with in a blanket note such as this (from the *Concise Oxford*): '. . . verbs that contain the suffix *-ize* . . . are all given without the alternative forms in *-ise*, although these are still the commoner British (as opposed to American) printing'. The note tells us that, in other words, that we can spell *specialise* either *-ise* or *-ize*.

It is important to be consistent. The publishers of this book, for example, point out to their authors that 'the copy-editor will usually apply certain conventions for the sake of consistency', and instance the following: '*-ise* spellings (e.g. organise, organisation) in all cases where *s* and *z* are alternatives'.

Use *judgement* or *judgment*, but stick to your chosen alternative. It is not sensible to jolt your reader's attention away from the content of your writing by presenting him with *judgement* in one place and *judgment* in another. (The latter form is habitually used in legal works.)

If you follow your dictionary's spelling you will know that you are right. You cannot always be sure that somebody else's spelling is wrong – not until you have studied all that your dictionary tells you about the spelling(s) that it uses and the way(s) in which it deals with accepted alternatives.

(f) Making a wordbook of your own

If you try to do this as a duty – a painstaking attempt to enlarge your vocabulary – that will be laudable, but you will not keep it up for long. It is too laborious a task unless you bring a collector's zest to it.

If you can collect words, as a keen train- or plane-spotter collects trains or planes, you will equip yourself with a most valuable tool, the use of which will do wonders for your word-power.

A small notebook that you can carry around is ideal. Allow plenty of space for each word – a page for each is not too much. Jot down any word that you hear or see each day that attracts your attention because:

   (i) it is new to you;
  (ii) it is not new to you *but* you have never heard/seen it used in that way before;
 (iii) it makes a pleasant noise;
  (iv) it makes a horrible noise;
   (v) it strikes you as being perfectly, uniquely, *right* for the purpose for which it is being used;
  (vi) it is funny;
 (vii) it is sad;
(viii) any other reason that seems good to you.

As soon as possible, look it up in your dictionary. Note the meaning that it had in the context in which you heard/saw it. If you think that it was a misuse of the word, note that. Note any interesting points about its history – where did it come from? – has it changed its meaning as it got older? Note any points that interest you in relation to the occasion on which it was used and the purpose for which it was used. Check on its subsequent uses when it appears again in your growing linguistic experience.

A wordbook can be the basis of an absorbing, lifelong hobby, and a very profitable one.

The final advice must be: read widely and listen attentively. Good readers and listeners usually become good writers and speakers.

8.4   Word-formation

(a) Syllables

You learnt early on in your study of English that your spelling improves if you pay attention to the syllables that form words. For example, it is easy to spell cup/board if you think of its two syllables; and you will not mispell im/me/di/ate/ly if you break it up into five syllables.

Improved spelling is not the only advantage. Study of the syllabic formation of words makes it easier to grasp their meaning. In this way you add rapidly to your vocabulary and learn to make apt use of your growing word-power.

(b) Prefixes and suffixes

There is no mystery about this topic. We use words containing prefixes and suffixes every day of our lives – we have to. If a friend spoke this sentence to you it would not seem remarkable: 'It's nonsense to expect justice in a dictatorship.' Use your dictionary to help you to identify the prefixes and suffixes in those words, and you may be surprised to see how many there are.

Again, it is unlikely that there are any words in the following list that are not already part of your vocabulary: abject; inject; object; project; reject. But you may not have realised that, although each word means something different, they all *stem from* a common (Latin) *root*. It is the different prefixes (*ab-*; *in-*; *ob-*; *pro-*; *re-*) that give the words their different meanings. Use your dictionary to discover the meaning of their common element (*-ject-*).

You already know that many English words form their opposites by adding a prefix (able/*un*able; possible/*im*possible) and you know that many English adverbs are formed by adding the suffix *-ly* to the adjective.

It is not difficult to familiarise yourself with the meaning of the common prefixes and suffixes used in English. Indeed, competent performance demands that you know their meanings – that you can distinguish between, say, *ante-* and *anti-*.

The best way of learning what prefixes and suffixes mean is to pay careful attention to the separate elements of each word that you look up in your dictionary.

The list of prefixes and suffixes printed at the end of this section will give you a useful start, but before using it you must remember two things.

First, remember that the list is merely a *selection* of the prefixes and suffixes that you will encounter. We have drawn your attention only to the commonest examples. (We have indicated the various languages from which the prefixes and suffixes come, not because you necessarily need to remember their origins, but as an interesting illustration of the point made earlier about 'imports' and 'blendings'.)

Second, remember that a prefix often changes its spelling when it is joined to a stem. For example, the (Latin) prefix *in-* means 'not'. So, when it is joined to *distinct*, we have the word *indistinct*, meaning (not distinct). Similarly, we join *in-* to *legal* to make a word meaning 'not legal'; but there is no such word as *inlegal* in English. The word we use is *illegal* (*in-* + *legal* = 'illegal').

This often happens. The spelling of the prefix is changed to bring about a more comfortable grafting of the prefix on to the stem.

When the spelling of the prefix is thus changed ('by assimilation') we get a double consonant at the join (the 'graft') between the prefix and stem. This is a point to look out for in spelling (see Chapter 8).

The word *assimilation* is itself an example of 'assimilation'! It means 'being made like' or 'being absorbed into'. This is how it is formed.

stem: 'similis' (from a Latin root, meaning 'like')
prefix: 'ad-' (Latin prefix, meaning 'to')
suffix: -'ation' (Latin suffix, indicating abstract noun)

But when the word is formed out of these elements the *d* of *ad-* is 'made like' the first letter (*s*) of *similis*. The prefix is assimilated into the stem, and so we have 'assimilate' (*not* 'adsimilate').

PREFIXES

1   English

a-	on
	e.g. aboard; ashore
be-	by, on, around, on all sides (used in many ways)
	e.g. bestride; befriend; belabour; behead; beside
for-	away
	e.g. forgive; forbid; forget
fore-	before (of time or place)
	e.g. foreleg; foretell; forerunner

mis-	wrong
	e.g. mistake; misdeed; mishap
un-	not, reverse
	e.g. unripe; undo; unwind
with-	against back
	e.g. withstand; withdraw

2 Latin

a-, ab-, abs-	away from
	e.g. avert; absolve; abstract
ad-	to
	e.g. adhere; accede; admit; adverb; aggregate
am-, amb-,	round about, both
ambi-	e.g. ambidextrous; ambiguous
ante-	before
	e.g. antecedent; antechamber; anticipate
bi-, bis-	twice, two
	e.g. bicycle; biscuit; bilateral
circu-, circum-	round about
	e.g. circumscribe; circuit; circumnavigate
co-, con-	with
	e.g. concoct; conform; collect; correspond
contra-, contro-,	against
counter-	e.g. contradict; controvert; countersign
cum-	with
	e.g. in certain English place-names such as Chorlton-cum-Hardy
dis-, di-	apart, away, in two
	e.g. dissent, dispel, divide
ex-, e-, ef-	from, out of
	e.g. elect; extract; efflux; eject
extra-	beyond
	e.g. extravagant; extraneous; extraordinary
in-	not, in
	e.g. invade; impose; ineligible; impossible; irregular
non-	not
	e.g. nonsense; nonentity; nonplus
ob-	in the way of; towards, against, in front
	e.g. obstruct; occur; offer; oppose
post-	after
	e.g. postpone; postdate; postwar
pre-	before
	e.g. predict; prefer
re-	again, against, away, back
	e.g. rejoin; rebel; remove; retrace

retro-	backwards
	e.g. retrospect; retrograde
sub-	under
	e.g. submit; succumb; suffer; suspend
super-, supra-	over, above
	e.g. supernumerary; superpose; superfluous
trans-	across
	e.g. transatlantic; translate; traverse
vice-	instead of
	e.g. viceroy; vice-chairman

3   Greek

a-, an-	not
	e.g. atheism; anarchy; atom
anti-	against
	e.g. anticlimiax; antidote; antipathy
auto-	self
	e.g. autograph; autobiography; authentic; automobile
mono-	single
	e.g. monograph; monarchy; monotheism; monoplane
pan-, panto-	all
	e.g. panacea; panorama; pantomime
para-	beside, as, beyond
	e.g. parable; parody; paramilitary
peri-	around, about
	e.g. perimeter; periphrasis
poly-	many
	e.g. polysyllabic; polyglot; polytechnic
syn-	together, with
	e.g. syntax; sympathy; syllable; symbol; system
tele-	far
	e.g. telephone; television; telepathy

SUFFIXES

Denoting abstract nouns
1 *English*
   e.g. man*hood*; God*head*; wis*dom*
2 *Latin*
   e.g. wast*age*; priv*acy*; prud*ence*; just*ice*; cult*ure*
3 *Greek*
   e.g. sarc*asm*; hero*ism*; monarch*y*

Denoting agent or doer
1 *English*
   e.g. fath*er*; costermong*er*; pok*er*; shov*el*

2 *Latin*

e.g. occup*ant*; antiqu*ary*; vic*ar*; chancell*or*; ward*en*

3 *Greek*

e.g. mani*ac*; crit*ic*; royal*ist*

Adjective suffixes

1 *English*

e.g. feather*ed*; wood*en*; leath*ern*; mani*fold*; merci*ful*; fiend*ish*; penni*less*; child*like*; friend*ly*; end*most*; loath*some*; wind*y*

2 *Latin*

e.g. aud*acious*; ment*al*; hum*an*; cert*ain*; hum*ane*; err*ant*; provid*ent*; angul*ar*; desol*ate*; host*ile*; flex*ible*; pens*ive*; peril*ous*

3 *Greek*

e.g. gigant*ic*; eulogist*ic*

Verb suffixes

1 *English*

e.g. glimm*er*; spark*le*; quick*en*; har*k*; length*en*

2 *Latin*

e.g. infl*ate*; coal*esce*; puri*fy*; abol*ish*

Adverb suffix

English loud*ly*

(c) Word-borrowing and word-coining

A living language is changing all the time. The way we use English words in phrases and in sentences (the grammar of the language) has evolved over centuries and it is still changing. Changes in vocabulary have been equally remarkable.

Growth has come from literary influences (words from Latin, Greek, and the modern European languages); from war (especially Dutch, German, and French words); from trade (words taken from Arabic, Malay, Spanish, Turkish, and almost every spoken tongue); from word-coining to express new ideas, especially in science, philosophy, and psychology (such coined words are often based on foreign roots which are added Greek, Latin, French, or German prefixes and/or suffixes.

Again, words change their meaning and the ways in which they are used. In the seventeenth century *conceit* had a different meaning from the one we give it today. Shakespeare could use *fool* as a term of endearment, as well as in disparagement; and *naughty* meant 'worthless' and 'wicked'. For centuries *bloody* was not 'impolite'. Words go up and down the social scale and the scale of formality. They come into and go out of fashion.

The chief sources of vocabulary growth and word formation are:

1 by the addition of prefixes and suffixes to a stem (see Section 8.4) (b)).
2 by direct 'importation' from other languages. For example: *Dutch* – spool, trek, skipper; *Arabic* – coffee (*via* Turkish), algebra; *German* – waltz, swindle; *Hebrew* – jubilee, amen; *Italian* – sonnet, stanza; *Persian*

– bazaar (*via* Turkish and Italian), caravan; *Russian* – bolshevik, steppe; *Spanish* – armada, banana.

3 by joining two or more words together (with or without a hyphen), for example: looking-glass, outlaw, God-fearing, nationwide, underwrite. (See Chapter 7, section 7.12, where the use of the hyphen is discussed.)

4 by the invention or coining of words for special purposes, usually to describe inventions or new scientific developments or fields of study. For example: *geology* was coined from two Greek words, *gē* (earth) and *logos* (discourse); *psychology* was coined from the Greek word *psukhē* (soul or mind) plus *logos*; *bicycle* was coined from the Latin prefix *bi-* (twice or two) and the Greek root *kuklos* (wheel); *television* was coined from the Greek prefix *tele-* (far) and the Latin root *videre* (to see), when coined words contain elements from more than one language, they are called 'hybrids'.

5 by derivation from proper names, either in English or in foreign languages. For example, *academy* comes from the Greek name for the garden near Athens in which Plato taught; *boycott* comes from the name of a certain Captain Boycott, an Irish landlord who was ostracised by his neighbours in 1880.

We hope that you will follow up this fascinating subject of vocabulary growth and word-formation. Find out all that you can about the words you use. There are many books about words and the English language. We recommend as a starter *Our Language* by Simeon Potter (Penguin), especially Chapter VII, 'Word Creation'.

8.5   Synonyms, antonyms and homophones

It is useful to study the meaning of these terms before tackling the kind of vocabulary and word-usage tests that are involved in examinations. A knowledge of the synonyms, especially, suggests approaches to language that add to your understanding of how words work.

(a) Synonyms

The word 'synonym' comes from Greek (*syn* plus *onoma*) and it means 'with the same name'. Synonyms are words that mean the same thing, or very nearly the same thing. (Examples are: leap/jump; slay/kill; start/ begin). For the reasons set out earlier in this chapter the English language is rich in synonyms.

However, synonyms are *not* instantly interchangeable words. Whenever you want to substitute one word for another, as you often do in composition, comprehension, or summary, you have to decide whether the word that you are considering as a substitute carries the particular *shade* of meaning that you require.

Your choice involves the following considerations:

1 Words arouse and convey feelings as well as ideas (see Section 8.6). So, for example, although *slay,* 'means' *kill* and *kill* 'means' *slay* no competent writer would substitute 'slain' for 'killed' in this newspaper headline: 'Fifteen Killed on County's Roads in Bank Holiday Black Week.'

2 Very rarely do two words mean exactly the same thing, though they may mean something very similar. For example, although *start* and *begin* can 'mean the same thing' you would choose 'started' rather than 'began' to fill the gap in this sentence: 'The mayor — the 3.30 race at Sandwood, run over two and a half miles for the newly presented Borough Trophy.'

3 Words must be appropriate to the context in which they are used. The context is not merely the sentence in which the words occur but the whole of the paragraph of which that sentence forms a part. Indeed, the *passage*, as a whole, must be taken into account when a choice of words is being made. For example, although *buy* 'means' *purchase* and *live* 'means' *reside*, you cannot just shuffle them around and slot one in instead of the other. There are contexts in which 'purchase' and 'reside' would be the wrong choices. They are *not* simple alternatives for 'buy' and 'live' (see Section 8.6).

4 Words have sounds – even written or printed words are 'heard' by a reader. The sound of the words you are using is an important consideration. No writer sensitive to the sounds of his words would permit himself to write a 'jingle' such as this: 'The general generally expects his subordinates to report their major decisions to him in writing.' (And having substituted 'usually' for 'generally', would you be happy about 'major', later in the sentence? Surely 'chief' would be better *in that context*? The point is a different one, but important.) *Euphony*, then, is to be considered when choosing words.

(b) Antonyms

The word 'antonym' also comes from Greek (*anti-* plus *onoma*) and means 'against a name'. Antonyms are words of opposite meaning: long/short; difficult/easy; known/unknown; good/bad. Many of the considerations that apply when choosing among synonyms apply also when selecting antonyms.

A long journey is (in respect of length) the opposite of a short journey, but opposites are not always quite so straightforward. These two sentences do *not* express a *simple* contrast – they are not 'black and white' opposites: 'I think this fish is good.'/'I think this fish is bad.' Think about them.

(c) Homophones

Greek again: *homos*, 'the same' plus *phonē*, 'sound'. Homophones are words having the same sound but different meanings. For example: gait/gate; fare/fair; be/bee; would/wood. The identity of sound can lead to careless slips, though a little thought should keep you strait/straight in this sentence: 'You would be stopped at the ticket-collector's gate if you had not paid your railfare.'

8.6   How words are used

(a) Sense of purpose and sense of audience

Success in using words depends on having:

- a clearly-thought-out purpose;
- a clear sense of audience.

Get into the habit of asking yourself:

- *Why* am I saying/writing these words?
- *To whom* am I saying/writing these words?

If you ask (and answer) those questions your choice of words (and the order in which you use them) will improve.

  For example, the practical writing question in the examination could well offer this this kind of choice:

Write a letter suitable to the circumstances described in *one* of the following situations:

(a) As secretary to your school current affairs society you have been instructed by the committee to write to the chairman of your local education authority asking him to speak at a meeting of your society. Write the invitation, remembering to give full details of time, place, data, and of suggested topics.

(b) You read in your local paper that the mother of a friend of yours has been awarded a degree by the Open University. Write a letter of congratulation that conveys a sense of admiration for her achievement and that shows your understanding of the hard work and determination called for by the years of study.

  The two tasks have some features in common. They are practical writing exercises. They are letters written by a younger person to an older reader. They demand a knowledge of the conventions of letter-writing.

  However, the differences between the two are at least as important as their similarities. Sense of purpose and a sense of audience should alert the writer to the need to draw on different areas of his vocabulary according to which of the two letters he is writing.

  The *purpose* of the first letter is to invite somebody to accept a speaking engagement. Such a purpose is best fulfilled by the use of crisp, clear-cut business-like language. The utmost clarity is required.

  The *purpose* of the second letter is to convey the writer's feelings of shared pleasure in an achievement and his/her admiration of the qualities of mind and character that made the achievement possible.

The *audience* for the first letter is a stranger, occupying an important position. The writer's choice of words should reflect the degree of formality required, and – though a favour is being asked – an impersonal tone is to be maintained, appropriate to the official nature of the correspondence.

The *audience* for the second letter is well-known to the writer. As the mother of the writer's friend, she has social relationships with the writer. The language must be appropriate to a personal correspondence. The tone should be warmer than would be acceptable in the first letter.

● *Remember*, you cannot choose *appropriate* words unless you keep your mind clear about your *purpose* in using them, and the *audience* for whom they are intended.

(b) Literal and figurative use of words

Everyday speech and writing provide ample proof of the frequency with which words are used figuratively. Expressions such as 'having a finger in the pie', 'over the moon', 'cooking the books' are in everyone's vocabulary.

We do not suppose that someone described as having 'cooked the books' has been boiling books in a saucepan. We all know that the expression means 'falsifying the accounts'. Similarly, we do not interpret 'having a finger in the pie' as meaning *literally* what it says. We know that it means having a share in some action or enterprise, and that it describes an officious person, a meddler, and one who, as a rule, interferes to seek his own advantage.

Unfortunately, a sloppy-minded habit has arisen of seeking to emphasise these figurative (or metaphorical) expressions by qualifying them with the word *literally*. The following example typifies this misuse of language. A pools winner, interviewed on television, and asked how he felt when he learnt of his good fortune, answered: 'Literally, over the moon.' – a nonsensical statement, of course.

The objections to this habit are not trivial. First, it is never desirable to utter nonsense. Second, the misuse of 'literal' weakens the legitimate exployment of language figuratively (or metaphorically). Third, if you acquire this silly trick, you will lose marks in the examination by failing to distinguish between words and expressions used literally and those used figuratively.

The examining boards do not, as a rule, ask candidates to identify 'figures of speech' (see below), but they test their use of words in a way that makes a knowledge of the commonest 'figures' very useful; and they do expect candidates to have a clear understanding of the distinction between the literal and figurative uses of words. An example of the type of question set will make the point clear.

Select three of the following words and use each in two sentences in which the word is (i) used literally; (ii) metaphorically; 'sweets; straw; knot; golden; pastures.

Example: leaden
 (i) The outer shell of oak, reinforced by a leaden lining, had preserved the contents of the coffer through three centuries of exposure to the elements. (literal)
(ii) My enduring memory of that period of waiting for news from the hospital is of the hooting of the passing trains by which the leaden hours were punctuated. (metaphorical)

(c) Imagery and figures of speech

Words can be used to appeal to the reader's (or hearer's) sense of sight, or sound, or touch, or smell, or taste. By appealing to the senses in this way the writer (or speaker) makes his language more vivid. We describe this use of language as the use of *images* – or the use of *imagery*. (NB *Images* and *imagery* – despite their names – do *not* appeal *solely* to the sense of sight. An image may appeal to any one, or more, of the senses, as just described.)
    Each of the following sentences contains an image:

1 The *rosy* clouds of early morning are held to be a warning of rain later in the day. (sight)
2 Away in the distance we heard the *stuttering* of light machine-gun fire. (sound)
3 The neat borders and *velvety* lawns were the park-keeper's pride. (touch)
4 As a conversationalist she is handicapped by her habit of talking nonsense and seeking of *nicotine*. (smell)
5 We woke to the sound of the sea and we drew in great gulps of the *salty* morning. (taste)

As those examples show, an image is a figurative (or metaphorical) use of language.
    Though images can, and often do, consist of a single word, they are frequently part of what are called 'figures of speech'. Even though you may not be asked to *identify* the precise figure of speech being used, questions on language often draw attention to their presence, because they play an important part in conveying shades of meaning – *nuances* of language.
    The list that follows defines and illustrates each of the figures of speech that you are likely to encounter in English-language questions.

Alliteration   The repetition of *consonant* sounds. 'Two toads totally tired trying to trot to Tuttlebury.'
Assonance   The repetition of *vowel* sounds. 'The half-heard word stirred a response from the semi-conscious man.'

Euphemism   The expression of a harsh truth in language that is designed to soften its impact. 'He passed away [died] yesterday.'

Hyperbole   A deliberate and obvious exaggeration to achieve emphasis and force. 'I was so hot at the end of the walk that I drank gallons of lemonade.'

Litotes   Deliberate understatement to achieve emphasis. 'He averaged over 80 per cent in the three papers, so we may guess that he knows a bit of maths.'

Paradox   An apparent contradiction, expressing a truth. 'It was often said of the law of libel that the truer a statement was the more libellous it was.'

Metaphor   A comparison of one thing with another *without* the use of *like* or *as*. 'That foolish economic policy yielded a meagre harvest.'

Onomatopoeia   A deliberate echoing of the sound of the object or action being described by the sound of the words used to describe it. 'The deluge had made a morass of the track over which our squelching footstops wearily fell hour after hour.'

Personification   Non-human objects or abstractions are given human characteristics. 'The weeping skies depressed me and I was thankful when, at journey's end, hospitality smiled and my friends welcomed me.'

Simile   The comparison of one thing with another, introduced by *like as*, *such as*. 'He ran like a deer. (NB Simile says that one thing is *like* another: *metaphor says that one thing is* another. In simile, the comparison is open, confessed, highlighted. In metaphor, the comparison is concealed. The two objects, qualities, actions are fused together.)

Used appropriately, and with originality, imagery and figures of speech add life and lend imaginative power to writing. Misused, they degenerate into stale, secondhand imitations of what the speaker or writer has heard or read. A deliberate attempt at 'fine writing' usually conveys a feeling of artificiality and affectation.

(d) Idioms and proverbial expressions

An idiom is a form of expression (or of grammatical usage) peculiar to a particular language and often having a meaning other than the one that it appears to have.

All languages have their own idioms. For example, in English we say that someone is 'as deaf as a post'; but the French expression (to convey the same sense) is '*sourd comme une pioche*' – 'as deaf as a pickaxe'.

Similarly, in English we say, 'It's ten francs *a* bottle.' In French, the idiom is '*C'est dix francs* la bouteille'.

Mastery of any language demands a fluent use of idiom. That is why *literal* translation from one language into another often results in gibberish. We have to find equivalent idioms when translating.

There are hundreds of idioms in the English language. Here is a selection of the idiomatic expressions that include the word 'head': head and shoulders; heads I win, tails you lose; to have a head on one's shoulders; to lose one's head; to have one's head turned; to make neither head nor tail of it; to be off one's head; over head and ears; to come to a head; to head off; to hit the nail on the head; to keep one's head . . .

Obviously, nobody can sit down to learn all the idioms in the language by heart. You pick up the idioms as you learn to use the language. Idioms have arisen from a multitude of human activities and occupations, from the accumulated experience of generation after generation, until this very moment – and they continue to multiply.

The kind of examination question that involves a knowledge of idiom is illustrated by this test.

__ Test 8.2 _____

(Answers in Answers Section at the end of the book.)
Rewrite the following sentences without using idiom. Do not change the sense.

1 I had not planned to take a holiday just then, but the offer was so good that I decided to make hay while the sun shone.
2 After a game lasting nearly three hours, Jones lowered his sail.
3 A man on the make is not to be trusted.
4 You cannot have much respect for a leader who passes the buck.
5 They were not enthusiastic about the scheme, but his forceful personality and eloquence roped them in eventually.

Proverbs and proverbial expressions are like idioms in that they are the distillation of centuries of general experience. Their sources are as varied as those of idioms. Books, the remembered sayings of famous people, the customs and traditions of particular groups of people, the tackle, conventions, and methods of a multitide of occupations – all provide us with familiar, everyday expressions: a stitch in time saves nine; Homer sometimes nods; it's hard to teach an old dog new tricks . . .

In using proverbial expressions we must be on our guard. Expressions that were fresh, vivid, and exciting when they were first used may well have been dulled with over-use. They have generated into clichés (see Section 8.7). They are then used by lazy thinkers and bad writers. One cannot say that this particular proverbial expression is 'good', whereas that is 'bad'. The judgement of whether or when to employ them is more complicated than that.

As a *general* guide, George Orwell's famous advice about the use of figures of speech may be applied to the use of proverbial expressions:

● Never use a metaphor, simile, or other figure of speech which you are used to seeing in print.

Orwell was encouraging writers and speakers to 'cut out all prefabricated phrases'. Excellent advice. However, proverbial expressions have been, and still are, much used, and comprehension demands that you know the meaning of a great many – even if you are (rightly) fastidious about using them yourself.

(e) Thinking and feeling

Words are used to make their readers/hearers think and/or feel. It is important to be clear about this fact, for in every situation in which we use language (and especially – as examination candidates – in composition, comprehension, and summary) both the meaning of what we write and our understanding of the meaning of others is profoundly influenced by this dual function of words.

A simple everyday example illustrates the point. Observe how the word *red* 'changes meaning' in these sentences:

1 When you're in a hurry all the traffic lights are red.
2 Red is the colour seen at the least refracted end of the spectrum.
3 Don't mention the end-of-term party to him – it's like a red rag to a bull, just at present.
4 We though the committee could carry that motion, but the AGM was packed with Reds and they threw it out.

It is not really the word itself that 'changes meaning' in those sentences. All the meanings that it has are 'built in' to the word. It us *used* in different ways to convey different meanings.

In some of the sentences it was employed so as to emphasise its 'reference'. In others, it was employed so as to emphasise its 'emotive meaning'.

Summary

- Words can be used as 'labels'. They then name and describe *things* and their attributes. This is language used factually and objectively. It is language used to convey 'referential' or 'denotative' meaning. The writer/speaker is saying to his reader/hearer, 'I am dealing with things as they are.'
- Words can be used to 'signal' feelings 'emotional attitudes' which the writer/speaker wishes to communicate to his audience. This is language used subjectively. It is language used to convey 'emotive' or 'connotative' meaning. The writer/speaker is saying to his reader/hearer, 'I am concerned with the emotions that I feel about these things and I wish you to share in my feelings about them.'

In scientific writing and in the practical business-like writing of transactional prose the reference of words is (or should be) uppermost.

In creative writing (and especially in poetry) the emotive meaning of words is as important as their reference.

Reference (denotation) is not 'better' or 'worse' than emotive (connotative) meaning. Sense of *purpose* and sense of *audience* must be your guides to the appropriate use of words.

What – as writers/readers, speakers/hearers – we all have to look out for is dishonest use of language. If you study advertisements and political speeches or articles with a critical eye you will become aware of how often writers and speakers pretend that they are dealing with facts when they are, in reality, peddling emotions. They pretend that they want us to *think*, but they are using language to make us *feel*.

8.7   How words are misused

A common and deliberate misuse of words has just been illustrated. The errors are, of course, not always deliberately committed. The following guidelines will help you to avoid traps into which we all fall from time to time.

- Choose plain words in preference to far-fetched words.
- Choose words drawn from the general vocabulary of the language in preference to words drawn from specialised vocabularies.
- Choose short expressions in preference to long ones – never use more than one word *where one will do*.

Failure to observe those three rules leads to pompous, turgid, windy writing and speaking.

(a) Plain words

As you have seen, the English language draws its vocabulary from many sources and has an abundance of synonyms. In Section 8.5(a)3 we used 'buy/purchase' and 'live/reside' to illustrate that care must be used when making a choice of words. Unhappily, many people honestly believe that the bigger – the more 'important' word – is somehow 'better' than the shorter and more common word. Consequently, the plain, simple word often drops out of use and the once-far-fetched word replaces it. The 'big' word then loses the usefulness – the precise meaning – that it once had.

Your judgement of which word to select when you have a choice should be based on the context in which you are going to use it and the purpose for which you want it. Sense of audience and sense of occasion must guide you.

The young reporter on a local paper who writes: 'The bride's father has purchased a property to present to his daughter and her husband as their future residence' should be 'blue-pencilled' by his subeditor. What he means is: 'The bride's father has bought a house which he has given to his daughter and her husband to live in.'

That does not mean to say that 'reside' and 'residence' have no useful part to play in our vocabularies. There are contexts in which they are 'right'. For example, 'Ranpoor House was the provincial governor's residence in the days of empire.'

The word 'house' would not be an appropriate synonym for 'residence' in that context. But the indiscriminating use of 'residence' instead of 'house' devalues the former word. It loses its special meaning and then ceases to be available for use in the appropriate context.

That simple example illustrates the principle on which you should base your choice between the plain, everyday word and the less familiar, more important-sounding word. Whenever you are about to use the latter ask yourself if it is right for the context in which you are going to use it. 'Do I want its special meaning here'. If the answer is 'yes', then go ahead and use it.

There is nothing 'wrong' with the polysyllabic Latin-derived words of the English language. It is just that they are often misused by people who think that their use lends importance and dignity to their writing.

You do not make yourself important by inflating your style – merely ridiculous.

(b) Jargon

The word 'jargon' comes from a French word meaning 'twittering'. A great deal of twittering can be heard in radio and television interviews and read in reports of the speeches and pronouncements of 'public men'. Take care that it cannot be read in your examination papers.

Jargon is a mode of speech or writing full of unfamiliar terms – words drawn from specialised vocabularies and then used in contexts in which they are not appropriate. Jargon words may come from the specialised vocabularies of science, or sociology, or economics, or the law – or any of the special fields of human knowledge and activity.

There is nothing wrong with the jargon word in its proper context. *There*, of course, it is *not* a jargon word! But in general use it loses its precise meaning and becomes merely trendy; and the jargon-user loses the respect – and often the attention – of his audience.

Examples of current jargon words are: parameters; paradigm; viable; scenario; orientated; escalate – just half a dozen selected from the vogue words of the day. Look each of them up in your dictionary. Then think about the contexts in which they can be used with precise meaning and in which they are, therefore, at home.

The two chief objections to the use of jargon words are: first, out of their appropriate context they are usually inaccurate; second, they give the audience an unfortunate impression of their user. He sounds phoney. He is trying to look tall by walking on tiptoe.

(c) Cliché

A cliché is a hackneyed expression, one that has been used so frequently that it has lost its force. Some clichés have lost their meaning. They are so wearisomely predictable that they succeed only in boring the reader. Cliché-users proclaim their dullness, their lack of originality.

Here is a brief selection of clichés, just to put you on guard against them. I cannot list more than a handful of the thousands in common use, but if you have a look at this list you will be better able to recognise a cliché when you see one. The words that could be used instead of the clichés are printed in brackets.

> abject terror (panic); an ample sufficiency (plenty); at a loose end (with nothing to do); be that as it may (nevertheless); a bolt from the blue (an unexpected misfortune); in the cold light of reason (examined intelligently); common or garden (ordinary); cut to the quick (deeply hurt); done to a turn (perfectly cooked); eat out of someone's hand (be subservient to); fall on deaf ears (to be heard but ignored); in fine feather (in good health and/or spirits); first and foremost (most notable, outstanding) . . .

It would be tedious to continue – just as it is tedious for your reader when you use clichés.

(d) Slang

Words and phrases that are used in colloquial speech are often unsuited to standard English. The *degree of formality* that is appropriate to the particular occasion is the measure of whether slang is permissible or not.

For instance, in a story composition it may be 'in character' for people to use slang in their dialogue. It may be effective for one character to tell another to 'pack it in'.

But if (in the practical writing exercise) you were writing a letter requesting an important person to speak to a school or college discussion society, you would not inform him that 'we usually pack it in at about 7.30'. You would inform him that 'the society's meetings are timed to end at 7.30'.

I am sure that you would not be guilty of a gross use of slang such as that; but we all have to be careful to adjust our vocabulary (and our sentence constructions – see Chapter 5) to the occasion. Our sense of purpose and sense of audience, are, once again, involved in the ways in which we select the appropriate words.

(e) Gobbledegook

Gobbledegook (defined in the *Concise Oxford Dictionary* as: 'pompous official jargon') is found not only in the language used by bureaucrats, but in the language you and I use when we strive to be important, to sound 'learned', to impress. It is then that we make 'turkey-cock noises' – for that is what 'gobbledegook' means.

Gobbledegook is the product of some of the linguistic sins described earlier. It arises from the following bad habits:

- using big words – to try to impress;
- using more words than are necessary – either to give extra 'dignity' to our utterances or to prevent our reader from understanding us quickly and clearly;
- using long-winded, roundabout expressions instead of direct ones – again to increase our importance;
- using passive and impersonal constructions instead of active and personal ones to give an air of authority to our pronouncements.

Here are some examples:

Big-word gobbledegook   My career with Phipps & Co was terminated in the September of that year, when I was translated to Hokums Limited at an enhanced remumeration. (. . . ended . . . moved . . . better pay).

Redundant-word gobbledegook   The congestion on several of the motorways during the Bank Holiday was such that the traffic circulation flow was periodically frozen and brought to a standstill. (. . . at times traffic stopped).

Roundabout gobbledegook   In so far as they can be projected, the adverse economic factors in the immediately foreseeable future are likely to be of the order presently pertaining. (The writer of that sentence cannot get off his verbal roundabout. Not only is he using superfluous words, but his sentence construction is circular. The virtues of plain, direct statement are beyond him. Recast into English, this is what he is trying to say: 'It is unlikely that present adverse economic factors will soon change.'

Passive and impersonal gobbledegook   It is desired to draw attention to the necessity that the regulations governing procedures established to ensure safety in the event of fire should be observed by all residents. (I/We/The manager remind(s) residents that they must obey the fire-drill regulations.)

As you can see from those examples and the comments on them the various kinds of words misuse often occur together. A writer who thinks that plain words will not serve his purpose is usually given to using too many words, roundabout – 'circumlocutory' – expressions, and unwieldy passive constructions.

(f) Danger signals

Whenever you are about to use one of the words and phrases in the following list, stop and think hard.

Far-fetched words (plain equivalents in brackets)

acquaint	(inform; tell)
advert	(refer to)
ameliorate	(make better; improve)
assist	(help)
blueprint	(plan)
ceiling	(limit)
eventuate	(happen; occur; result)
evince	(show; display)
in isolation	(by itself; on its own)
initiate	(begin; start)
locality	(place)
materialise	(come about; happen; occur)
a percentage of	(some)
state	(say)
visualise	(imagine; picture)

Inflated phrases

The use of these almost always brings out the worst in the writer or speaker. If you use any of the following you are usually heading for trouble.

in/with regard to	in the majority of
in the case of	in a position to
in relation to	will take steps to
in connection with	it should be noted that
as to	it is appreciated that
in respect of	a crisis situation

8.8   Good style

(a)   What is style?

The word 'style' is used in many different ways. We talk of a batsman's style; we say of a coat, a dress, or a car that 'it has got style'; we say that a man or a woman 'has style'; we talk of somebody's 'life-style'.

Above all, of course, we speak of a writer's style. It is not only the makers of literature and professional writers who have style. You, too, have style – good *or* bad!

The style in which you write is the *way* in which you carry out any piece of writing; and, as this has been stressed, the way in which you do it must be suited to your purpose in doing it and to the audience for whom it is intended.

Your style, then, is a reflection of your ability to choose appropriate means to achieve given ends. If the means you choose are appropriate you will have a good style.

One purpose is common to all the writing you do. Your purpose is to be understood. Therefore, the virtue common to all the writing you is clarity.

Your style is revealed in your choice of words and in the order in which you arrange your own words. Order and arrangement are discussed in Chapter 5.

(b) The elements of good style

Good style is, obviously, the antithesis of the faults discussed in Section 8.7. There you were encouraged to *avoid*:

- long windedness;
- pompousness;
- affectation;
- slang, jargon, and cliché;
- passive and impersonal constructions.

Put positively, to achieve good style *you must try to*:

- be plain;
- be direct;
- use no more words than are necessary;
- search your vocabulary for the *right* word;
- use active verbs whenever you have a choice.

Those are useful guides to good style, but they will come alive for you only as you deliberately use them in practice.

Reinforce the lessons of this chapter (and those of Chapter 5) by referring to the following books:

H. W. Fowler, *A Dictionary of Modern English Usage*
Sir Ernest Gowers, *Plain Words*
George Orwell, 'Politics and the English Language', *The Collected Essays, Journalism and Letters of George Orwell*, vol. 4
Eric Partridge, *The Concise Usage and Abusage*

8.8 Testing your vocabulary

Try to work through all these tests in the course of your preparation for the examination. Many of them will send you to your dictionary for the answers. Some you should work through on your own. Others are suitable for team work – tackle them with a friend or as part of a small group, discussing them as you go along. Often a test serves its purpose best when it encourages you to look out for similar uses (or misuses) of words in the English of your daily life. It is only through your readiness to apply the lessons of this textbook to your experience of everyday English that you will get the help that we have tried to offer.

Test 8.3

(Answers in Answers Section at the end of the book.)
Fill the blank in each of the following with a word opposite in meaning to the italicised word.

1 He is a *profound* not a . . . thinker.
2 Early on it seemed that he might be good at mathematics, for he tackled *simple* calculations successfully, but his limitations were revealed when he was faced with . . . problems.
3 The old manager's methods were *rigid*, and all the employees hoped for a more . . . approach when his successor arrived.
4 The examiners were surprised by his bad performance in the *compulsory* question in view of his good showing in the . . . section of the paper.
5 The dealer was delighted to be offered a *genuine* antique after seeing so many . . . in the course of a busy day.

Test 8.4

(Answers in Answers Section at the end of the book.)
Express in *one* word the meaning of each of the following.

1 causing, sufficient to cause, or designed to cause death
2 respect highly, confer dignity upon
3 preliminary discourse, sometimes in verse, introducing a play
4 put right, correct, amend, reform
5 immediately, without delay

Discuss your answers when you have completed the tests.

Activities 8.1

Use each of the following expressions in a sentence in such a way as to make its meaning clear.

1 to harp upon
2 to ride roughshod over
3 a square peg in a round hole
4 to look askance at
5 a *quid pro quo*

___ **Activities 8.2** ___

The words paired up in this list are often confused. Use your dictionary and then write a sentence for each word, bringing out the different meanings.

1 practical/practicable
2 uninterested/disinterested
3 intelligent/intelligible
4 ingenious/ingenuous
5 cultured/cultivated

___ **Activities 8.3** ___

Use your dictionary to discover the sense of the prefix in each of the following words.

1 cyclonic
2 expatriation
3 generation
4 hippopotamus
5 hexagon

___ **Activities 8.4** ___

Without changing the sense, rewrite the following in plain English.

1 The Medical Officer of Health extended assurances to the subcommittee to the effect that the occurrence of one isolated case of typhoid was no necessary cause for undue alarm.
2 Speaking in this very same council chamber some twelve months ago I stressed emphatically, and with all the seriousness at my command, that the services of an outside expert engineering consultant should be called in to assist with advice the surveyor's department with the serious problem situation of subsidence in Chapel Street.
3 The Trustees have decided and come to the conclusion that residence within the boundaries of the borough for a minimum period of five years is going to be for the future an essential condition of qualifying to be considered for the award of grants that are within their disposal as Trustees.
4 The treasurer reported that there were serious financial considerations involved in respect of the prospect of completing the new housing estate by the target date that had been set and that a crisis situation could eventuate.

5 In the majority of instances householders who were tenants of the council informed the council's investigating officers in response to the questions put to them that they were satisfied with regard to the scheme for differential rents operative with respect to the rented properties within the council's jurisdiction.

⑨ Spelling

Good spelling creates confidence. It impresses the reader and enables the writer to feel that he is in control. The essential feature is that it shows efficient management of words and control of communications.

Marks are deducted in the GCSE, Advanced Level and professional examinations for bad spelling. It is in our own interests to develop an awareness of the spellings of words and of the damage that poor spelling can do to our images as proficient users of the language.

The main source of help is your own determination to become a good speller and a sense of embarrassment when you discover that you have misspelt a word. These concepts of 'pleasure-in-achievement' and 'pain-through-mistakes' will do much to boost performance.

This chapter contains some useful tips to make it easier for you.

9.1   General advice

1 Read a lot. Then, when you want to use words that you have read, attempt to visualise them. Try to recall what they looked like when you say them in print.
2 Think hard about spelling. You know which words you find difficult to spell. Pinpoint where you go wrong in the words that you misspell. Concentrate on your errors in a methodical way. You will soon find that you are making fewer mistakes.
3 Take an interest in looking at other people's spelling of words – on notices, in shops, advertisements and signs. Do not be too critical of errors, but learn to compliment yourself on mastering difficult words and take pride in using them . . . with confidence.

9.2   Specific and technical advice

(a) Syllablising

Revise Section 8.4. Good examples of the help that the habit of syllablising gives are: vet/er/in/ary; tem/per/at/ure; Feb/ru/ary.

(b) Prefixes and suffixes

Revise Section 8.4. If you notice word formation you will not go wrong, for example: disappoint (dis + appoint); dissatisfaction (dis + satisfaction); innocent (in + nocent − *nocere*, Latin = 'to hurt'); unnatural (un + natural).

Double consonants at the 'joint' of some words will be far less trouble-some if you remember the effect of 'assimilation'. See Section 8.4 – i*l*legal; co*l*lapse a*t*tract'; a*cc*ommodation.

(c) The spelling rules

Although English spelling is not very 'law-abiding', there are some rules that you should know.

Rule 1   *i* before *e*, when the sound is *ee*, EXCEPT after *c*.

> *For example*: piece; grief; achieve; siege; wield; relieve; shield; priest; mischief.

REMEMBER, *after c* – receipt; receive; receiver; deceit; deceive; deceiver; conceive; conceit; conceiver.

BUT when the sound is NOT *ee*; deign; reign; feign; rein; vein; skein; neigh; weigh; weight; veil; feint; eight.

AND some more *ei* words with other sounds: heir; their; sovereign; foreign; height; sleight; forfeit; leisure.

Rule 2   When a word ends with *e* and you add to it:
(a) DROP the *e* when the addition begins with a vowel.

> *For example:* wake/waking; hate/hating.

(b) KEEP the *e* when the addition begins with a consonant.

> *For example*: wake/wakeful, hate/hateful.

EXCEPTIONS: awe/awful; true/truly; due/duly; paste-pastry/ argue/ argument.

Rule 3   When a word ends with *ce* or *ge* and you add to it keep the *e* when the addition begins with *a* or *o*.

> *For example*: peace/peaceable; outrage/outrageous.

Rule 4   When a *stressed* syllable with a *short* vowel precedes a consonant, double the consonant when adding to the word.

> *For example*: mat/matting/matted; rat/ratting/ratted; begin/beginning; dim/dimming/dimmed; transmit/transmitting/transmitted; propel/ propelling/propelled/propeller.

Rule 5   When an *unstressed* syllable with a *short* vowel precedes a consonant *do not* double the consonant when adding to the word.

> *For example*: profit/profiting/profited; limit/limiting/limited.

Rule 6 When the vowel before the consonant is *long* double the consonant when adding to the word.

    For example: refer/referring;referred; prefer/preferring/preferred.

Rule 7 Singular words ending in *vowel + y* (e.g. donkey) form their plurals by adding *s*.

    For example: donkey/donkeys; chimney/chimneys; valley/valleys; alloy/alloys.

Rule 8 Singular words ending in *consonant + y* (e.g. baby) form their plurals by changing the *y* into *i* and adding *es*.

    For example: baby/babies; lady/ladies; territory/territories; parody/parodies.

Rule 9 Most words ending in *our* drop the *u* when the suffix *-ous* is added.

    For example: humour/humorous; labour/laborious; valour/valorous.

Rule 10 Most words ending in *double l* drop one *l* when combined with other words.

    For example: cup + full = cupful; skill + full = skilful; well + come = welcome; all + ways + always; all + though = although; all + together = altogether; all + so = also; all + ready = already; full + fill = fulfil; cheer + full = cheerful.

There are other spelling 'rules', but they have so many exceptions that we do not think they are very useful.

    The ten rules just given are helpful. At least, if you obey them you will be right far more often than you will be wrong.

(d) Groups of words

We all use our own mnemonics to help us to avoid our own habitual spelling mistakes. Many a pupil has mastered 'Mississippi' by chanting the word to himself rhythmically: 'M–i–*double s*–i–*double s*–i–*double p*–i'.

    Grouping words according to their similarities of spelling is a useful way of tackling your own 'pet' mistakes. Here are some suggestions. Add words to each group as you come across them.

Group 1 verbs with an 's' and nouns with a 'c'
verbs: advise; devise; license; practise; prophesy.
nouns: advice; device; licence; practice; prophecy.

Group 2 words ending in '-ence'
convenience; difference; experience; pestilence.

Group 3   words ending in '-ible'
accessible; admissible; audible; contemptible; convertible; eligible; feasible; flexible; forcible; imperceptible; incredible; indefensible; inedible; intelligible; invincible; invisible; irresistible; legible; permissible; plausible; reprehensible; responsible; sensible; susceptible; tangible; terrible.

Group 4   words ending in '-ness'
cleanness; greenness; keenness; meanness; plainness; sternness; suddenness.

Group 5   words ending in '-age'; '-ar' and '-or'
average; courage; damage; sausage; village; calendar; circular; grammar; particular; author; councillor; radiator; surveyor; mentor.

Group 6   plural in '-oes'
cargoes; mosquitoes; potatoes; tomatoes; volcanoes.

Group 7   plural in '-os'
commandos; dynamos; photos; radios; solos.

Group 9   common confusables
accept/except; access/excess; affect/effect; allusion/illusion; altar/alter; ascent/assent; capital/capitol; choose/chose; clothes/cloths; coarse/course; complement/compliment; conscience/conscious; council/counsel; descent/decent; desert/dessert; dairy/diary; dual/duel; dyeing/dying; formally/formerly; later/latter; lead/led; loose/lose; peace/piece; personal/personnel; principal/principle; quiet/quite; respectfully/respectively; stationary/stationery; their/their; to/too; weather/whether.

10 Practical writing and imaginative writing

10.1 Different kinds of composition

(a) Composition in the examination

All examination boards require candidates in English Language to write a composition, and most of them allot more marks to this than to any other question. The composition is sometimes called an 'essay', sometimes 'continuous writing'. Whatever name is given to it, the question requires the candidate to write in 50 to 60 minutes an answer consisting of two or three pages of prose.

Most examining boards include another kind of composition question. This is given various names, of which the most common are 'practical writing' and 'factual writing'. This kind of writing is tested in a separate question – and sometimes in a separate paper – but, like the 'essay' question, it is primarily a test of the candidate's ability to write good English prose.

These two kinds of writing are discussed in this chapter, and the different demands that they make on the candidate are thoroughly explored.

Do not forget that, in your answers to both kinds of question, the examiners are looking for:

- correctness of grammar, punctuation and spelling;
- well-made and varied sentences;
- a piece of writing that shows management of structure and tidiness.

Lively and imaginative work will always be given extra marks, but it is the candidate's ability to write well-organised, clear and accurate English that is the examiners' first concern.

(b) Imaginative writing/practical writing

Bearing in mind that the qualities of good English (as described in the paragraph you have just read) are required in all writing, it is useful to consider composition under the two headings:

- 'Imaginative' (or 'Creative');
- 'Practical' (or 'Factual').

Those terms describe the two different kinds of writing for which the examiners are looking. They also point to the different mental activities that the different kinds of question demand.

Here, for example, are two examination questions that illustrate the two different kinds of writing expected of candidates:

1 Write a story entitled 'A Narrow Escape'.
2 Write a series of instructions of how to operate a cassette tape recorder. Your information should be written for the benefit of a reader who has never come across such a machine.

Clearly, Question 1 is a subject for imaginative or creative composition, while Question 2 is a subject for practical or factual composition.

In answering Question 1 the candidate must imagine or create material that he uses in the composition. In answering Question 2 the candidate must draw on his knowledge of the facts and his practical experience of how the thing is done.

Another difference between the two is the degree of control that each question imposes on the candidate. Question 1 leaves the writer with a lot of freedom to make his own personal response to the subject. Question 2 defines the subject clearly and strictly and, by the way in which it is worded, exercises considerable control over the writer's response to the subject that has been given.

The examining boards emphasise the difference between imaginative or creative writing on one hand and practical or factual writing on the other. The latter is sometimes described as 'transactional' because it stresses the transactions or dealings between people. It is often concerned with tangible objects, while the former is often about conceptual matters.

The essential difference between the two kinds of composition that the examiners demand can be summed up like this:

Imaginative composition	Practical composition
Free treatment of created material	Controlled treatment of factual material

It would, however, be a mistake to think that an imaginative composition does not demand careful planning or that a practical composition does not demand imagination. In this chapter and in the next we discuss the planning and the imaginative demands of both 'free' and 'controlled' writing of the kind that examination candidates are required to undertake in composition questions.

___ **Test 10.1** ___

(Answers in Answers Section at the end of the book.)

Which of the following composition subjects are imaginative (or creative) and which are practical (or factual)? Mark each with an *I* or a *P* to indicate your answer.

1 Describe a pocket calculator. Assume that the reader of your description is not familiar with this kind of machine. Do not exceed 250 words.
2 Describe the sounds of early morning either in the country or in the town. Your composition should be about 500 words in length.
3 Write, in not more than 250 words, instructions to enable a stranger to find his way from the nearest rail or bus station to your home.
4 Give an account of a television programme that you have enjoyed and describe those qualities of the programme that you found especially pleasing. You are allowed up to 400 words.
5 In not more than 500 words write a composition entitled 'The Pleasures of Travel'.

Your work in this Activities section has meant that you have had to make judgements and look for key words in the instructions. These words are the guides as to whether your writing will be 'Practical' or 'Imaginative'.

1 In this question the term 'pocket calculator' suggests something that is relatively standard regardless of the manufacturer. You have to tailor your thoughts to fit in with the specifications of the product and the ignorance of the person whom you are addressing. Practical advice is needed.
2 'The sounds of the early morning' vary considerably. They differ according to the time of year, urban or rural setting, country of the world. The feature that matters is your location, frame of mind and imaginative response.
3 The key words 'instructions' and 'stranger' indicate that practical considerations are necessary. Ingenuity may be helpful; inventiveness will hinder.
4 Here the key words are 'you have enjoyed'. You as a person and a viewer are the main features of this imaginative composition. The television programme itself is of secondary importance.
5 There may be many practical suggestions to enable 'travel' to become associated with 'pleasures'. However, the subject of enjoyment does depend primarily on the way in which you approach life and how your imagination copes with it.

10.2   Planning your time in the composition question

Many examining boards allow one hour for the composition question. Some allow 50 minutes. You must find out how much time your own board allows and then practice writing compositions within the specified time limit.

When an hour is allowed a composition of two to three sides of examination paper is expected. When 50 minutes is allowed a slightly shorter composition is looked for, but it is inadvisable to write much less than two sides.

You will find it helpful to think in terms of a composition consisting of five or six paragraphs. You can then keep this useful structure in mind as you plan your composition.

Introduction: Paragraph 1
Body of composition: Paragraphs 2, 3, 4 (and 5)
Conclusion: Paragraph 5 (or 6)

Do not aim to spend all your time in writing the composition. To do so would be to invite failure. There are other stages in the production of a good answer that are as vital to success as the actual writing. These stages are selection, planning, and revision.

The reasons for spending time on selection, planning, and revision lie in the syllabus requirement for success in the composition question. The various boards word those requirements differently, but the sense of them all is the same:

- plan your composition carefully, so that it has unity;
- paragraph clearly, so that your material is presented in a logical sequence;
- write in a style appropriate to your subject;
- be accurate in punctuation, spelling, and grammar;
- remember that marks are given for quality, not quantity – provided that you write a composition of the minimum length, as stipulated.

When answering a question for which one hour is allowed the time allocation should be of this order:

- reading through the instructions at the head of the paper and making sure that you know exactly what you have to do – one or two minutes;
- reading through all the questions and making your choice – not more than five minutes;
- finding your material, selecting your 'angle of attack', planning your composition – not less than ten minutes;
- writing your composition – about 40 minutes;
- reading through your composition and correcting careless slips – not more than five minutes.

If your board allows less than one hour for the composition question it is the writing time that should be reduced, since in that case a shorter composition will be expected. The other stages described above are as important for a success in a 50-minute question as in a 60-minute question *and they must not be skimped*.

10.3   Imaginative or creative compositions

(a) The personal element in imaginative writing

You may have found the answer to Question 4 in Activities 10.1 surprising. The instruction 'Give an account of a television programme' seems to suggest that a factual composition is expected. If a witness of a road accident was asked to give an account of what he saw, a factual answer would certainly be expected. The question, however, introduced a personal element. The full instructions were: 'Give an account of a television programme *that you have enjoyed* and describe those qualities *that you found especially pleasing.*' The words in italics show you that the material for the composition is to be found in a personal experience.

Consider these instructions:

1 Give an account of how a television programme is produced.
2 Give an account of how a television programme is transmitted.
3 Give an account of a television programme that you have enjoyed.

You can see that 3 introduces a personal element that is not present in 1 and 2, both of which require factual, *objective* treatment. You would need to know a lot of technical facts to write on those subjects, and *you would be expected to confine your answer to those facts*.

When writing about 3, on the other hand, a personal approach is required. You would not be able to carry out the instructions without stating what it was that *you* enjoyed and describing the various ways in which the programme had given *you* pleasure: the excitement of the plot, or the quality of the acting, or the interest of the subject, or the delight of the humour – and so on, according to the kind of programme that *you* had chosen to describe and *your own reactions* to it.

In other words, 3 requires a mainly *subjective* treatment, whereas 1 and 2 require *objective* treatment. That contrast is fundamental to the distinction between imaginative or creative composition on the one hand and practical or factual writing on the other. The imaginative composition always demands that the writer *puts something of himself* into his writing.

(b) Different kinds of imaginative composition

Examination syllabuses refer to different kinds of imaginative compositions. Here are some examples: 'The subjects will normally be narrative, descriptive, or discursive.' 'The subjects may be descriptive, narrative, or controversial.' 'There will be opportunities to write a narrative, descriptive, discursive, or argumentative composition.' 'Dramatic, impressionistic, narrative, and discursive subjects will be included.'

Analysis of all the syllabuses and of past papers shows that the subjects set for composition may be classified under these headings:

1 Narrative
2 Descriptive
3 Discursive or argumentative or controversial
4 Dramatic or controversial
5 Impressionistic.

The alternative names in common use are given in 3 and 4, above.

The requirements of each kind of imaginative composition are discussed, each in a separate section of this chapter. Before that, however, we will study a typical English Language Composition Paper.

COMPOSITION

Time: one hour

Write on one of the following subjects. Pay careful attention to punctuation, spelling, grammar, and handwriting.

1 Write a story entitled 'A Narrow Escape'.
2 Describe the sounds of early morning, either in the country or in the town.
3 Describe a visit that relatives or friends have paid to your home.
4 What are the advantages and disadvantages of computers?
5 Magic.
6 An employer and one of his employees have had a disagreement.
  Outline the circumstances. Then write a conversation between the two in which they settle their differences.
7 What do the following lines suggest to you:
      And hushed they were, no noise of words
        In those bright cities ever rang;
      Only their thoughts, like golden birds,
      About their chambers thrilled and sang.
8 Write a composition about the ideas that this photograph brings to your mind.

(Candidates are supplied with a photograph – which may be a real life scene or a reproduction of a painting or a drawing – to enable them to answer Question 8.)

How do you decide which of those subjects to choose? You will recognise that different kinds of writing are called for by the different subjects set – narrative, descriptive, discursive, etc. – and in preparing yourself to take the examination you will probably have discovered that you are better at some kinds of writing than others. Even so, it would not be wise to choose, say, the discursive subject (4) just because you have generally gained good marks for discursive writing. Consider all the subjects carefully before you make your choice. It may be that you have no very clear ideas about this particular discursive subject and you may do better to choose, say, one of the descriptive subjects.

Remember, the prerequisite for a successful composition is to have a lively interest in your subject. You will do good work if you have personal experience of your chosen topic. Your imagination will then work on that experience to round it out into full and lively material which can be shaped into a well-planned piece of writing.

Test 10.2

(Answers in Answers Section at the end of the book.)

Identify the kind of writing – descriptive, discursive, etc. – that each subject in that examination paper calls for.

As your answers to Test 10.1 will have shown, some subjects can profitably be given a mixed treatment. The important thing is to think hard about each topic and to decide on your 'angle of attack' in the light of the subject-matter and the way in which the question is worded.

⬡11 **Writing letters**

11.1 Introduction

If you are taking an English Language examination, there is a strong
chance that you will be faced with questions involving letter-writing in its
various forms. Whether you have qualified or not in the field of examina-
tion-taking, you will be confronted with letter-writing for the rest of your
life. At the beginning of the 'telephone era', it was forecast that letter-
writing would become moribund. The advent of computers was supposed
to herald a time when communication by paper would wither away.
Neither has happened. The Post Office carries more and more letters;
businesses need people who can read and write letters effectively. In short,
to be able to earn a reasonable salary you have to be able to put pen or
typewriter key to paper, word-processor components to disc. The customary means of communication remains the letter. To neglect it can be a
costly business.

11.2 Different kinds of letters

The are three main kinds: formal letters; informal letters; business letters.
Although in the general English examinations you will not be asked to
write a business letter, in the strict sense of that term, you will probably
have to write a formal letter. A formal letter has some of the qualities of a
business letter, so we shall look at business letters later in Section 11.4.

Many of the letters that we have to write can be described as 'business/
formal' letters. They are letters to business firms written by private
individuals. For example, we write letters to firms that have advertised
their products in newspapers and magazines. The purpose of such letters is
to order goods, or to request free samples, or to ask for further information. Or we may write to a firm to complain about delay in supplying
goods, or to express dissatisfaction with goods that we have bought. Or we
may write to a business firm replying to a letter that we have received from
one of the firm's employees writing on the firm's behalf.

Another kind of formal letter involves correspondence with people who
have an official position. We ourselves may be writing to them in an official
capacity of our own or simply as private individuals.

For example, as secretary of a school debating society you might have to
write to a councillor inviting him or her to take part in a debate on some
topic connected with local government. In those circumstances you would

be writing to the councillor in his/her official capacity and you would be writing in your own official capacity.

Or, as a private individual, you might write to the secretary of your examining board enquiring how to obtain a copy of the board's regulations and copies of past examination papers.

In those cases the letters that you would write would be formal. Efficiency in the writing of formal letters depends on the writer's ability to be 'business-like' (we shall return to that quality) and to 'hit the right note' (achieve an appropriate style of writing).

Informal letters are letters to friends and relatives. Business-like qualities are not the first consideration in such letters, which are much more 'free and easy' than formal letters. Hitting the right note is the first consideration in informal letter-writing.

11.3 The conventions of letter-writing

All letters – formal, informal, business – must obey certain conventions. These conventions serve certain useful purposes. They are not time-wasting, old-fashioned devices, retained out of mere habit. They are used because they increase the efficiency of correspondence by providing a framework for essential information.

However, the designs for the frameworks change according to the fashions of the time, the styles of publishers and the requirements of individual companies. If you are learning your skills of letter-writing from a company or organisation, you may find that their basic page-designs differ from ours. Do not worry. You will find that the all-important matters involve clarity and consistency. Advice from your employer or college must be followed – for their particular interests and your future development are closely linked.

Our intention is to guide you along certain well-defined and recognised lines, but we are aware that changes in style are occurring all the time. Allow common sense, the directives from those for whom you are working, as well as your own personal judgement to influence the style that you develop.

(a) The writer's address

Unless you are using writing-paper on which the address is printed you must always write your address on the first sheet of your letter. The customary place for your address is at the top of the sheet and at the right-hand side. There is a choice of styles, as the following examples show, but some examining boards insist on Style 1. You *must* find out whether your board lays down a rule about this. If it does, then – of course – you must use Style 1 in the examination and in all your preparatory practice.

Style 1

                                                51 Oldport Street,

                                                Midford,

                                                Midshire.

                                                MD16 10S

Notes on Style 1

1 Each line of the address (except the postcode line) is indented – i.e. it begins nearer to the right-hand edge of the sheet than the line above. It is customary to set each line back at an angle of 45 degrees.
2 The postcode line is not indented. It begins at the same distance from the edge of the sheet as the county line.
3 Each line of the address ends with a comma, except the county line (the last line before the postcode) which ends with a full stop. The postcode line is *not* punctuated at all.
5 Some writers insert a comma after the house number (51, Oldport Street) but that is not obligatory. The line looks less cluttered if that internal comma is omitted.

Style 2

                                                51 Oldport Street

                                                Midford

                                                Midshire

                                                MD16 10S

Notes on Style 2

1 There is no indentation. Each line of the address begins at the same distance from the right-hand edge of the sheet.
2 There is no punctuation. Those who favour Style 2 argue that there is no need to pepper an address with either end-of-line or internal punctuation. Each separate item of the address is written on a separate line, so why use end-of-line commas and a final full stop?

Advice on the choice between Styles 1 and 2
The sole (and, of course, vital) purpose of writing your address on the first sheet of your paper is to enable your correspondent to reply. Style 2 gives him all the information that he needs. It provides that information in a less-cluttered (and, therefore, clearer and more attractive manner) than Style 1, as you can see when the two styles are set out side-by-side.

Style 1

```
51, Oldport Street,
    Midford,
        Midshire.
        MD16 10S
```

Style 2

```
51 Oldport Street
Midford
Midshire
MD16 10S
```

(b) The date

Letters must always be dated. In formal correspondence it is frequently necessary to refer to an earlier letter and to identify it by its date: 'Thank you for your letter of 31 May. I have given much thought to your proposals for rearranging the programme but . . .'

Informal letters that are undated can inconvenience and sometimes infuriate their recipient: 'I'm going to stay with Jean the day after tomorrow, so let me know before I go if you want me to give her a message.' An undated letter containing such a statement causes confusion and worry.

It is thoughtless and inefficient not to date letters. That is why you will lose marks if you forget to date your letter in the examination.

The date is written immediately under the address like this:

```
51 Oldport Street,
    Midford,
        Midshire.
        MD16 10S
    21 June 1992
```

Notes

1 The form of date used there – 21 June 1992 – is the form that is nowadays favoured. No punctuation. No 'st' after 21. Similarly, there would be no 'rd' after 3 and no 'th' after 5, etc.
2 These date forms are also acceptable:

```
21st June, 1992.
June 21st, 1992
21/6/92
21.6.92
```

We do not think that any of those is as clear as the preferred form used above. They are all fussier. We have set them out in order of preference.

(c) The salutation

A letter is written to somebody and it must, therefore, begin by naming that person:

```
Dear Mr Jones,

      I am writing to ask you if you will . . .
```

```
Dear John,

      Have you made up your mind about . . .
```

This initial naming of the recipient of the letter is a sort of greeting and it is called *the salutation*. Every letter must begin with a salutation.

   The correct salutation for all formal letters, for all business letters, and for most informal letters is *Dear* . . .

   Very informal letters marked by a close friendship or loving relationship can, of course, have warmer salutations than *Dear* . . . Such salutations are not your concern for examination purposes.

   You must observe all the conventions that regulate the placing and capitalising of the salutation.

```
                                              51 Oldport Street

                                                     Midford

                                                     Midshire

                                                     MD16 10S

                                              21 June 1992
```

```
Dear Mr Jones,

      When I wrote to you on 20 May I . . .
```

Notes

1 1 Capital D for *Dear*.
2 Salutation ends with a comma – *Dear Mr Jones*, (the absence of a full stop after *Mr* is explained in Chapter 8).
3 The salutation begins close to the left-hand edge of the sheet.
4 The first line of the letter itself is indented. (All subsequent paragraphs in the letter begin with an indented line.)
5 The first word of the first line of the letter begins with a capital letter.

There are *no* exceptions to any of these rules. Failure to observe these rules in the examination will cost you marks.

Test 11.1

(Answers in Answer Section at the end of the book.)

What mistakes are there in the following salutations?

1   Dear Mr White

     Can you please let me know . . .

2   Dear Mrs Robinson, I hope that . . .

3   Dear June

  What are you going to do at half term?

4   dear Miss Green –

     The next committee meeting will be . . .

(d) The formal close

The writer of a letter 'signs off' at the end of the letter. The formula used in this signing-off is called *the formal close*.

Yours sincerely,

J. White

Yours faithfully,

T. B. Robinson

Yours,

Jane

Yours ever,

Betty

Notes

1 The formal close is placed at the bottom of the letter and on the right-hand side of the sheet.
2 *Yours* begins with a *capital* letter, but *sincerely* or *faithfully* or *ever* (or whatever word is used after *Yours*) begins with a *small* letter.
3 The formal close line ends with a comma.
4 There is no full stop after the writer's signature.
5 NB *spelling*: sincerely (*e* between *r* and *l*).
       faithfully (double *l*).

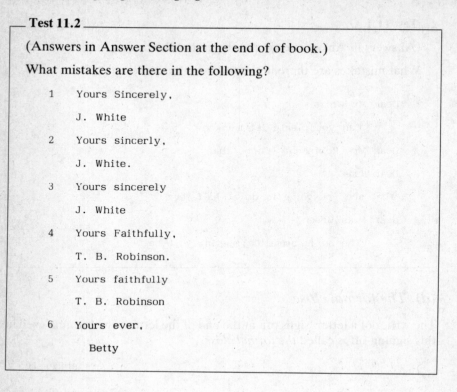

Test 11.2

(Answers in Answer Section at the end of of book.)

What mistakes are there in the following?

1   Yours Sincerely,

    J. White

2   Yours sincerly,

    J. White.

3   Yours sincerely

    J. White

4   Yours Faithfully,

    T. B. Robinson.

5   Yours faithfully

    T. B. Robinson

6   Yours ever,

    Betty

(e) Signing the letter

Never write Mr or Mrs or Miss or Ms *before* your name. The rules are these:

> Male writer signs Alan B. Jones – no Mr needed
> *or* A. B. Jones (Mr)
> Female writer signs A. B. Jones (Mrs or Miss or Ms)
> *or* Ann B. Jones (Mrs or Miss or Ms)

(f) Matching up the salutation and the formal close

When the salutation *names* the recipient the writer of a formal letter must always close with *Yours sincerely*. When the salutation does *not* name the recipient the writer of the letter must always close with *Yours faithfully*. So, when the salutation is, for example.

    Dear Mr Brown,

or

    Dear Mrs Green,

or

    `Dear John,`

the formal close must be

                          `Yours sincerely,`

and when the salutation is

    `Dear Sir,`

or

    `Dear Madam,`

or

    `Dear Sirs,`

the formal close must be

                          `Yours faithfully,`

and there are no exceptions to that rule.

    An alternative formal close for *Yours faithfully* is *Yours truly*, but that is less used now than *Yours faithfully*.

    An *informal* letter may, as we have seen, be closed *Yours*, or *Yours ever*, or with whatever close the degree of warmth between writer and recipient makes appropriate.

    A letter written to the editor of a newspaper for publication in the correspondence columns of the paper usually begins with the salutation *Sir* and ends with the close *Yours faithfully*.

11.4 Planning the letter

Like any other composition a letter must be clearly planned. The three-part structure recommended earlier makes a good basis for a clear, easy-to-read letter: introduction – body of letter – conclusion.

    Because the conventions of letter writing must be observed the full plan for a letter is:

                                         `Address`

                                       `Date`

`Salutation`

    `Introduction`

      `Body of letter`

        `Conclusion`

                                `Formal Close`

                                     `Signature`

Use that plan as a checklist when you are practising.

As in other compositions, each paragraph in the letter must deal with one aspect of the subject. The paragraphs must be linked and must be arranged in a logical sequence.

(a) A formal letter to study

Figure 11.1 illustrates the points discussed so far. Study it carefully and use it as a working model when you are practising letter-writing.

Westcross College of Art,

Bank Street,

Westcross,

Westshire.

WS8 1BS

2 November 1991

Dear Professor Hands,

    I am arranging next term's programme of weekly meetings for the Discussion Society of this College and I have been instructed by the Committee to ask if you will very kindly agree to be our guest speaker at one of those meetings.

    We meet in the College Library at 7.30 p.m. each Wednesday. I should be grateful if you could speak to us on one of the following dates: 22 or 29 January; 19 February; or any Wednesday in March.

    Naturally, the choice of subject is yours, but many students here have been following your current research into the later work of John Constable. If you were willing to speak on that subject you would, I know, give great pleasure to all our members.

Yours sincerely,

Jane Brown (Miss)

Hon. Sec. Westcross College Discussion Society

Figure 11.1 a formal letter

(b) An informal letter to study

As we have said, an informal letter is more free and easy than a formal letter. Even so, the writer of an informal letter must take care to hit the right note. Many a friend and relative has been put out by receiving a letter written in an ill-judged style and, consequently, conveying an unfortunate tone. Again, when there are arrangements to make, the writer of an informal letter must be business-like – in other words, clear and crisp.

Study the informal letter in Figure 11.2. It provides guidance for your own practice.

26 Charlesworth Road,
Holly Bank,
Marden,
Northshire
NH11 16HB

3rd August 1992

Dear Jill,

I hope you're enjoying yourself, though I'm not writing this merely to wish you a happy holiday.

The point is this. You return on 15th, I think. Well, I've just seen in the local rag that the Festival Ballet is at the Hippodrome from 17 August to 23 August. Booking opens on Monday 10th.

Do you want me to get a seat for you? I'm hoping to book for myself for Wednesday 19th ('Giselle'). If you want me to book for you as well, let me know by return. The seats will go like hot cakes, so I must be at the Box Office when it opens on 10th.

I do, of course, hope that you are all having a splendid time – and better weather than here at home. Give my love to your parents, please.

Yours,

Mary

Figure 11.2 an informal letter

(c) A business letter to study

Although, as has been said, you will not have to write a business letter (in the strict sense of the term) in the examination, you often receive such letters and have to reply to them. Some of the features of business letters are also found in formal letters, and the crisp clarity of a *good* business letter is a quality that you should try to achieve in your own formal letter. Figure 11.3 is an example of a business letter.

Highlands Camping Equipment Ltd.,
Unit 17 - The Crask,
Allerton   IB12 6TX

Tel. 6725-43817
Fax. 6725-94318   10 July 1992

Our ref. IM/OS

T.W.Aston, Esq.,
70, Woodbridge Road,
Myerston,
PT23 2EU

Dear Sir,

Re. Two-berth Alness Tent - order number AN 547

We thank you for your letter of 6 July, together with your remittance of £59.95.

We regret to inform you that stocks of the Alness tent that you ordered were exhausted within a few days of our special offer appearing in Outdoor Life.

However, we have ample stocks of the Durness range of tents and are prepared to offer you the two-berth model (order no.DN347), which is normally sold at £69.95, for the price of the equivalent Alness tent.

If this is not acceptable to you, we will, of course, refund your money promptly. Perhaps you will let us have your instructions.

Yours faithfully,

Ian Matthews

(Ian Matthews)

Manager - Mail Order
Highland Camping Equipment

Figure 11.3 is an example of a business letter

Notes

1 The letterhead is printed so that the typist need fill in merely the details that apply to this particular letter – i.e. the date and the reference.
2 The reference – IM/OS – consists of the initials of the sender of the letter and those of the typist. This is a common reference system for business letters.
3 Although Mr Aston's name is typed in above his address at the top of the letter the salutation used is the impersonal '*Dear Sir*'. This is the correct form in a business letter concerned with buying and selling.
4 The form 'Esq.' is used (see Section 11.5, 'Addressing the envelope').
5 The letter begins with a heading – *Re* (short for 'in the matter of') – Two-berth Alness Tent – order number AN547 – so that its subject-matter is clearly announced for the benefit of both the sender and the recipient. Such a heading is a sensible device to assist in keeping a business letter short and to the point.
6 The sender introduces his letter with a reference to the letter from Mr Aston that initiated the correspondence. In this way, he 'tunes in' his reader, making it easy for him to comprehend the purpose of the letter. In that same introductory sentence he acknowledges that Mr White's order and money have been received. All this is crisp and business-like.
7 In the body of the letter the writer explains clearly what the difficulty is, suggests a way out, and offers a refund should the recipient not wish to accept the suggested solution.
8 He ends with a courteous request for Mr Aston's instructions.
9 The formal close is 'Yours faithfully,' since Mr Aston is not named in the salutation.
10 The letter is signed, and the writer's name and official position in the firm are typed in below his signature. This gives the recipient the assurance that his reply will be dealt with by the responsible person. It will not wander aimlessly around an impersonal organisation, hoping to be dealt with by somebody.

Altogether this is a good business-like business letter. (Not all business letters succeed in being business-like!)

(d) A reply to a business letter

Figure 11.4 is an example of a reply to a business letter.

70, Woodbridge Road,
Myerston,
PT23 2EU
14 July 1992

Mr. Ian Matthews,
Manager - Mail Order,
Highlands Camping Equipment Ltd.

Dear Sir,

<u>Two-berth Alness Tent</u> - order no. <u>AW547</u>

Thank you for your letter of 10 July.

I am sorry that you have sold out of the stocks of the Alness tent, but am happy to accept your offer of the alternative - the Durness (order no. DN347)

Yours faithfully,
Tom Aston.

Figure 11.4 a reply to a business letter

Notes

1 Mr Aston chooses to use progressive indentation for his address and no indentation for the address of the recipient. Closed punctuation is used in both cases and commas are used to end the salutation as well as the formal close.

2 He does not write out the firm's address in full, but does identify the person to whom he is writing by his name and his position. This is a sensible precaution. In many firms all incoming mail is opened in a post-room, and a letter identifying its addressee will get on to his desk more quickly than one that is simply addressed to the firm.

3 He sensibly repeats the heading that appeared on the firm's letter. This is good practice: both parties to the correspondence are 'tuned in' to the matter being dealt with. The heading makes for economy of words.

4 Although he knows the name of his correspondent he quite rightly uses the impersonal salutation 'Dear Sir'. This is a reply to a business letter about buying and selling. He does not know Mr Smith personally. Nor is their correspondence likely to develop. 'Sir' (or 'Madam') is correct.

5 He signs his letter with his forename as well as his surname. It gives a personal touch and acknowledges that the Manager himself used his forename, 'Ian'.

11.5   Addressing the envelope

The rules that apply to the writing of addresses in the letter apply also to the writing of the address on the envelope. Care must also be taken to place the address so that the cancellation of the stamp does not obliterate any item of the address. A good working-rule is to consider the top half of the envelope as 'Post Office Property' and the lower half as yours. Place the address either towards the left-hand edge of the envelope or directly in the centre of the bottom half. Always leave generous margins.

When addressing a man, business firms often use *Esq.* ('Esquire') instead of *Mr.* The practice is by no means universal, and it is decreasing both in business and in private correspondence.

When Esq. is used two rules must be obeyed:

1 Never use Mr as well as Esq. (One *or* the other is sufficient.)
2 'Esq.' can be used *only* when the initials of the addressee are known: 'J. A. E. Brown, Esq.'

11.6   Postcards

They are useful for brief messages, but they are not suitable for correspondence on matters involving any degree of privacy. Postcards are a very public form of correspondence.

A postcard message does not begin with a salutation nor does it end with a formal close. It is usually signed with the initials or the forename of the sender.

Business firms make use of postcards for '*pro forma*' communications: 'Date as postmark. We acknowledge your order dated _____. The goods will be despatched on _____. Please inform us if not received within 14 days of despatch.'

―― **Activities 11.1** ――――――――――――――――――――

When you have written your replies to these suggested topics exchange them with fellow-students, colleagues or friends with whom you are working. Give one another the benefit of friendly criticism.

Write a letter suited to one or more of the following situations:

1 As secretary of a fund-raising effort write to a television personality asking him/her to donate a small personal possession to be auctioned at an event that you are organising.
2 Imagine that you are the secretary of an organisation that wishes to meet or to know the views of your local MP. Write to him or her.
3 Imagine that you have been given a large sum of money as well as the opportunity to spend some of it on a holiday. Devise an unusual holiday for yourself and write to a specialist tour-operator that you believe will be able to help you.
4 A friend of yours has moved away to live in another part of the country. You have written to him/her once, but have not received a reply. Some months after his/her departure you hear a rumour that his/her partner, though now recovering, has been seriously ill. You do not know any details. Write a suitable letter to your friend.
5 The offer detailed in this advertisement is of interest to you, as you have been trying without success to obtain some books locally. Write a suitable letter to the firm.

Paperbacks Unlimited
Book House　60 Chase Street　Milltown MT4 4CS

Frustrated by difficulty in obtaining that book you specially want? Even 'the latest' paperback is often unobtainable from your local bookshops. Send us a list of your wants. We invoice you when your order is ready for despatch. We charge £1.00 postage and packing on each parcel, regardless of the number of books enclosed. Please give full details: title, author, publisher.

6 You wish to open an account with a Bank that has recently set up a new branch in your area. Give details of the services that you want – current account/high-interest deposit account/credit card/ travellers' cheque facilities – and of the income and/or borrowing needs that you have.

Remember that in these exercises you do not have to worry about the details of the material in these letters because this is a make-believe activity. However, you can demonstrate your mastery of the skills of presentation. Good lay-out creates favourable impressions. When you have to write letters in 'real life', you will be judged, and your requests determined, partly by the ways in which you *present* your requirements.

12 Notes, memos and reports

12.1 The problems

The volume of information that we receive from other people – spoken instructions in the classroom or lecture hall, communications from the radio, programmes from the television, entertainment from videos, advertising matter, millions of words from newspapers, magazines and books – has increased remarkably during the twentieth century. The problem is that our brains have not altered in size in order to cope with the increased flow of material that is literally around us all the time – in the streets, shops, sound waves and television signals.

What we have learnt to do is to assimilate or incorporate these new, powerful stimuli into our ways of life. One method that is necessary to protect ourselves against excessive interference by these 'outside forces' is to disregard much of what we hear and see. Imagine what a mess we would be in if every sound or sight that we experienced had a profound effect upon us. Our tendency is to use our minds to 'filter' information in order to accept whatever gives us immediate pleasure or appears to have some meaningful application to ourselves.

These protective mental processes seem to be a part of human nature. We do not need lessons in being inattentive! What we need to acquire – and this is the essential problem – is the ability to *retain* whatever is of use to us or those paying us. Added to this are the problems involved in being able to *convey* what we have retained so that the relevant information is shared and leads to the right actions being taken.

Notes, memos and reports are among the methods used to undertake these tasks and overcome some of the problems of human communications.

12.2 The requirements

The skills of being able to retain information and convey it effectively can be acquired by training. The very act of training the mind – in this case of leading it along simple, well-defined lines – is not just the teaching method, it is the target in itself. The elements that are needed are:

logical thought – clarity of purpose – reduction of material – simplicity

The obstacles that have to be overcome are:

   inaccuracies – irrelevant details – inattention

Obviously we can train our minds and discipline ourselves in many ways, but the problems that we encounter in any act that demands change of behaviour are overcome more easily if the following conditions exist.

- Desire to succeed
- Needs to be fulfilled
- Devices to assist
- Confidence

If these are considered in relation to these two skills mentioned – retaining and conveying – a number of features become evident.

1 The desire to succeed is of paramount importance. There are many jobs in which there is little pressure to retain ideas in a formal way. However, there are few well-paid jobs in which the keeping of written records and the communication of information plays little part. Self-interest is therefore a vital factor, However, consider the ways in which memory works when people are engaged in activities about which they feel enthusiastic and for which pay is not a primary factor. Hobbies, pursuits and passions promote levels of recall and standards of articulate response that do not require any special training. For example, bridge-players, motor-racing followers, hockey-umpires, wine-connoisseurs, religious devotees are usually, by nature, enthusiasts. Their minds are able to assimilate information and they are eager to share it. The skills are intuitive. There would appear to be some sense in the saying – 'Make your job your hobby.' It will help you succeed.

2 The human mind will find many excuses to avoid confrontation, especially when the encounter is with work that involves new concepts and adjustments to change. Few people relish the thought of having to apply the mind to a task that demands concentrated effort. Yet most individuals are well aware that the ability to concentrate, assimilate information, retain it and then recall it when required is a gift or a learned activity worth cultivating or acquiring. There are obvious needs for these skills. Job satisfaction as well as financial reward are motivating forces. Management of people, time and opportunity depends upon performance-related skills, especially of communications. The abilities to note effectively, to inspire others through effective memoranda, and to report in a memorable way is a series of skills that we should strive to attain.

3 Just as there are many desires to achieve these abilities, there are countless devices to assist the human mind. Every bookshop has a section in which there will be texts on mind-improvement techniques. The work of Tony Buzan in the BBC series is well-worth exploring. These books will help you to develop the potential powers of your mind. They all have one thing in common. They encourage you to see and hear

ordinary sights and sounds in *extraordinary* ways so that you will be able to recall them effectively. They suggest particular patterns or help you to 're-frame' the picture of something that could have become a stagnant image. This pursuit of the vivid is an essential part of the note-making scheme that will be revealed in the following sections.

4 It has been said that only 10 per cent of the mind's capacity is used by individuals. If we can harness our powers a little more and become aware of our improvements, our confidence will increase accordingly and we shall find it easier to accomplish our tasks.

12.3 'Overview' and 'insight'

The fundamental principles on which professional communicators depend – and into this category come those whose livelihood depends on taking notes, making memos and report-writing – involve the creation of an 'overview' of a subject and an 'insight' into a few aspects of that particular topic.

Remember that you do not need to know everything about a subject and that you are not expected to be an expert on it. You are, after all, only an observer.

What is required is that you can appreciate the gist of a theme or the core of an argument. The easiest way is to strive to see the subject in a clear, easy-to-manage way. The Germans have a word – *gestalt* – which means 'whole or complete'. As we progress through infancy we are able to identify the shapes, sounds and sights with greater effectiveness. Our development is partly influenced by our ability to witness objects and matters around us as a *gestalt* or whole. The details increasingly fit into place and are not mistaken for complete entities in themselves.

So, by the time we have matured, the ability to see a subject in a wide perspective is a vital one. Some years ago an expert on water conservation in the Dakotas and Montana was asked the question, 'What is the drainage pattern of the United States?' Now that is a question that could merit a long answer . . . and in some classrooms would receive one. He merely put his hands together, palms upwards and, at first, tilted them away from him. 'This is the south, with the Mississippi–Missouri flowing into the Gulf of Mexico,' he explained. Then his left hand tilted sideways. 'Here's the Hudson going into the Atlantic . . . and here is the Colorado,' he indicated as his right hand twisted, 'on its way to the Pacific.' Finally he brought both his hands up, palms facing his chest, with the remark, 'And this is the Red River going into Canada.' A continental drainage pattern brilliantly encapsulated with a simple 'overview'.

The nationalist troubles in Yugoslavia take and deserve a lot of explaining. One local commentator, quoted on the television news, made a memorable observation with the remark, 'The jug is broken; it will be difficult to put it together again.' At first, the metaphor appeared to be an ordinary one. Then it dawned that the alternative spelling for that country's name is '*Jug*oslavia.' The symbol of the broken container stuck in the mind. It was an 'overview' of a potential political disaster.

Whenever journalists write their copy for newspapers they are not able to detail every aspect of the topic that they have been asked to 'cover'. That may become the task of academic writers at some time in the future, if the subject merits that sort of attention. The reporters are required to 'angle', 'slant' 'pitch' or 'present' their story in such a way as to capture the imagination of their readers. They have to reveal a view, a pattern or, perhaps, a previously undetected dimension of the subject – in short, to have 'insight'. This does not mean that they have to go on at length, but rather to abbreviate and reduce a complex series of concepts to a simple idea. There are dangers here, of course, and yet anyone who has to read reports knows that the concentration span of the human mind is limited. Brevity is the key to success.

12.4   Details

Life consists of trillions of working parts. It is mind-boggling to contemplate the complexity of existence on this planet. There are times when the sheer size, number and mass of people, places and things could absorb us to the point of complete distraction. Fortunately our minds have a way of avoiding this abyss and we are forced to concentrate on preserving our own identity. The details of day-to-day existence become manageable and we are able to survive without 'breaking down'.

It is the same with our management of the welter of ideas, the thousands of words and the pages of paper that sometimes confront us. They can appear to be overwhelming . . . and sometimes do get the better of us, but the successful note-maker and reporter is keen to break them down into parts that can be handled.

We are like an angler sitting on the bank of a river, unable to resist the flow of the water, but able to control our line and catch something that will give us satisfaction. Notice how this metaphor contains some essential 'insights'. The word 'angler' here means fisherman, but it also has the journalistic interpretation of seeing something from a different angle. 'Flow' suggests the constant stream of stimuli referred to in 12.1, while 'control' and 'line' have their alternative meanings of 'management' and 'viewpoint'. If the desired aim is to 'catch' other people's attention by our use of ideas, then 'satisfaction' is the result when we are successful.

Our mastery of the note-making, memo-creating and report-writing techniques depends on our abilities to see, capture and record the following –

Essential meanings or overviews – patterns or insights – points of interest.

12.5   'Trigger' devices

In the processes of sorting out the patterns from the mass of details in the presentation of these ideas it is necessary to devise a system that will help us to control the flow. It will also be a way of assisting our memories to recall what we want, when we want. This book has attempted to break down the information that we wish to convey by dividing ideas into chapters, topics, paragraphs and sentences. This is a standard, formal technique. It may be helpful and it may enable you to refer quickly to relevant parts and to skip back and forward through the text according to your needs. It is not designed, for example, to assist you to *memorise* many features of the English language. If that had been the case, we would have devised a different format.

Note-making, memo-creation and report-writing invariably demand shorter, more concentrated forms. Systems that divide, highlight, emphasise and show sequences are necessary. They help us to 'trigger' our necessary tendencies to impose a sense of order on the task in hand. They also assist us in that complex task of recalling what we have noted, of 'triggering' our memories. Here are some of them in this list of 'Twenty Ways of Note-taking':

1 'Single-page operating' – try to condense what is necessary onto one sheet of A4 paper.
2 Number sequence, as used here.
3 Alphabetical approach – with the added help that individual letters may link with the actual topic – e.g. A – Alphabet, B – Best order.
4 Subdividing using combinations of numbers and letters – 1.1, 1.2; 1i, 1ii; A.1, B.2; A.a, B.a; Ai, Ciii, etc.
5 Underlining key words.
6 Creating a box for vital topics.
7 Using a marker pen that will highlight aspects that you wish to stress.
8 Headings and subheadings.
9 Pyramid-shaped diagram with the vital points at the top and the less vital topics in descending order.
10 A 'pie-chart' with a segment for each significant feature.
11 A 'snakes and ladders' formation with the advantages and disadvantages of the topics being placed in the strategic positions.
12 Outline material arranged on cards that can be carried in the pocket and used for reference at any time.
13 The themes and ideas presented as positions of football, rugby or hockey players on a diagrammatic field of play.
14 Impose the ideas on a roughly-sketched world map with the more important features in the positions of the powerful nations and more outlandish suggestions in remote places.
15 Draw a quick diagram of a tree with the trunk containing the vital information while the branches and twigs hold relevant, but less significant points.

16 Devise the front page of a newspaper using your own headlines and material to give prominence to the topics that you feel need to be emphasised.
17 Take the main themes, reduce them to single words and place them in a rough crossword layout so that the words interlock.
18 Link each of the topics to be remembered with pop-songs in the current Top Twenty or in an all-time-favourite list of your own and by recalling the one, remember the other.
19 Take the name of the subject to be noted and use each of the letters to be the first letter of the subdivisions on that subject.
20 Use the 'brainstorming' pattern suggested in Chapter 3.

12.6   The lay-out of your notes

Once the ideas have been gathered either from the lecture or briefing or from the written source it is necessary to recast them in your own words. You have probably transformed the order in which the ideas have been presented by using your own system of 'triggering' the important features. Once you have imposed your own structure and have 'broken the mould' of the original you are well on the way to having a series of ideas that will lend themselves to effective notes.

The main thing to remember is that these notes are primarily *for your own benefit*. Another person who reads them does not need to know your short cuts, abbreviated forms, patterns of presentation because it is essentially your way of looking at things. You may prefer to use several of the twenty methods presented above and may like to ring the changes with a code of your own. The important element is for you to be consistent and not to confuse yourself.

Incidentally one of the major problems with note-making involves handwriting. At the time of committing your original words to paper you will have full powers of recall. Within a day you will have forgotten over 70 per cent of the material and the words that looked so meaningful, even when scribbled, take on a distinctly mysterious element. It pays to write more clearly even if it takes longer. You are not going to write down everything and so you had just as well understand what you have written.

Activities 12.1

Attempt a variety of note-taking approaches. Select one or more of the following topics and then devise methods based upon two or more of the 'Twenty Ways of Note-taking' to show how you can fit ideas into patterns that will help you to retain and convey the information that you consider to be important.

1 Choose the main story from a daily newspaper and reduce it to a series of brief and effective notes.
2 Watch the first parts of the consecutive news programmes on rival

television channels when their lead items coincide in content. Look for the different pieces of information that are broadcast.

3 Make notes on the first sections of this chapter.

4 Pick up a few holiday brochures from a travel agent. Compare and contrast the holiday-packages, the destinations and the bargains that are on offer.

5 Attend a public meeting or lecture in order to test your skill at being able to assimilate the information given. If this is not possible, watch a television programme in which the technique known as 'talking heads' is the primary production feature – in other words where the presenter or interviewee is talking directly to the camera.

12.7 Memorandum

This word comes from Latin and means, literally, 'a thing to be remembered'. In legal terms it refers to a brief note of some transaction; in diplomacy it is a summary of the state of a question. For us it means a note that we write either to remind ourselves of something or, more likely, to draw the attention of others to a specific matter.

The correct plurals of the word are either memorandums or memoranda, but the abbreviated forms are memo (singular) and memos (plural).

Note-making is, as stated previously, primarily for ourselves. It is a personal form of shorthand that we devise to reduce the mass of information to manageable proportions. Memo-writing is primarily for the eyes of other people. In consequence it has a different set of guide-lines.

The 'Twenty Ways of Note-taking' emphasised the ordered approach as well as the vivid, the standard as well as the unorthodox. It was meant to contain methods that would appeal to a range of personalities. With memo-writing there is less scope for choice.

Within our daily lives – in schools, colleges, offices and home – we may encounter many different types of people. Those to whom we have to send messages will respond to a wide range of remarks and styles, but the memo is not a message. It is a formal statement of what we wish to be noted, observed or obeyed. It demands a different type of treatment.

The fundamental principles behind memo-writing are the same as for any form of writing. They are, in ascending order of importance:

Euphony – Simplicity – Clarity

Euphony This may not be a commonly used word, but it expresses a much-needed quality – 'to be agreeable in sound'. Although memos will often have to indicate unpleasant matters and reflect disagreements between people, it is important that the actual words do not jar or give offence in themselves. The tone of writing should be harmonious and avoid the high-sounding effect, patronising air or self-important manner. In short, the memo should be courteous, polite and business-like.

Simplicity   Often the purpose of the memo-writer is to reveal the straight-forward plan of action that has to be taken despite the complexities of a given situation. There are enough obstacles to prevent clear-cut approaches without complicating them with intricacies of our own. Remember the American directive – 'KISS' – 'keep it simple, stupid!'

Clarity   This is the most vital ingredient. Although simplicity is important, there are occasions when full explanations have to be given to avoid misunderstandings and ambiguity. The meanings of words may be listed in dictionaries and appear to be used with precision. Yet human beings have ways of interpreting them that reflect different cultural backgrounds, upbringings, self-interests and wilfulness. Recall the story of the Scottish minister of religion who suggested to an unwell and elderly lady who was a lifelong teetotaller that she should observe St Paul's advice to 'take a little wine for the stomach.' 'Ah!' she replied, 'but he didn't mean drink it, he meant "rub it on."' It is the unexpected interpretation that will show the flaw in the memo.

12.8   The form of the memo

It is obvious that great care has to be taken when devising the form as well as the words of the memo. Many organisations produce basic outlines as part of their stationery as, for example, the memo shown in Figures 12.1 and 12.2. However, you will probably have to work out something for yourself and here it is worth noting that there are five basic matters that need attention. These involve:

Time – People – Places – Points to make – Numbering points

Time   reference has to be made to (a) the date and perhaps the actual time, and (b) when the response to the memo is required.

People   a memo should make clear (a) who sent it, and (b) for whom it was sent. In a letter the signature and name of the sender traditionally come at the end, but in a memo the name of the sender should come at the top together with the name, names or group of people to whom it is to be despatched (see Figures 12.1 and 12.2).

Place   the memo should show (a) where it originated, and (b) where the reply should be sent.

Points to make   this is the 'body' of the memo and normally it is about things to be noted/things to be aware of/things to be avoided/things to be thought about/things to be done. In fact, any number of things.

Numbering points   to avoid confusion and to encourage systematic working through the points you have made, it is a good idea to number each of the topics. It makes it easier to check later that all the necessary action has been taken.

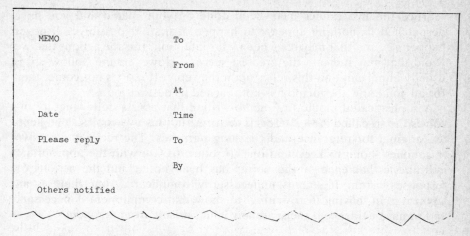

```
MEMO                    To

                        From

                        At

Date                    Time

Please reply            To

                        By

Others notified
```

Figure 12.1 A typical pro forma memo sheet

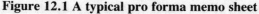

```
MEMO                    To      Mark Deacon

                        From    Simon Johnson

                        At      Despatch

Date  24 Oct '92        Time    11.30 am

Please reply            To      My Secretary

                        By      3.30 p.m.

Others notified                 All Control clerks
```

1) From tomorrow the Post office at Parcelforce will be collecting mail at 4.30 not 5p.m.

2) Securicor will be here for cash collection at 5p.m.

3) Please ensure that mail is here by 4p.m.

4) We shall be establishing an 'emergency only' message service for vital letters or parcels that have to be despatched in the last hour.

5) Any problems?

Figure 12.2 A typical memo

Once the five checks have been done on your memo and you have despatched it, nothing appears to happen at first. It possibly will never happen . . . and that may have been your intention. It is the actions that we avoid that may indicate the greatest success. However, the 'follow-up' is usually important and this relies upon the reply. If it does not come, then for all you know the memo has not reached its destination.

A sophisticated method of memo-writing that assists 'following-up' involves the so-called 'O + 2'. This is the orginal, plus two copies. You keep the original for reference and checking purposes. The recipients receive two copies – one to keep and one to return to you with the appropriate indications that each of the points has been noted and the actions or responses taken. It sounds unnecessarily complicated, but there is an advantage in 'having it in writing' to show that commitment is necessary and to have evidence if there are any issues arising from the memo.

Activities 12.2

If a group of you are able to take part in a role-playing game which features memo-writing, it could be useful. The topic to be explored concerns a bypass that is being considered for your village. Here are the facts.

The projected length of the bypass is $1\frac{1}{2}$ miles and there are two possible routes. The route to the north of the village would pass within earshot of the council estate and affect 250 residents with its noise. The route to the south passes relatively close to an expensive housing development and would affect 30 residents. It also cuts into a small part of a nature conservation area and could affect some of the habitat of the rather rare raft-spider.

Shopkeepers, who realise that there will be loss of passing trade, are pleased that the starting-date for the project looks likely to be delayed. The contractors are anxious to move their plant and machinery from a similar scheme that has just been completed nearby. Parents of children at the village school, which is situated on the main road, look forward to there being less traffic.

Cast members of the group into various roles – The planning office responsible for village development/A spokesman for the council residents/The local councillor who has a house to the south of the village/The newsagent/The warden of the Nature Conservancy/The Head-teacher/Parents. Write a series of memos to the Chief Planning Officer.

Then study the individual memos and think of ways in which the Chief Planning Officer could phrase his statement about the proposed development.

12.9   Reports

There is, perhaps, a tendency to think of reports in the way that is intended in schools – that is, as a direct, rather personal statement about an individual's performance. These reports may claim to be 'objective' by giving a detached view of the student, yet they are normally 'subjective' in tone and reflect the teacher's feelings towards the student's response. In the same way, the newspaper 'reporter' is supposed to give an unbiased judgement and appear to be above personal involvement. Yet the demands of this job involve having to 'angle' the news story in order to present it in an attractive way for the reader. An individualistic style and a distinctive approach are inevitable. As there are no set rules for report-writing, it may be best to draw up some guide-lines.

As with memo-writing, reference to the three requirements –

An Attractive Tone – Simplicity – Clarity

should be displayed prominently on the wall facing the report-writer. It may also help to have the word B–A–T–T–I–N–G appear on a notepad that's at hand. This word can act as a good memory-jogger so that the vital guide-lines are followed. Good report-writing should take the following into account:

*B*usiness-like   Most reports that you will write will be connected with aspects of business. The tone should be brisk and the lay-out easy to follow so that time is not wasted.

*A*udience   Think of the people for whom you are writing. On this assessment depends the amount of jargon you can use. A specialist, knowledgeable audience will be treated differently from members of the general public.

*T*arget   Remember that you have to convey information to people who will probably have to try to retain it. (These are the two features stressed in the section on note-making in 12.1.)

*T*opics   Work out in advance the individual topics so that your report is well-defined, has a strong sense of order and uses space. The reader wishes to be led along paths that are comfortable on the eyes.

*I*llustrations   Give examples or references to specific matters in order to avoid sounding vague.

*N*umbering topics   This will assist the sequence of ideas and reinforce the impression that you have imposed a sense of order.

*G*oal   Attempt to assess your own report by asking yourself the question: 'Had this come through my letter-box or dropped onto my desk, would I feel encouraged to read on, or be daunted by the prospect of having to look into it?'

—— **Activities 12.3** ——————————————————————————

Report-writing demands the stimulus of compulsion or self-interest. Few people write reports for pleasure. However, attempt to produce a short, 400-word report on each of the following three topics which represent the main divisions into which reports can be classified – personal, factual, opinion.

1 Write about the significance, as you see it, of the next three years of your life. Consider: qualifications – residence – finance – work or study – possessions – holidays.
2 Report on the state of your city, town or village. Make reference to its history, recent developments, current prosperity, future plans and potential.
3 Give an account of the ways in which the beginning of the Third Millennium (from the year 2000 onwards) should be commemorated or celebrated. Your report could consider, among other topics, what objects could be placed in a time-capsule to indicate the main advances and weaknesses of the Second Millennium.

Finally, check you work against the B–A–T–T–I–N–G order:

*B*usiness-like – *A*udience – *T*arget – *T*opics – *I*llustrations – *N*umbering – *G*oal.

12.10   Ideas into action

The successes of a series of notes, memoranda or reports are judged by the influence they have on our ability to think and retain ideas, on other people's positive reactions and on the actual actions that they stimulate. They are, essentially, a means to an end.

Activities 12.3 and 12.4 are meant to promote the techniques described in the various sections of this chapter. They are intended to combine the strategies of note-taking, memo-writing and report-making. Ideally you should work with a number of others in a group so that you have both an audience and sympathetic critics on hand. However, if working on your own, you can probably make a fair assessment of the quality of your work by referring to the number of ideas that you have generated and by the way in which you have presented them.

—— **Activities 12.4** ——————————————————————————

Notes/Memos/Report on Prospective House Purchases

Imagine that you have been asked by a wealthy friend, who lives overseas, to search on his behalf for two houses situated in the English countryside. One should be large enough to accommodate his family of five, as well as his elderly mother, and also be suitable for housing his office and entertaining business clients. He has had some thoughts about eventually converting a large house into a small hotel. The other should be an 'interesting property' that he can use as a 'retreat' to get away from family and business demands.

Study the two photographs of houses in Figures 12.3 and 12.4. Then undertake the following exercises, using your imagination to supply the details of the properties, i.e. number of bedrooms; sizes of the hall, living rooms and kitchen; features of the kitchen; number of bathrooms; heating methods; outdoor facilities such as size of grounds, extent of garden, swimming pool and tennis courts; proximity to town, railway and motorway.

1 Write a series of notes outlining the position, features and potential of these two houses so that you can use them to conduct a business-like, informative, international phone call with your friend.
2 Devise memos to be sent to the estate agents in order to ask them if they could indicate whether the larger house is likely to be allowed planning permission to convert it into an hotel and whether the smaller house is likely to be very expensive to insure because of its unusual construction and thatched roof.
3 Write a formal report for your friend in which you give details of the properties (using some of the information that you have worked out for the notes) and suggest the advantages and disadvantages of the houses in question.

Figure 12.3

Figure 12.4

Activities 12.5

Notes/Memo/Report on Transport Changes

Imagine that you have to take part in a television programme about the changes in Britain during the twentieth century. Your 'brief' is to speak about the way in which developments have taken place in East Anglia and, in particular, the ways in which the railway network has been altered. The producer of the programme has written to ask you to supply him with the information that you intend to use. Here are some aspects of the subject in addition to the map that appears in Figure 12.5.

East Anglia is a distinctive area of England, well-defined historically by its agricultural tradition and geographically by the railway line from London to King's Lynn on one side and the North Sea on the other.

There has been a rapid increase in population in the final quarter of the century, with many people moving out of London to work in Cambridge, King's Lynn, Thetford and Bury St Edmunds.

The towns of Braintree, Colchester and Ipswich, as well as the villages around them, attract many commuters who go daily to London for their work. Norwich has grown substantially and 'London's Third Airport' has been developed at Stansted.

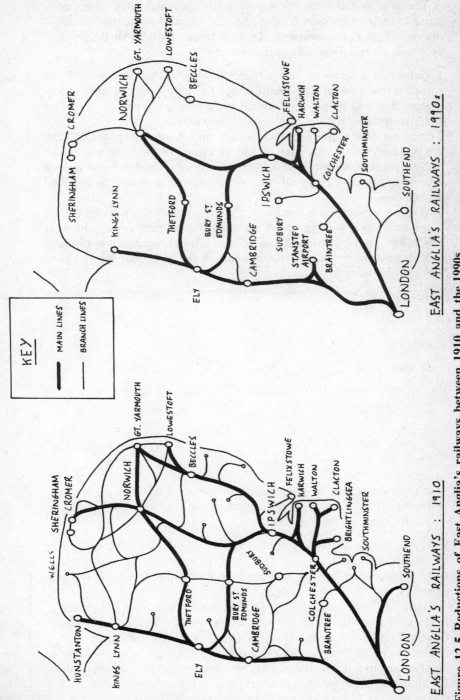

EAST ANGLIA'S RAILWAYS : 1990s

EAST ANGLIA'S RAILWAYS : 1910

KEY

MAIN LINES
BRANCH LINES

Figure 12.5 Reductions of East Anglia's railways between 1910 and the 1990s

The port at Felixstowe has grown from a small quay to a vast handler of international freight. Several car and passenger ferries operate from Felixstowe and Harwich to destinations in Belgium, Holland, Germany and Scandinavia.

1 Construct a series of notes that will inform the producer of the topics that you will be mentioning. Develop them in such a way that they will help you to recall what you are going to say when confronted by the interviewer and the camera.
2 Imagine that you are the person in charge of planning the development of this part of the country. Write a memo to the Government Minister who is ultimately responsible for decision-making advising him that the railway network should be reduced no more.
3 Write a report for a company that is considering developing an existing large, but run-down leisure-complex near Sheringham. It was built in the 1920s and is in need of either investment or closure. You have been asked to comment on the potential for business from rail-users.

13 Writing a summary

13.1 The importance of a summary

A summary of one kind or another is required by all the examining boards and, whether it is based on the comprehension passage or on a separate passage, the summary exercise carries a high proportion of the total marks. A good performance in this branch of English language work is crucial to success in the examination as a whole.

The importance that the examiners attach to summary reflects its importance in everyday life. It is one of the mental activities in which we are all frequently involved, whether we realise it or not.

A few examples will readily illustrate how often the need to summarise occurs. A letter arrives for you from a firm to which you have applied for a job. As you are reading it, your mother asks, 'What do they say?' She is asking for a summary. So is somebody who comes into the room half-way through a news item on television and says, 'What's that all about?'

More obviously, a summary is required when, at work, your boss pushes a newspaper across to you and says, 'There's a report on page four of objections to the council's outline development plan. Let me have the gist of it by lunchtime. I'm meeting the borough surveyor at 2.30, and those arguments may bear on our proposed extension to the paint shop.'

Thus, the summaries required in the examination are a way of testing skills that you need in daily life.

13.2 The skills involved

Summary involves all the skills required for general competence in the use of language. Far from being an artificial exercise designed by examiners as a test for candidates, it is an accurate measure of your *ability to communicate*. It tests you in comprehension and in composition, demanding:

- first, that you can understand what you read;
- second, that you can express that understanding.

For the moment, we will assume that you have completed the comprehension of the passage that you are about to summarise. Here is a breakdown of the skills that are needed, whether you are required to make a summary of the whole passage or of selected parts:

- the ability to *organise* your answer in a *coherent* and *logical* manner;
- that, in turn, requires competence in *sentence* and *paragraph* construc-

tion and a thorough knowledge of punctuation;
- the possession of, and the judgement to make use of a large *vocabulary*, so that you can *condense* the passage that you are summarising and choose *appropriate* words to reflect its spirit and its writer's intentions.

Each of those requirements is discussed later in this chapter.

13.3   Different kinds of summary

(a) Précis or full-length summary

Précis is a synonym for 'summary'. The word 'précis' came into the English language from French. It is useful to bear in mind that, in French, when *précis* is used as a noun it means 'summary', and when it is used as an adjective it means 'precise, accurate, definite'.

For that is what a précis is: a precise, accurate summary – and it is 'definite' in the sense that it *must* be written to the *exact* number of words stipulated in the examiner's instructions.

When précis is required in the examination the instructions generally follow a well-established pattern. A separate passage is usually set and the candidate is instructed to reduce that passage to a third of its length (in the case of longer passages) or to a quarter of its length (in the case of shorter passages). Usually, the permitted number of words is stated: 'not more than 300 of your own words'; 'in about 200 of your own words'. When an approximate number of words is given you should aim at being not more than five words above or below the stated figure.

Nowadays, we tend to use 'précis' to describe the summary of a whole passage, and to use the word 'summary' for the kind of selective summary and the short summary questions that most examining boards now set.

Typical précis instructions

Make a précis (summary) of the following passage in not more than 150 words. You may have to retain some words or brief expressions from the original passage but, as far as possible, *use your own words*. State at the end of your précis the exact number of words that you have used. There are 455 words in the original passage.

(b) Selective summary

Instead of being asked to summarise a whole passage the candidate is instructed to select from its contents the items that bear upon a specified subject and to summarise those.

The set passage may deal with two main themes, and the instructions may require a summary of one of the two. For example, in a passage describing the progress of an invention from the laboratory to commercial use the subject-matter may divide into an account of the early experiments and the development of those to the production stage, followed by an account of the way in which, and with what success, the product was marketed. The candidate may be asked to summarise one or the other.

A less straightforward exercise will involve the selection and summarising of material that is found here and there throughout the set passage. For example, an account of a politician's life may include references to various periods of his career during which his particular qualities of character and temperament were exercised in different ways with varying degrees of success. The candidates may be asked to select and summarise those qualities that were either of enduring advantage or of sporadic disadvantage to him.

As those illustrations show, the examiner is testing the candidate's ability to 'see through' the material and to reach the heart of the matter *as specified in his instructions*. Much that is important in the original has to be disregarded in the summary because it is *irrelevant* to the job that the candidate has been told to do.

Again, the material for selective summarising may not be a single passage of continuous prose. It may take the form of a conversation, or of a series of letters, or of notes or memoranda.

But, whatever the form, the candidate will be clearly instructed what aspect of the subject-matter to select and how many words to use.

Typical instructions for selective summary

Study correspondence between Mr Brown and the Westshire County Planning Officer. Then, in one paragraph of about 100 words, summarise the points at issue over access to the garage, for the building of which Mr Brown is seeking planning permission.
Use your own words as far as possible, though it may be necessary to employ some of the technical terms used in the letters.
(NB   Other subjects may well be discussed – colours, kinds of doors, building materials, etc. – but they are not relevant to the summary that has been specified.)

(c) Short summary questions

These are a particular kind of selective summary. They occur among – and as part of – the comprehension questions set on the given passage. They do not differ *in kind* from any other exercises in the summary, for they involve the same kind of mental processes and the application of the same skills. But they do not always contain the instruction 'summarise', and this can confuse an ill-prepared candidate.

You can recognise that they *are* exercises in summary by the number of words permitted in the answer. Whereas a comprehension question can be answered briefly, the answer to a summary question is allowed (and expected) to contain more words. Also, of course, more marks are given for a summary question than for a single comprehension question. Some examining boards indicate on the examination paper the marks given for each question. Whether your board follows that practice or not, you may be sure that examiners will allot more marks to a question requiring, say, a 60- or 70-word answer than to one that can be answered in one word, or one phrase, or one short sentence.

Typical short summary question
Note   This example is presented in the kind of context in which it would be found in an examination paper. It is accompanied by 'straight' comprehension questions.

> Read the passage carefully and then answer the questions. Be sure to use your own words wherever you are instructed to do so. When you are asked to quote from the passage be careful to quote only the relevant word or words.

[Imagine that the passage follows here]

1 Quote from the first paragraph the two words that indicate that the narrator was nervous. (4 marks)
2 Give one word meaning the same or nearly the same as the following as used in the passage: (i) devious; (ii) premature. (2 marks)
3 Set out clearly, and in not more than 60 *of your own words*, the reasons that Jan gives for being suspicious of Blenkinson. (10 marks)
4 Write down two of the things that you learn about Henry Jones's previous career. Indicate briefly the evidence on which your answer is based. (4 marks)

[Question 3, above, is a short summary question.]

13.4   Practice in précis

Although only a minority of the examining boards test candidates in summary by setting a full-length summary of a whole passage, a study of précis is the best way to learn how to summarise. All the skills demanded by every kind of summary are involved in the making of a précis.

(a) Stage 1: Getting the gist of it

1 Read the passage right through once, concentrating your attention on what seems to be its main theme. In other words, *get the gist of it*. As soon as you have completed this first reading make a note of the main drift of the contents, like this:

> Writer argues that pace of industrial development must be slowed to conserve world's resources of minerals and fuel.

A similar note encapsulating the theme of a descriptive passage read:

> Description of the changes in the Soviet Union during the last decade of the twentieth century and of its effects on the more prosperous Western economies.

2 Read the passage right through a second time, bearing in mind the main drift as discovered through your first reading. During this second reading, pay attention to the spirit of the passage, noticing the key words and phrases and opening your mind to their implicit meaning as well as their explicit sense. You are 'reading between the lines' now, entering into the author's intentions, and noticing not only *what* is said but also *how* it is said. Notice, too, how the passage is developed. Trace the stages through which the writer's subject-matter is unfolded. Attention paid now to the structure of the passage will yield dividends later.

(b) Stage 2: The spirit of the passage and the writer's intentions

With your statement of its chief theme in mind you now work through the passage, attempting to deepen your understanding of it.

As you read, you note key words, phrases, and sentences that indicate the spirit in which the passage was written and the author's intentions when writing it.

You can note these key expressions either by underlining them in the passage or by jotting them down on your rough paper.

If, as you read, you ask yourself these two questions you will pick out the key points:

- *What* is the writer trying to do?
- *How* is he using language to achieve his aims?

Reading like that is 'reading between the lines'. The reader is entering into the writer's mind and perceiving his intentions.

This is stage 2 of précis, Let us see how it works. Suppose that the passage you are preparing to précis is an account of the invention of gunpowder. You have completed the second stage of your work when you have the answers to these questions:

- Is this a 'scientific' account of the invention, employing technical terms and written for a special readership?

or

- Is this a 'popular' account of the invention, written in language that anybody can understand?
- Does the writer simply give an account of the invention?

or

- Does he introduce other topics?

- Does he write about the effects of the invention?
- Does he say whether he thinks that it was a beneficial or a harmful invention?
- Does he give reasons for his opinions and, if so, what are they?

Asking (and answering) such questions provides you with a full understanding of what the writer was doing. Once you have that deep understanding you know what ground your précis must cover.

(c)　Stage 3: The structure of the passage

Stage 3 of your work is an analysis of the structure of the passage. In stages 1 and 2 you discovered what the passage is about and what the writer was trying to do. Now, in stage 3, you take the passage to pieces, noting the steps by which it passes *from* its beginning *through* its middle *to* its end.

Of course, you will not include in your précis everything that the passage contains, nor will you necessarily present the items in your précis in the same order as that in which they occur in the original.

You have to *condense* to write a précis. To condense, you have to:

- omit any material that is not essential to the main theme;

and

- save words, by reducing longer expressions to shorter ones with equivalent meanings (a point developed later in this chapter).

Your précis must also present its summary of the main theme of the original in a *coherent* and *logical* way. When you are shortening the subject you may find that you need to rearrange the order in which the items occur in the original. An order that is satisfactory in the longer original *may* be unsuitable for your shortened version.

But, until you have noted all the items included in the original and the order in which those items are presented, you cannot decide what to include in your précis or in what order to present the items that you have selected.

(d)　Stages 1–3 in action

The passage chosen for this demonstration is short, because I want to make the method as clear as possible; but, as we shall see later, it works just as well with longer passages.

Henry Ford did more than any other man to make the motor car a popular and readily available means of transport. He was not an inventor, and he contributed nothing to the scientific evolution of the car; but he was a genius who applied the principles of mass-production to the making of cars, and so transformed what had been the sport and pleasure of the few into a useful vehicle for the many. Ford decided that cars must be tough enough to stand up to daily wear and tear on ordinary roads; that they must become cheap enough to be within the reach of ordinary people; that their construction must be simplified so that spare parts could be widely available and easily fitted. These aims were realised in his huge factories, where mechanised and highly organised car production was first undertaken.

Stage 1: Statement of gist of passage   Henry Ford's unique contribution to the development of the motor car.

Stage 2: Spirit of passage and writer's intentions   Writer gives a straightforward account of Ford's historical importance in development of car, and of methods he used to make the changes he brought about. No value judgements made by writer – concerned only with facts.

Stage 3: Analysis of structure of passage   One paragraph, the structure of which is:

Main point 1   Henry Ford . . . means of transport.
  1(a) . . . not an inventor
  1(b) . . . contributed nothing to scientific evolution . . .
Main point 2   . . . genius . . . principles of mass production . . . cars.
  2(a) . . . transformed . . . sport and pleasure of the few . . . useful vehicle for the many.
Main point 3   Ford decided that cars must be
  3(a) . . . tough enough . . .
  3(b) . . . cheap enough . . .
  3(c) . . . spare parts . . . widely available . . . easily fitted.
Main point 4   These aims were realised . . . first undertaken.

As you see Stage 3 produces a 'skeleton' of the original passage. You dissect the passage and lay bare the bones of its structure.

(e) Stage 4: Selecting the key points

This is Stage 4. With the skeleton in front of you, you can decide what items to include in your précis and the order in which you will present those items.

To guide your selection refer to your brief statement of the gist of the passage (Stage 1). Items that are directly relevant to that statement *may* be included in your précis: any that are not *must* be excluded.

When, as often happens, an item has relevance to the main theme of the passage but seems of minor importance, you can usually decide whether to include it or not by referring to the writer's purposes, as discovered in Stage 2. An item may bear on the main theme but be of comparatively small importance to the writer's chief intentions in writing the passage. It has a part to play in the original, where the writer was free from the pressure on space that you have to contend with. You are looking to save words, so a doubtful item that does not seem to be essential to the writer's purposes must be excluded.

Applying those considerations to the passage 'skeletonised' in 13.4(d) Stage 3, we find that the key points are: 1–2–3–3 (a)–3(b)–3(c).

Those key items – and only those – will be included in the précis.

It is instructive to study the omitted items and the reasons for their exclusion.

Points 1(a) and 1(b) are excluded. The writer's chief intention in the passage is to describe what Henry Ford did – to emphasise his positive achievement, *not* to dwell on the qualities that he did not possess.

Point 2(a) is excluded. Its substance is adequately represented (for the précis-writer's purpose) in 1.

Point 4 is excluded. It is an expansion of 2. It makes a useful 'rounding off' for the original passage, but it is not a sufficiently separate and distinctive item to merit including in the précis.

(f) Stage 5: Making a plan for the précis

When you have decided on the key points you are ready to write out a plan in note form from which you can write your précis. This is Stage 5.

Bear the following advice in mind as you make your notes:

- use *your own words* as far as possible;
- include sufficient detail to enable you to write the *first draft* of the précis *from your notes* and without referring to the original passage.

There are two good reasons behind that advice. First, if you use the writer's words (instead of your own) in your notes you will be in danger of incorporating them in your précis. Second, if your notes are too thin and you have to keep referring to the original as you write your first draft, you will be in danger of departing from the scheme of key points worked out in Stage 4. You will then lose sight of the priorities and the scale of relevance that govern the inclusion or exclusion of items. The resulting muddle will ruin your précis.

(g) Recap – the first five stages in précis writing

Stage 1 Study the subject matter of the original passage. Discover its gist. State its gist in your own words.

Stage 2 Discover the writer's purposes. Get clear in your own mind what he was intending to do.

Stage 3 Analyse the structure of the passage, noting the separate items and the order in which they are presented. Make a skeleton of the passage.

Stage 4 Decide which items are fundamental to the writer's theme and purpose. List those key points.

Stage 5 Use your list of key points as the framework for a *detailed* plan on which to write the first draft of your précis. Check each item in your plan to make sure that it is an accurate representation of the item in the original to which it corresponds. Use your own words wherever possible throughout your plan.

(h) Stage 6: Pruning and polishing the first draft

Having written your first draft from your précis plan you have still got a lot of work to do before your can write out on your answer sheet a fair copy of your final version. This is what must be done when the first draft is complete:

1 Count the number of words in your first draft. You will almost always find that you have exceeded the permitted work limit. So, usually, the first thing to do is *prune*. (NB If you find that your first draft is comfortably under the permitted length, do not be comforted! That is a danger signal. You have almost certainly omitted essential points from the original passage.)
2 Check that your draft is a *connected and readable composition*. A précis is a shortened version of the original, but it is not to be written in note form or in a series of jerky sentences. Nor should its style be informal. Avoid all colloqualisms and slang.
3 Check for errors in punctuation, spelling and grammar.
4 Check that you have provided a suitable title.
5 Check that you have stated *accurately* the number of words used in your précis. The examiner has a pretty good idea of how many words occupy how many lines of the answer sheet. If the number you state at the end makes him suspicious, he will count every word in your précis, and he will not be pleased at being put to the trouble.

When all that pruning and polishing has been completed you are ready to write the final version on the answer sheet.

Set out in its successive stages and discussed in detail, the writing of a précis seems a time-consuming and daunting task. 'How can I possible get through all that exam?' you may be saying. Well, you must – and you *can*.

Remember that method is essential – and the method that has been set out here is a well-tried and successful one. To attempt to write a précis (or any other kind of summary) 'off the cuff' is to court disaster.

Remember, too, that describing the successive steps and illustrating how they work takes longer than actually carrying them out.

Above all, remember that regular practice in preparation for the examination will speed you up. You should practise précis-writing, using the method set out here, once a week during your examination preparation. Then you will answer your summary question with confidence and efficiency. You will also find that this regular summary practice brings about an improved performance in every other branch of your English Language work. (And that, of course, means that your work in all subjects will improve.)

In the next section one of us will work through a complete précis to show you how to apply the method advocated in this book. Pay close attention to the comments on the various stages. They are meant to take you right into the workshop.

(i) Worked example of précis, with a commentary

Note   A short passage has been chosen so that each stage can be fully discussed and illustrated within the space available in this chapter. Short though the passage is, the exercise is an example of full-length summary (or précis), since the summariser (the précis-writer) is instructed to deal with the contents of the whole passage.

Summarise the following passage in not more than 65 words. You may have to employ some words or brief expressions from the original passage but, as far as possible, *use your own words*. State at the end of your précis the exact number of words that it contains. There are 250 words in the original passage. Provide your précis with a suitable title. The words of the title do *not* count towards the word total permitted.

Stanley Spencer never looked on his writing as something private; he intended to publish what he wrote. His autobiography was to be a fulfilment and rounding-off of his painting. But as a writer he lacked the discipline which made composition the outstanding feature of his painting. He wrote with wonderful freshness, but could not cut or select or prune; everything was of equal importance. When Maurice Collis received the two trunks and the large wooden box on castors, containing these papers he was appalled. To read every word, let alone sort, select and arrange in chronological order this mountain of papers which, taken out of their trunks, filled an entire room, seemed at first an impossible task.

With the help of his daughter, a writer herself and used to research, he set to work. Often he worked seven days a week and sometimes late at night, not because he was being pressed by his publishers, but because he found the material engrossing. The occasional reports he sent at this time were all the more interesting because we knew that he was not a man of gushing or even ready enthusiasm. A selection of these bulletins reads:

'Stanley Spencer is a wonderful original, a far more remarkable man than I supposed before I read the papers.'

'The drama increases the more one reads.'

'New and extraordinary material goes on appearing.'

'The whole of Stanley Spencer's life is revealed in his pictures if one has the key.'

Irene Stirling: 'The Spencer Papers' (in *The Bookseller*)

Stage 1: statement of main theme (gist) of passage
The enormous quantity of Stanley Spencer's writing gave Maurice Collis (his biographer) a difficult and laborious task, which he tackled with enthusiasm because the material fascinated him.
Comments
1   I had to decide whether the subject matter of the first four sentences of the original made a major contribution to the theme. In the end I decided that their contents were *introductory* to the main theme. It was *because* of Spencer's qualities as a writer, as set out in the first four sentences, that he produced such an enormous quantity of papers. The fact that matters (to the précis writer working on this passage) is that he *did* produce so much (not *why* he produced so much) and that, in consequence, Maurice Collis was faced with a huge task.
2   I had to decide what Maurice Collis's role was, since that is not directly stated in the original. Careful 'reading between the lines' revealed that he was writing a life of Spencer. Evidence:

  (i) Spencer 'intended to publish what he write'. Something – presumably death – prevented him from doing so. Consequently, his *autobiography* will not be written, but a *biography* is being prepared.
 (ii) Maurice Collis received all the Spencer papers, which he had to 'read . . . sort, select and arrange in chronological order'. That is a description of the task of a biographer.
(iii) Collis is working for publishers (see second paragraph of passage).
(iv) All of Collis's 'bulletins' (quoted at the end) refer to aspects of Spencer's life, work, and personality, so he is obviously discovering all that he possibly can about the man.

Stage 2: the writer's purpose
To communicate two things to the reader as vividly as possible:
 (i) the enormous labour that faced Collis;
(ii) the enthusiasm with which he undertook that labour, fired by the fascination of the material.

Stage 3: skeleton outline of contents of original
1 Spencer's qualities as a writer
   1(a) did not see his writing as private – intended to publish
   1(b) importance he attached to his proposed autobiography – fulfilment of his painting
   1(c) an undisciplined writer
   1(d) a fresh and lively writer, incapable of selecting and pruning
2 Enormous quantity of papers received by Collis
   2(a) Collis's initial reaction – 'he was appalled'
   2(b) task of reading and sorting papers seemed impossible
3 His daughter, experienced writer and researcher, helped him – he got down to it
   3(a) Ceaseless labour – 'seven days a week and sometimes late at night . . .'

3(b) Labour sustained because material was engrossing
4 His 'bulletins' to his publishers quoted to illustrate his enthusiasm for work

Stage 4: key points selected from skeleton
Before selecting key points I referred to my statement of the main theme and my descriptions of the writer's intentions. Guided by those I decided that the following were the key points: 2–2(a)–2(b)–3–3(a)–3(b)

Stage 5: a detailed plan for the précis
1 Spencer's papers filled two trunks and a large wooden box on castors when they reached Maurice Collis, his biographer
1(a) Collis horrified at first by sheer bulk of material
1(b) Task of reading, sorting, selecting, and arranging in chronological order all those papers seemed impossible
2 Aided by his daughter, an experienced writer and researcher, he got down to work
2(a) He had to work extremely hard – every day and late at night
2(b) He was sustained in his labours because – as his reports to his publishers showed – he found the Spencer material engrossing.

Comments
1 I was not entirely happy with that plan when I had finished it. I felt that I had got the order of the précis right, but I was not too sure that the balance of the contents was an accurate reflection of the key points that I had selected. I knew, too, that here and there I had copied words from the original. Consequently, I was uncomfortable about one or two of the expressions in the plan and knew that I ought to find substitutes for them.
2 However, since I was aware of the weaknesses in the plan, I decided to go ahead with my first draft, working entirely from my notes. Then, when I knew what pruning had to be done, I could pay special attention to balance and vocabulary, checking back with the original passage.

Stage 6: first draft of précis

Spencer's writing was not very disciplined, and his papers filled two trunks and a large wooden box on castors when they reached his biographer, Maurice Collis. They filled a whole room when they were unpacked.

At first, Collis was horrified by the sheer bulk of the material. The task of reading, sorting, selecting, and arranging in chronological order all those papers seemed impossible. With the help of his daughter, an experienced writer and researcher, he got down to work. He had to work extremely hard every day and late into the night. He was sustained in his immense labours because – as his reports to his publishers showed – he found the Spencer material engrossing.

Stage 7: pruning and polishing the first draft

1 *The word count* showed that I had used nearly double the number of words allowed! There were 113 words in my first draft, and the instructions stipulated not more than 65. A most thorough revision was clearly essential.

2 *Pruning* involves two operations:

(i) Strike out material that is irrelevant to the main theme; strike out material that plays no major part in achieving the writer's purposes.
(ii) Substitute brief expressions where longer ones have been used. Try especially to find single compendious words to take the place of phrases (*compendious* means 'containing the substance within small compass').

The précis writer needs a large vocabulary, with the aid of which he can make one word in his précis do the work of several words in the original.

3 *Pruning the contents of the first draft.* I looked at the first paragraph of my draft, then compared it with my précis plan and with the original. I had slipped up there. The point about Spencer's writing was *not* included in my plan. Obviously, I had allowed a memory of the original passage to upset the balance of my key point selection as I wrote the first draft.

Again, why include those details about the trunks and the wooden box on castors? They appeared in my plan. This was one of its faults, for I certainly had not the space to include details in the précis. In the original, those details provide a vivid illustration of the massive quantity of the Spencer papers, but the précis-writer cannot afford to include illustrative details. He has to concentrate on the bare essentials. In any case, I had made the necessary point by using the words 'sheer bulk' in the second paragraph of my draft.

Another reference to my key points showed that, in the draft, I had spent far too long in getting to the first main point. It was apparent to me now that I must cut right through the first paragraph of the draft – probably discard it – and get at 'the meat' of the précis straight away.

I then revised the opening to read:

Maurice Collis, the biographer of Stanley Spencer, was horrified by the sheer bulk of the material when the huge collection of Spencer's papers reached him.

What other material could be struck out? I had achieved a much crisper and better balanced opening for my précis, but I had saved only 22 words. Where else had I used unnecessary details?

An obvious example occurs in paragraph two of my draft, where the statement 'He had to work extremely hard every day and late into the night' says far more than is needed. The point to be made is that the biographer had to work extremely hard. The précis-writer does not have to *prove* the point by using details.

On checking with the original, I found that I had not been accurate in my use of those space-wasting words. The original does *not* say that he worked every day and late into the night. It says that he *often* worked seven days a week and *sometimes* late at night. So, I had used unnecessary details, consumed precious words, *and* I had committed the worst fault that a précis-writer can commit – I had distorted the meaning of the original passage.

Next, I realised that the material in parenthesis in the last sentence of my draft was unnecessary. Again, I was using details to illustrate or prove facts that, as a précis-writer, I needed only to state. The point that the précis must make is that Collis's enthusiasm saw him through the heavy task. There is no need to waste words in explaining how that enthusiasm was made plain to the publishers.

Finally, I considered whether the material about the biographer's daughter was necessary ('herself an experienced writer and researcher'). I decided that it served a useful purpose in the précis, for the fact that he had to have help emphasises the laborious nature of his task, and the fact that he needed skilled help backs up the statement that it was a difficult task. Also, I had reworded the original, turning 'a writer herself and used to research' into an equivalent expression in my own words.

4 *Word-pruning and substitution in the first draft.* I saw that I had used words wastefully in my first draft. In the second paragraph 'The task of reading, sorting, selecting, and arranging in chronological order' is almost a transposition from the original and it is very word-consuming. Surely I could think of a compendious word to do the work that those words do? What does the expression 'sorting, selecting, and arranging in chrono-logical order' mean in this context? It means *editing*. So, one word does the work of seven. *And* I was now using my own language instead of words copied from the original.

Again, I noticed that I had lifted the word 'engrossing' straight out of the original passage. It is a key word, so I had to find a word of my own that meant the same – or nearly the same – and the use of which would show my reader that I had understood one of the main points made by the original. I thought of 'fascinating' (which I had already used in Stage 1) but it did not seem quite right. It gave a sense of the attraction that the material had for the biographer, but it did not convey the sense of being totally immersed in the task – of being willingly 'up to the neck' in it. It is important that the précis should reflect the spirit of the original, so I wanted to do better than 'fascinating'. In the end, I decided that 'absorb' and 'engross' were truly equivalent in this context.

Stage 8: writing the final version
By now, I felt that I had been as critical of my own first draft as the examiner would have been had he seen it. I hoped that I had identified its chief faults. I had used my knowledge of précis-writing technique in my attempt to improve the draft. I could move on to my final version.

Maurice Collis, the biographer of Stanley Spencer, was horrified by the sheer bulk of the material when the huge collection of Spencer's papers reached him. Even just to read them all, let alone edit them, seemed impossible. With the help of his daughter, herself an experienced writer and researcher, he worked hard and long, sustained in his immense labours by his absorption in his subject.

(65 words)

There are, as you see, exactly 65 words in the final version, so the examiner's word limit has been met.

The précis seems to me to be accurate, to cover the main points made in the original passage, and to accord with the purposes that the writer had in mind.

It is, I think, a clear and connected piece of writing, and its style is appropriate.

All in all, it is now as good as I can make it in the time available.

Stage 9: fair copy and title for précis
All that remains to be done is to write out a fair copy on the answer sheet, *remembering to provide a suitable title for the précis.*

The test for a good précis is this:

- Would a reader of this précis *who had not seen the original passage* learn from the précis all the *essential* material contained in the original?

That test indicates what kind of a title you must provide for a précis.

The précis title must give the *source* of material that has been summarised. If the précis title does not provide the source of the original material then essential information is withheld from the reader of the précis.

So, in the case of the précis just completed, the title is:

Précis of an extract from 'The Spencer Papers' by Irene Stirling (from *The Bookseller*).

13.5 Selective summary

Practice in making full-length summaries, using the techniques described and illustrated in this chapter, will give you the confidence and experience that you need to answer the selective summary questions. The same principles apply to both: only the scale of the operation is different.

The instructions for selective summaries direct your attention to a part (or parts) of the subject-matter, whereas in making a précis you take the whole of the subject-matter as your field of operations.

Of course, you cannot make a successful selective summary until you have studied the *whole* passage carefully, because you need to identify the selected area, picking out what concerns you and excluding what does not.

You also need to have a good understanding of the whole passage in order to understand fully each part of it. Words, sentences, and paragraphs take a large part of their meaning from the whole of their context, not just from their immediate surroundings.

Nevertheless, it is important to be clear that you are instructed to operate on different areas of the original passage when selective summary is called for.

- When making a précis you identify and then present in your own words and in shortened form *the major points of the main theme* in the passage *as a whole*.
- When making a selective summary you identify and then present in your own words and in shortened form *the major points* made in *a specified part* of the passage. *Or* you may be required to deal with *the major points* made on a *specified topic*, the relevant material occurring *in various places throughout* the passage.

Some selective summary tasks are straightforward. For example: 'Explain in your own words the arguments advanced in favour of compulsory voting in paragraph three.'

But when, as often happens, the topic to be summarised crops up here and there throughout the passage you really do have to keep your wits about you.

Quite often, the topic specified for summarising is divided between various speakers, or treated from different points of view, or spread over more than one of several short passages that, together, constitute the material on which the summary is to be based.

In short, the material set for selective summary takes different forms, and the instructions are based on a variety of meaning. It is not possible to anticipate which of many variants will face you in the examination, but if you have a thorough grasp of the summarising techniques taught in this chapter, and if you *study carefully* the *particular instructions* that you find on your paper, you need not fear this kind of question.

--- Test 13.1 ---

Read this passage carefully. Then make a plan for a précis of the passage. Use your own words when making the plan and remember to head your plan with a brief statement of the gist of the passage. (Revise 13.4 (f) and 13.4 (i) before starting work. Our suggested answer is in the Answer Section at the end of the book. Do not turn to it before working out your own answer.

Perhaps it has never struck you that scientific inventions can be very helpful to the artist? Then the following story may be of interest. The horse has always been a favourite subject but have you ever realised that it was not until the closing years of the nineteenth century that a galloping horse could be truthfully depicted? The reason is that the human eye is not quick enough to observe accurately the movements of a horse's legs when in rapid motion. The consequence was that, until the invention of slow-motion films, no artist had any idea what a galloping horse really did with its legs. So, for centuries, the moving horse was painted, either rearing up on its hind legs and pawing the air with its front hooves (which, of course, it may do, but not when galloping), or in the celebrated 'flying gallop', its front legs extended forward and its hind legs extended backwards. This flying gallop posture was suggestive of great speed and was very successful artistically, though a little thought will show that a horse in such a position would be an anatomical impossibility. The convention lasted, however, until slow-motion pictures enabled artists to achieve realism without loss of movement in their studies of galloping horses.

13.6 Direct and indirect (reported) speech

The rules for the correct punctuation of direct speech are set out in Chapter 7, section 7.8, but it is necessary to deal with indirect speech in this chapter on 'Summary' for this reason:

- All *direct speech* in the original passage *must be changed into indirect speech* in the summary.

(a) Definitions

Direct speech is a *direct representation* in writing of the words *actually spoken*:

John said, 'I'm late because I overslept.'

Indirect speech is a *report* in writing of the words *actually spoken*:

John said that he was late because he had overslept.

That is why *reported speech* is the alternative name for 'indirect speech'.

(b) The use of reported speech in summary

It used to be obligatory to write all précis in reported speech. The précis writer was expected to begin his précis with a 'formula' introduction such as this:

The writer states that there were three reasons for the decline of rural transport in the mid-twentieth century.

Examiners no longer insist on this. Nowadays you are encouraged to express the writer's material directly, as if it were your own – provided, of course, that you do not copy out the writer's actual words. So, the accepted presentation of the above is:

> There were three reasons for the decline of rural transport in the mid-twentieth century.

However, the use of reported speech is still compulsory in the following circumstances:

(i) When the examiner's instructions say, 'Make a précis of the following passage in reported speech.' Examiners do, from time to time, insist on this. They are perfectly entitled to do so. Candidates are expected to be capable of using reported speech *and* they are expected to read the instructions.

(ii) Whenever direct speech occurs in the original passage, and you need to include that material in your summary because it is a key point, you *must* change it into reported speech. You must never quote in a summary.

Suppose that the following seems to you to embody a key point in the passage that you are summarising:

> 'I'm perfectly certain', said Councillor Jones, 'that the ratepayers will get steamed up about this proposal.'

The remark must be *reported* in your summary, like this:

> Councillor Jones said that he was convinced that the ratepayers would be angry about that proposal.

Notes on the above example

1 'perfectly certain' becomes 'convinced'. The précis-writer is using his own words and condensing.
2 'I'm' becomes 'he was'.
3 'will' becomes 'would be'.
4 'steamed up' becomes 'angry'. The style of a summary is always formal. Figures of speech are not used.

Those notes draw attention to some of the rules for the writing of reported speech, which are discussed now.

(c) The rules of reported speech

1 A 'saying' verb followed by 'that' introduces reported speech, as in the example given earlier:

> John said that he was late because he had overslept.

The 'saying' verb is not always 'said'. It can be an 'expressive' saying verb, useful to the summariser because it conveys swiftly and economically the tone or purpose of the speech that is being reported:

The prisoner protested that he had been denied access to his solicitor.

Robinson objected that the item had not been discussed in committee.

2 The tense of the 'saying' verb governs the tenses of all the verbs used in the reported speech. This, if you look at it realistically, is just a matter of common sense. You cannot put your meaning across if you jumble up the tenses. These examples illustrate the tense rules which are shown immediately before them.

The 'saying' verb is often in the past tense. When it is, the verbs in the reported speech must be in the past tense, too:

The chairman reported that his committee had given the fullest consideration to that point but announced that it had felt unable to change its recommendation.

If, however, the 'saying' verb is in the present tense, then the tenses of the verbs in the reported speech are adjusted accordingly, like this:

Our special correspondent writes that conditions in the devastated area are improving slowly and that it should be possible to restore railway communications fairly soon.

3 When direct speech is turned into reported speech all pronouns and possessive adjectives must be changed into the *third person*. For example:

Direct speech The rebel leader announced his acceptance of the terms of the truce, saying: 'It shall never be asserted that I prolonged this struggle uneccesarily. The lives of my men are precious to me, and the cause has always been that of the people of our country.'

Indirect (reported) speech The rebel leader announced his acceptance of the terms of the truce and declared that it should never be asserted that he had prolonged that struggle unnecessarily. The lives of his men were precious to him, and their cause had always been that of the people of their country.

4 The necessity of using only third-person pronouns and possessive adjectives can give rise to ambiguity – a fatal weakness in any writing, and especially in summary. A competent summariser avoids this fault by substituting appropriate nouns for pronouns and possessive nouns for possessive adjectives. Here is an example of how it can be done:

Ambiguous He said that he had followed his proposals carefully and his objections to them would be quite clear to them when they had heard what he had to say in his speech.

Improved He said that he had followed the last speaker's proposals carefully and his objections to them would be quite clear to the members of the audience when they had heard what he had to say in his own speech.

5 Adjectives and adverbs indicating nearness in place and in time in direct speech are changed in reported speech into adjectives and adverbs expressive of a 'distancing' effect. For example, 'this' becomes 'that'; 'today' becomes 'that day'. Like the tenses, these adjectives and adverbs 'go back one', so to speak – as in this passage:

Direct speech   The delegate said: 'My union sent me here to find a solution to this long-standing problem. We have set ourselves a time limit for the conclusion of this troublesome business, but we are prepared to be patient until it becomes clear to us that the will to succeed does not exist on your side. We want an agreement by the end of next month.'

Reported speech   The delegate said that his union had sent him there to find a solution to that long-standing problem. They had set themselves a time limit for the conclusion of that troublesome business, but they were prepared to be patient until it became clear to them that the will to succeed did not exist on the other side. They wanted an agreement by the end of the following month.

6 Colloquialisms and contractions are not used in reported speech.

Direct speech (extract from a letter)   'I'd better tell you that I've decided not to be your candidate at the next election – whenever it comes – and I'll probably get it off my chest at the committee meeting next Jan.'

Reported speech   The writer informed his correspondent that he had decided not to be their candidate at the election, whenever that occurred, and that he would take an early opportunity of announcing that decision. He would probably do so at the committee meeting in the following January.

As the above example shows, slang is not used in reported speech, either.

Test 13.2

Re-write the following passage in reported speech before looking at our version in the Answers Section at the end of the book.

The chief opposition spokesman for education said: 'I have listened to the minister's speech with care but I find nothing new or constructive in his proposals. Indeed, I regard his speech as a flagrant betrayal of his party's election promises. Far from spending more on education, he proposes to hold expenditure at this year's level. In a time of rising prices that is tantamount to reducing the money spent on education, and I accuse him of weakening the service that it is his duty to strengthen.'

⑭ Understanding and response

14.1 The key issues

For many years the examination boards tested candidates' skills in understanding by a series of formal, carefully structured exercises called 'Comprehension Passages and Questions'. In recent years the demands on examination candidates have been different. 'Understanding' has been assessed as an integral part of the skills of reading and writing.

It is important for people in general, and candidates in particular, to recognise that understanding is not only about the *meaning* of a piece of writing, but about the purpose and intentions of its author as well as some of the methods used in its construction.

The range and extent of our appreciation of these features of writing determine the quality of our response. The level of interest that we show and the extent of our experience in judging such matters are vital factors. However, do remember that candidates are not expected to be experts.

The ways in which we progress in these skills of understanding and response are determined by the tuition that we receive and by the intuition that we develop.

Tuition is available to all – by listening to teachers and lectures at school, college or evening institute; reading the observations of reviewers and critics in newspapers and magazines; by watching and noting the commentators on television and radio.

Intuition is a more complex matter, but suffice to say that within us there are many areas of 'awareness'. These differing areas are used for survival, advancement and pleasure. As we mature it becomes obvious that people have an instinctive need for communication with one another. The particular skills of reading, writing, speaking and listening that we develop, depend upon and, perhaps, grow to love, are part of these evolving forces within human beings. The seeds of understanding are planted within us. Exposure to words stimulates growth and assists the development of intuitive powers.

14.2 Understanding of meaning, purpose and method

(a) Meaning

The word that was frequently used to express our understanding of meaning was 'comprehend'. It is a verb concerned with 'the ability to grasp with the mind, to take in'. Comprehension, then, is 'the act of grasping with the mind, taking in'. It is understanding in *depth*.

Not many candidates scored high marks in the Comprehension tests that were widespread at one time. This generally poor performance was due to widespread failure to appreciate what is meant by 'comprehension', in the full meaning of that word. Too few candidates learnt to read with the concentrated and directed attention that is essential.

Very careful reading of any passage that is to be 'tested' is the first requirement. By 'careful reading' we mean reading with insight and imagination. Lazy-minded, superficial reading is of no use. Anybody can skim over the surface of a passage . . . and fail to appreciate its essentials. When you are confronted with a piece of writing that requires your full attention, you must read with complete concentration, determined to master the meaning of the passage in front of you – determined to grasp it with your mind.

You must also read it sympathetically, entering into its spirit and working *with* the author. That is what is meant by 'reading with imagination'.

(b) Purpose

All authors have a purpose or intention. At one level they are, perhaps, writing for financial gain, at another because it is part of their job. In literary terms their intentions vary considerably. The point is that the reader should, at a fairly basic level, be able to determine something of the motives that inspire the writer.

A simple way of assessing and pinpointing the intentions of an author is to apply the letters P–L–E–A–S–E to a section of his or her work. The letters stand for the following features that can apply either singly or in combination with others:

Persuasion	the intention of the politician, preacher or advocate
Listening	the desired achievement of the story-teller or fiction-writer
Education	the motive of the documentary or textbook writer
Advice	the driving force behind the manuals and practical guides
Stimulation	the purpose of the author who wishes to elevate his readers
Entertainment	the wish to create within others feelings of pleasure

(c) Methods

It is obvious to any reader of this book that the assessment of a writer's method or use of language is a very complicated matter. Again, expertise is not expected of the candidate in an examination, but the application of common sense and the understanding of a few basic considerations is required. In order to assess the approach of an author to the subject under review, read the chosen passage carefully and note the following:

1 First or third person? Is the 'I' form used to denote the more personal involvement of the author or his characters?
2 Subjective or objective? Does the author or his views *directly* participate in the matters of the text or does he try to be *detached*?
3 Narration, description, analysis or comment? Is the author attempting to tell a story, set a scene, expose underlying reasons or make direct personal observations?
4 Emotional pitch? The ways in which an author approaches his subject vary. At one extreme there are intensity and feverish commitment to the theme; at the other extreme the tones of indifference and casual detachment are evident. In between there is a complete range of emotions and mental states involving such feelings as: optimism – pessimism – depression – cheerfulness – detachment – bitterness – encouragement – restraint – effusiveness – carefulness – abandon – humour – austerity – frivolity – seriousness – reverence – respect – provocativeness – calmness – coolness – awe.

___ **Activity 14.1** ___

Read the following passage taken from Fraser Harrison's autobiography study, *A Winter's Tale*. Study it closely to understand its meaning and to develop in your mind the image of the grandfather that the author wishes to convey. Then refer to the last two sections again and try to assess what you see to be the writer's purpose and his methods. Explore the relationships between the individuals involved:

the author – the author as a child – the grandfather – the other people present at the dining table.

You should see this passage as being about a domineering man who has a strong effect upon a child. Yet in retrospect this 'ceremony of mealtimes' indicates a strange ritual of adult prowess that is somewhat bizarre.

My Stackpole grandfather had huge, richly veined hands. His fingers and thumbs were stout and powerful, but what made his hands truly enormous was their breadth, for the span of his palm, held flat, was easily large enough to encircle a tea plate. When I try to reconstruct my childhood memories of him, it is his hands I chiefly recall, partly because they were remarkable in their own right, but also because I was afraid to look him in the eye. Most of these memories are gathered round the ceremony of mealtimes, which was, I suppose when he generally saw me and when he was at his most domineering. It was his presence that I, at any rate, was most conscious of, and so, rather than face him directly, I studied his hands, which in miniature I have inherited.

Despite their immensity, these hands could wield a carving knife and fork with the sweetest dexterity. He did everything with a theatrical flourish, and his performance over a roast chicken never failed to fascinate me. And when he tackled a job, he did it properly. There was no hacking or pulling: he shaved off the breast in perfectly proportioned wafers, and severed the joints of legs and wings with single, devastating strokes. He laid out the slices on each plate in an elegant pattern, nearly separating the white meat from the brown with a strip of crisp skin. He always adjusted his arrangement with a few delicate flicks from the point of his knife before passing on the plate for my grandmother to add the vegetables. When everyone was served, he would bend over his own plate and invade it with awe-inspiring heartiness. He had a way of piling up his food on the back of his fork, which I have never seen anyone else achieve. Every part of the meat – leg, breast and skin, potato, sprout and carrot – would be stacked up in little chunks, compressed into a solid, stratified block, drenched in gravy and briskly transported to his mouth, where it would be engulfed in one cavernous bite, leaving not a scrap or drop on his moustache. Having eaten everything else, he would scoop up his gravy with his knife, flattening its blade against the plate and leaning on it with all the strength of his formidable hands as he scraped off the last spots. He invariably left his place so clean it could have been put straight back on the shelf without being washed.

Although I have since grown to be just as robust an eater as he was, in these days I could never finish any but the smallest meals. This he saw as a weakness which he made it his business to correct by the simple method of doubling my rations. And so, while he scoured the glaze off his plate, I would still be nauseously confronting the mound of food on my overloaded plate.

Fraser Harrison A Winter's Tale

This is a closely-observed portrait with strong emotional under-tones. Your reading of this passage should have the same precision and enable you to share something of the author's feelings.

14.3   Appreciation of these features

The extent of our being stimulated by these literary matters depends upon several factors. The first is probably our wish to be involved. Second, we are influenced by the strength of our imaginative abilities. Third, the degree of open-mindedness and receptivity that we possess influences our response. Last, we have to be able to read effectively and to have a mind that actually enjoys words, their meanings and the impact that they make on ourselves and on others.

Our inadequacies are always evident. Words have a way of 'escape' for their meanings shift constantly and they have ways of slipping out of general use as well as in and out of our minds. Literary criticism is not an exact science. However, it appeals to many and does give an immense amount of pleasure. We probably have to bear in mind something that Auberon Waugh observed:

> Humanity has always divided between those who worry over the world's imperfections and those who are happy to celebrate its working parts.

Our response to words and the methods that are used to weld them into meaningful passages, articles, stories and books should be part of this 'celebration' of the working parts of life.

In order to succeed you should endeavour to find a teacher or textbook that appeals to you; join a class of like-minded students; be ready to respond to the stimuli; be aware of your own intuitive faculties; make a study of the art of reading (see Chapter 21); practise your own skills as a writer.

The next six chapters are about the various features of different types of writing and the techniques that can be used to produce them. The six that will be studied here are.

Chapter 15   Directed writing
Chapter 16   Discursive (or argumentative) writing
Chapter 17   Narrative writing
Chapter 18   Descriptive writing
Chapter 19   Impressionistic writing
Chapter 20   Dramatic writing

(15) Directed writing

15.1 The requirements

In the case of many English Language examinations you will be given, in certain sections, all the information that you need to know about a topic, the directions in order to fulfil the required task, and even suggestions about the lay-out and presentation. This approach is known as 'directed writing' and is frequently a part of the examination structure.

This may sound a particularly contrived situation. It could be considered that your creativity, inventiveness and imaginative qualities are being largely untested. In some ways this is true, but the requirements for 'directed writing' are only a part of the whole examination. However, this form of writing, in one way or another, constitutes much of the type of writing that you will have to do during your time at work.

Companies, organisations and employers demand the very skills that are required by the examiners in these sections of the examination papers. Think of the ways in which the work of the following groups of skilled employees is undertaken:

> Secretaries – Report-writers – Analysts – Consultants – Programmers
> – Researchers – Tax-officials – Printers – Accountants

They are all undertaking work that involves the arrangement of words and figures in ways laid down by tradition, accepted practice or management directive. There is no scope for radical innovation by the individual because the work has to be produced according to predetermined patterns. The skill is to be able to manage and manipulate the material efficiently in order to achieve the desired result with the minimum of effort and the maximum impact.

You are being asked either by the examiner or by your employer to *manage* words and numbers, facts and figures, ideas and illustrations. You are not being invited to devise them.

Emphasis is placed upon the following:

- identifying what matters;
- arranging the material in an appropriate sequence;
- expressing the ideas coherently;
- awareness of the audience for whom you are writing;
- appreciation of standards of presentation.

Do remember that in an examination much, if not all, of the material in this section will already have been shaped. The examiner will have 'fashioned' it in order to be helpful. You will have to 're-shape' some of it according to the question and in response to your personal judgement. This skill will reveal how effective you are in the management of material.

In day-to-day working life similar requirements will be equally clear-cut, but probably in a more extreme way. There will, perhaps, be an absolute sense of order with the company policy and the computers' demands determining the exact way in which the directed task has to be performed. On the other hand there could be chaos, an absence of data or a mass of apparently unrelated material, but the actual directives and the final required order for information and its presentation will have been determined beforehand.

15.2 An approach

There are, of course, many ways in which to approach the tasks of directed writing. Two things are necessary. One is to bear in mind the importance of the five features mentioned in 15.1. They are:

Identification – Sequence – Expression – Audience – Presentation.

The other is to have a systematic approach and to aim to structure your answer in such a way that the minimum effort is employed to achieve the maximum effect. Ergonomics – the study of our working habits – need not preoccupy us, but it is worth bearing in mind whenever problems have to be solved or tasks undertaken.

Take the sequence of letters Re–Ti–N–Dr–A–W. Hold them in mind and note them in the following way:

*Re*ad	It is necessary to do this twice. On the first occasion you are assessing the material; on the second you are studying it.
*Ti*tle	Devise a title that incorporates within it the demands and the requirements that the examiner wants. This is, in its way, your 'contract'.
*N*otes	You are not having to summarise the passage, but to indicate the main points of your answer that responds accurately to the requests of the examiner and to the demands of the 'contract' that you have just devised.
*Dr*aft	A quickly completed, rough copy of your piece of directed writing should be produced. Its length should approximate to that required.
*A*lterations	If time allows, re-read the original. It time does not permit this, study your notes carefully. Then make any necessary amendments to your draft.
*W*rite	Make an attractively-presented, completed piece of work.

Activity 15.1

Imagine that you have been asked to arrange an aspect of a holiday in London for a family of five. They will be staying in the capital for a week and have expressed an interest in taking part in a number of guided tours. They are active, have a basic knowledge of English culture and history, and want to undertake a variety of walks. Your requirement is to study the brochure, *The Original London Walks*, (see Fig. 15.1) that has been recommended to you, plan their choice of 'Walks' for one week, bearing in mind the following information, and present a clear, straightforward plan that outlines your proposals and, to an extent, justifies your selections.

Members of the Family:

Father	Peter (42)	Company Manager	Enjoys historical matters
Mother	Jenny (40)	Schoolteacher	Likes meeting people
Grand-mother	Doreen (65)	Retired legal secretary	Reads detective novels
Daughter	Lucy (17)	A-Level student	Wants a theatrical career
Son	Simon (13)	School-pupil	Sport and musical interests

Length of Stay:

One week   Sunday until Saturday

Number and times:

Five walks should be planned, spread throughout the week, preferably at different times of the day.

If you feel that you have presented a successful itinerary for this English family, try a similar exercise for a French or German family who have a knowledge of the language, but little awareness of the local cultural details.

You may need to be reminded of some of the places to be visited on the Walks described on page 166.

The West End – Where the theatres are situated.
Westminster – Famous for its Abbey and for Parliament.
The City and the Square Mile – the financial district.
Jack the Ripper – A notorious murderer of the nineteenth century.
Little Venice – A residential area close to a canal.
Mayfair – A residential area for the wealthy.
Covent Garden – A market-place for tourists where street-entertainers perform.
Hampstead – An attractive suburb famous for its writers and artists.
Soho – An area in central London well known for its restaurants and erotic entertainment.
Chelsea – A suburb that is fashionable and which attracts many young people.
'Blitz' – The bombing of the Second World War.

THE ORIGINAL
LONDON
WALKS

"If you want to know London better, if you want to learn some things about the world's most cosmopolitan city that most people who spend their lives there never learn ... I can think of no better investment than London Walks"   The New York Times

We're London's **longest established** walking tour group and, with over 20 years in the business, we think we've got it right!

In practice that means **superb guides** and **small groups** (we average about 15-20 walkers per tour). In other words, with London Walks you **will not** be herded round in a mob of 75 or even 100 or more other tourists. We don't go in for hype or slick, saturation advertising. And that keeps our groups down to a comfortable size for everybody—walkers, guide, and locals!

A word about our guides. We think that if you're doing a job like this 40 hours a week you get stale. So we don't use full-time guides—we don't want any "walking tape recorders". London Walks guides have other careers and guide as a labour of love, which means they look forward to each walk and conduct it with enthusiasm, flair, and genuine interest in their subject.

To go on a walk, just come along and join your guide and your fellow walkers at the entrance to the appropriate Underground station at the time stated. The walks last about two hours (pub walks take a little longer) and end near Underground stations.

Each walk costs **£4** (£2.50 for students). Children under 15 go free if accompanied by an adult. If you want to go on several walks, Discount Walkabout tickets are available.

The Original **LONDON WALKS**
PO Box 1708
London NW6 1PQ
Tel: **071-435 6413**
(or 071-794 1764 / 071-911 0285)

Figure 15.1a Details from front of brochure

THE WALKS

Time	Day & Walk	Underground
	MONDAYS	
11:00am	Legal London-Inns of Court	Holborn
11:30am	The Old Jewish Quarter	Tower Hill
2:00pm	Shakespeare & Dickens's London (the Bankside)	Monument
7:00pm	Along the Thames Pub Walk	Blackfriars
7:30pm	Ghosts of the West End	Embankment
	TUESDAYS	
10:30am	Sherlock Holmes & the Baker Street Beat	Baker Street
11:00am	"The London Nobody Knows"	Chancery Lane
2:00pm	"The Westminster Nobody Knows"	Green Park
7:30pm	Ghosts of the City	St. Paul's
7:30pm	Jack the Ripper Haunts	Tower Hill
	WEDNESDAYS *(except December 25th)*	
11:00am	Shakespeare's & Dickens's London (the Old City)	St. Paul's
2:00pm	Historic Westminster	Westminster
2:30pm	Little Venice	Warwick Avenue
7:00pm	An Aristocratic London Pub Walk	Sloane Square
7:30pm	Jack the Ripper Haunts	Tower Hill
	THURSDAYS	
11:00am	The Famous Square Mile (2000 Years of History)	Monument
2:00pm	Legal London-Inns of Court	Holborn
2:30pm	The Old Jewish Quarter	Tower Hill
7:30pm	Jack the Ripper Haunts	Tower Hill
7:30pm	Ghosts of the West End	Embankment
	FRIDAYS	
10:00am	Mayfair ("the best address in London")	Green Park
11:00am	Hidden London	Monument
2:00pm	In the Footsteps of Sherlock Holmes	Embankment
7:00pm	Along the Thames Pub Walk	Blackfriars
7:30pm	Jack the Ripper Haunts	Tower Hill
	SATURDAYS	
10:00am	Covent Garden	Embankment
11:00am	Shakespeare's & Dickens's London (the Bankside)	Monument
2:00pm	Historic Westminster	Westminster
3:00pm	Jack the Ripper's London	Tower Hill
7:00pm	A Hampstead Pub Walk	Hampstead
7:30pm	Ghosts of the City	St. Paul's
	SUNDAYS	
10:30am	Village London-Hampstead	Hampstead
11:00am	Historic City-Romans to the Blitz	Tower Hill
2:00pm	Little Venice	Warwick Avenue
2:00pm	Soho (the Infamous Square Mile)	Embankment
2:30pm	"From the Repertory"	(Changes Weekly, Ring for Details)
7:00pm	A Chelsea Pub Walk	Sloane Square
7:30pm	Jack the Ripper Haunts	Tower Hill

> **For a fully detailed description of our programme of walks, please write or telephone and ask for a copy of our main pamphlet.**

Figure 15.1b Details from back of brochure

16 Discursive writing

16.1 The requirements

A discursive composition is one in which the writer arrives at a conclusion by reasoning. He considers in turn various aspects of his subject-matter and then proceeds to make a statement of his own carefully-thought-out opinions about that subject.

The alternative names for discursive writing are 'argumentative writing' and 'controversial writing'. Those alternative names indicate what kind of subjects are set and what kind of treatment is expected.

There are many typical subjects for discursive compositions. As many, in fact, as the disagreements and alternative ways of doing things that there are in society.

Here are some examples, phrased in the ways that are usual in examination and coursework requirements:

The advantages and disadvantages of organised and packaged holidays.

The advantages and disadvantages of marriage.

State the arguments for and against censorship on television.

What is the case for compulsory school uniform and what are your views on the matter?

Do you think that smoking should be banned by law?

Do you think that potentially dangerous breeds of animals should be kept by private individuals? Should these animals be kept in public institutions such as zoos or safari parks, or does this raise problems?

The examiners and moderators of coursework are looking for certain qualities in discursive compositions. They are:

- a genuine interest in the subject under discussion and an adequate fund of information about that subject;
- the ability to see both sides of an argument and to present opposing views clearly, coolly and fairly;
- the temperament to take account of objections while calmly and rationally coming down in favour of a considered opinion;
- the determination to move steadily through conflicting arguments and to present a clear conclusion at the end.

16.2   The problems

These fall into two specific categories – technical and temperamental. The first concerns the lack of clarity in this particular division of writing that does demand a high standard of straghtforward and uncomplicated expression. The second is a more personal matter. Whenever people argue, certain features of personality often emerge. They include what we may call the 'don't-want-to-be-involved' approach, the 'you-just-listen-to-me' school of thought, and the 'know-it-all' syndrome. These features reveal themselves in ways of writing.

In this case the three defects that should be avoided are:

- *No conclusion* – you are expected to have a view and to express it.
- *One-sided presentation* – your opinion will carry more weight if you show an awareness of the arguments that are used against it.
- *Prejudice* – many of the topics are controversial and anger will be a strong element. It must be tempered with cool, reasonable judgement that avoids bitterness and prejudice.

16.3   An approach

Your approach to this aspect of written work will be determined by your skills in producing ideas and by your personality in being able to handle their presentation. It may be helpful to consider the following sequence.

A Three things to keep in mind:

  Conclusion – Choice – Coolness

1 Discursive writing depends upon bringing matters to a conclusion.
2 Argumentative writing requires expounding the arguments for and against and making a reasoned choice between them.
3 Controversial writing demands coolness and clarity when dealing with topics that will stir up strong feelings.

B Three things to plan on paper:

  Head – Body – Foot

1 Introduction: a brief lead-in to head the subject, stating its importance, topicality and, perhaps, an aspect of its history.
2 Body of composition: a series of paragraphs each dealing with a relevant topic that presents arguments for and against.
3 Conclusion: this is the 'bottom line' in which the considered opinion, based on cool, rational appraisal of the arguments, is delivered.

C Three things to aim for when writing: A–B–C

1 *Attractive*-sounding arguments. 'Listen' as you write.
2 *Be* simple in your approach and try to avoid complications.
3 *Clarity* matters more than anything.

Activity 16.1

The following article appeared in the *Daily Telegraph* during the summer of 1991. The weather had been remarkably varied, with many hours of sunshine, days of rain and a range of temperatures. During 1990 there had been weeks of continual sunshine that had made Britain appear to be 'Mediterranean' in climate.

The journalist, Cassandra Jardine, argues a case for taking holidays in the British Isles where, she claims, 'unpredictability means variety'. She indicates that she writes, 'as a convert' – in other words, as a person presenting a case strongly in order to convince others.

1 List her arguments for holidaying in the English county of Cornwall.
2 Find the concession that she makes for going abroad.
3 Imagine that you are the regular writer of the column, Oliver Pritchett, who is 'on holiday'. Write a reply from anywhere in the world, apart from in Britain, arguing that the real 'variety of a vacation' is to be somewhere different.

Oh, to be wet in England

Each morning in this much-maligned summer I feel a sense of relief that it is not like last year. Sometimes there's cloud, sometimes sun, occasionally even a downpour. Lovely, especially for those on holiday.

Sun, relentless sweltering sun, I have recently decided, looks best on a postcard. I speak as a convert who has made a long-delayed return to holidaying in Cornwall. It was heaven. Having followed fashion in recent years and headed for the hottest rays available, it was a joy to rediscover the pleasure of a holiday in a country that has weather instead of a climate.

Unpredictability means variety. During dull patches we walked or visited stately homes. When the rain came down we enjoyed getting soaked, or we read. This year I got through novels by the stack instead of the page. In the mindnumbing heat of foreign beaches, even an Agatha Christie becomes hard work.

Cornwall was not totally without sun. Most days there was an hour or so when it was fine enough to head for the beach and the pleasure of those patches was magnified by anticipation. It became a game in itself to be ready to seize on a

'British hotels are such bad value for money that going abroad makes economic sense'

chink in the clouds; the outcome was my best tan in years, since I didn't first shed 10 layers of skin.

It is possible to enjoy holidays in the sun if you are content to sit in the shade, only I feel a duty – no doubt induced by a childhood of Cornish holidays – to drop everything and catch each ray.

I have always felt that the perfect quantity of sun is that which can be absorbed in a lunch-hour. A day is too much, especially with children. By eleven o'clock you either have to devote yourself to non-stop application of Factor 23 and sunhat replacement, or think of an indoor activity (most of those involve a prolonged bake in a car to something that turns out to be shut). Blinded and sweaty, sleepless and bitten, the afternoon becomes a matter of waiting for the sun to set and the mosquitoes to come out.

I am not alone in being less critical about the British weather, "She had a lovely time," said my sister of her daughter's holiday in the south of France last week, "but it was very hot." Would we have heard that "but" a few years ago? Twice recently one-time sun-worshippers told me they "just love the smell of wet grass".

Two years of hotter summers and global warming talk has made us less wistful about non-stop sunshine. Edwardian picnickers on sunlit lawns don't look so enviable: not only must they have been boiled in all those frilly clothes and bloated from eating raised meat pies, they must have gone cross-eyed reading in the golden light.

The only shame about this reconciliation with delightful, unpredictable weather is that it is too expensive to enjoy except in your own or a friend's back garden. British hotels, boarding houses and restaurants continue to be such bad value for money that going abroad, almost anywhere, makes economic sense.

The graph which, each year, shows fewer of us holidaying at home, in 1990 showed a tiny reversal. Weekends away in this country are proving increasingly popular. But, from a glance at the empty beaches on which I sat, the revival of the British beach holiday remains only a Punch and Judy man's dream.

Oliver Pritchett is on holiday

17 Narrative writing

17.1 The requirements

Everyone has the material for dozens of stories – life sees to that. True, but what a mess most people make of telling their stories! Everyday conversations afford abundant proof that few people are natural storytellers. 'I should have explained that Mark's letter arrived after Jill saw Fiona. That made all the difference,' 'Of course, you really have to know my uncle to see how funny that was.' 'No, wait a minute . . . I'm forgetting. It was July just *before* we went away.'

In the time that an examination allows, and even under the restraints of course-work, it is a difficult task to write a successful short story. Even professional writers of fiction recognise that a short story is hard to write – and they are not tied down so firmly by limitations of time and length. Nor do they have either a title or some other rigid constraint laid upon them as the examination candidate does.

So the first requirement is actually to think hard before choosing a narrative composition. We are not saying that you should never attempt the story question. The examiners and moderators are not setting an impossible task, nor do they expect an impossibly high standard. They do not expect the candidate to reveal the talents of a professional. An interesting, well-planned story told in correct English will get a good mark. Just remember that a narrative composition is not an *easy* option.

The second requirement of a story composition is that it must interest the reader. This is true, of course, of other kinds of composition. The candidate who bores his reader is not making things easy for himself, whatever kind of writing he chooses; but a story is associated with leisure reading – with reading for pleasure. By choosing to write a story the candidate promises his reader an entertaining experience and so, consequently, something that fails to come up to the mark, in both the metaphorical sense of giving pleasure and in the literal, examination sense, will create a feeling of disappointment.

The third requirement is that, as in any imaginative composition, the writer must put something of himself into his writing. It is easy for the writer to reproduce the 'formula writing' from memories of television crime series or from newspaper reports on 'personalities' and sporting encounters. The unvaried diet of stale, secondhand material that is traded as fiction in some series of cheap books is to be avoided. Personal commitment and that genuine quality of experience will show through and give an authentic touch to a story, even when the style lacks the full professional skills.

An interesting story has originality; and originality does not depend on the frantic invention of far-fetched episodes and improbable details. It is achieved by springing out of your own experience, not somebody else's. It depends on your ability to be creative, inventive and use imagination to good effect. Your story should be as alive as you are.

17.2   An approach

Before you start writing at all, make an agenda for yourself – planning, writing, polishing.

17.3   Planning

Much planning is needed to turn the raw material for a story into a successful narrative. The writer can start work on his plan when he is sure that his material

- interests him and, therefore, stands a chance of interesting his reader;
- is rooted in his own experience (i.e. is firsthand and fresh, not secondhand and stale);
- is capable of being used for a story of the kind required.

Observation of these points does not guarantee success. It probably ensures that not too much time is wasted on failures.

(a) Plots

The first step in planning is to work out a *plot* for the story. This need not be elaborate. The examiner does not expect the candidate to be a professional writer of stories. But any story – if it is to be a story – must have a 'story-line'. It cannot be static. It must move towards a conclusion. It should include that all-important element – *change*. The situation depicted at the beginning must change into a different situation as the story unfolds.

The need for progression in the narrative is particularly important in the writing of 'puzzle stories' of the kind set in examinations. Typical instructions for the writing of such stories are: 'Write a story ending with this sentence, "She was thankful that she had not won that prize"' or 'Write a story ending with this sentence, "I never did discover the name of the girl on the train."'

Everything that happens in the story must be a development carrying the narrative forward. At the end, the situation depicted at the beginning has been resolved into a new state of affairs, linked to but different from the starting-point. Pace is therefore necessary to move the story towards its climax. At times the narrative lingers to set scenes or to build suspense.

Action and description alternate. The beginning, the middle and the end should be carefully proportioned to give the story shape.

To sum up this section here are some of the key words that should be jotted down at the head of the piece of paper on which the planning is being undertaken –

- Plot – Change – Pace – Shape

(b) People

Stories are invariably about people. They must contain 'characters', as they are usually called. The reader needs to recognise the people in the story as 'real' people. If he cannot do this he cannot get interested in them. He does not have to like them all. He may feel liking or disliking, admiration or contempt, friendship or enmity, etc., for any of them, but he must feel something about them. He must understand why they are as they are and why they do what they do.

To involve his reader with his characters the writer of the story must believe in his people and be interested in them. Then, he needs the technical skill to bring them to life. He has to describe what they feel and think as well as what they do. He has to give them motives for their conduct. He has to reveal their natures through their words as well as through their deeds. To do this involves the writing of credible dialogue as well as the ability to describe scenes and narrate events.

17.4 Writing

The story must have atmosphere. Stories do not happen in a vacuum peopled by shadows. There has to be a setting – places, houses, furniture, weather, cars, possessions. People have looks, voices, mannerisms; they laugh, cry, wear clothes, are old, young, thin, fat.

The blending of people, events and setting creates atmosphere; and the writer needs a vivid but controlled imagination to build up an atmosphere that makes an impact on the reader and draws him into the story.

A way of 'bonding' the interests of reader and writer is to realise just how much we all depend upon our five senses in assessing and capturing the essential feel for people, places and things. The story should incorporate, to varying degrees, references to sight – sound – touch – smell – taste. These are, by their very nature, shared experiences.

17.5 Polishing

Once the planning has been finished and the elements of plot, people and atmosphere worked out, it is easy to be carried away and to write furiously in order to complete the required task. Take care! Steady control of the pen, typewriter or word-processor is vital. The skills that are needed for a successful story of your own invention – the mastery of the narrative, dramatic and descriptive – apply equally to the story of your own development as a writer.

The skills that are needed for a successful story of your own involve endeavour, inventiveness and vision. The mastery of narrative, dramatic and descriptive writing will not come without many attempts. Revision of what you have written will take more of your time and need polishing, and that is hard work. Do not despair. It is a chore that is common to writers – whether amateur or professional, full-time or part-time.

The many small amendments and insertions that you make to your script should sharpen your style and give that polished effect. 'Trivialities make perfection,' somebody once suggested, before concluding that, 'perfection is no triviality'.

Activity 17.1

It helps to study a fine example of story-telling in order to see just how much can be conveyed about people, places, things and changes.

This short story by the French writer, Alphonse Daudet, has been translated by Professor J. C. Reid. It is set in a small French town within a rural environment. The military presence nearby means that the German authorities will continue to impose changes on the town in general and on the school in particular. The news of these changes, which have been occurring for about two years, is conveyed to people either indirectly through the notice boards outside the Town Hall or directly by sudden changes to long-established routines.

In this town people had respect for their school and schoolmaster, although children were often kept away from lessons in order to earn money by working. The last lesson of the French-speaking school-master is witnessed by Franz, to whom it is an unexpected change. Within the space of a few minutes he becomes aware of Monsieur Hamel's lifetime of service to a school that he loved, in which he lived and through which he had hoped to influence often reluctant pupils and their parents. His departure will be 'for ever'.

This is a story about a boy who becomes aware of life around him and feelings within him. As Franz, an expressive name in this story, appeals towards the end of his observations, 'Imagine it!'

The Last Lesson

ALPHONSE DAUDET

I was very late starting for school that morning and was afraid of being scolded, especially as M. Hamel had said that he would question us on participles, and I didn't know the first thing about them. For a moment, I thought of staying away and spending the day in the open. The weather was so warm, so bright! You could hear the blackbirds chirping away at the edge of the woods, and in Rippert's meadow, behind the sawmill, the Prussian soldiers were drilling. It was all much more enticing than the rule for participles, but I had the strength to resist and hurried along to school.

As I passed the Town Hall, I saw a crowd in front of the little notice-board. For the past two years, all our bad news had come from there – the lost battles, the requisitions, the orders of the commanding officer – and, without stopping to look, I thought to myself, 'What's the matter now?'

Then, as I raced across the square, the blacksmith, Wachter, who was there, with his apprentice, reading the bulletin, called after me, 'Don't go so fast, son; you'll get to school in plenty of time.'

I thought he was making fun of me, and I reached M. Hamel's little courtyard quite out of breath.

Usually, when school began, there was a tremendous commotion, which could be heard out in the street, the opening and closing of desks, lessons chanted in unison, very loud, with our hands over our ears to understand better, and the teacher's great ruler rapping on the table as he shouted, 'A little silence!' I had counted on the racket to get to my desk without being seen; but, of course, on that day everything had to be as quiet as on a Sunday morning. Through the open window, I could see my schoolmates, already in their places, and M. Hamel walking up and down with his terrible iron ruler under his arm. I had to open the door and enter in the middle of this vast silence. You can imagine how I blushed and how frightened I was.

But nothing happened. M. Hamel looked at me without anger, and said very gently:

'Go to your place quickly, Franz my boy. We were beginning without you.'

I jumped over the bench and quickly sat at my desk. Not until then, when I was beginning to get over my fright, did I notice that our teacher was wearing his fine green coat, his frilled shirt and the little black cap, all embroidered, that he put on only on inspection and prize days. Besides, all the class seemed so strange and solemn. But what surprised me most was to see, at the back of the room, on the benches that were always empty, the village people sitting silently like ourselves; old Hauser, with his three-cornered hat, the former mayor, the former postmaster, and several others as well. Everyone looked sad; and Hauser had brought an old primer, tattered at the edges, which he held on his knees with his large spectacles lying across the pages.

While I was wondering what all this meant, M. Hamel took his place in his chair, and in the same serious and gentle tone he had used to me, he said:

'My children, this is the last lesson I shall give you. The order has come from Berlin that only German shall be taught in the schools of Alsace and Lorraine. The new master arrives tomorrow. This is your last French lesson. I want you to pay close attention.'

His words were like a thunderclap. The wretches! *that* was what they had posted up at the Town Hall.

My last French lesson! And I hardly knew how to write. I would never learn now! How bitterly I regretted all the lost time, all the lessons missed to rob nests and go sliding on the Saar. My books that a while ago I had found such a bother, so heavy to carry, my grammar and my history of the saints, seemed now to me old friends that I couldn't bear to give up. And M. Hamel, too. The thought that he was going away, that I would never see him again, made me forget all the blows from his ruler and other punishments.

Poor man! It was in honour of this last lesson that he had put on his fine Sunday clothes, and now I understood why the old men from the village were sitting there at the back of the room. It meant that they were sorry, too, that they had not come more often to school. It was also a way of thanking our master for his forty years of faithful service, and of showing their respect for the country that was no longer theirs.

Suddenly, in the middle of my thoughts, I heard my name called. It was my turn to recite. What would I not have given to have been able to say that terrible rule for the participle right through, very loudly and clearly, and without a single mistake; but I became confused on the first words, and just stood there, holding on to the desk, my heart thumping, and not daring to raise my head. I heard M. Hamel say to me:

'I won't scold you, Franz my boy; you must feel bad enough. See how it is. Every day we have said to ourselves: "Bah! I've lots of time. I'll learn it tomorrow." And now you see what happens. Ah! that's the trouble with Alsace; she puts off learning till tomorrow. Now those fellows out there have the right to say to you: "What! you claim to be Frenchmen, and yet you can neither speak nor write your own language!" But you aren't the worst, my poor Franz. We've all a lot to reproach ourselves with.

'Your parents weren't anxious enough to have you learn. They preferred to send you to work in the fields or at the mills, so as to have a little more money. And aren't I also to blame? Haven't I often sent you to water my garden instead of learning your lessons? And when I wanted to go fishing, didn't I just give you all a holiday?'

Then, from one thing to another, M. Hamel went on to speak about the French language, saying that it was the most beautiful language in the world, the clearest, the most logical; that we must preserve it and never forget it, because, when a people became enslaved, so long as they held fast to their language, it was as if they held the key to their prison . . . Then he took up a grammar-book and read us our lesson. I was amazed to see how well I understood it. Everything he said seemed to be to be so very easy. I am sure, too, that I had never listened so carefully, and that he had never explained things with so much patience. It was as if the poor man wanted to give us all he knew before going away, and to force it into our heads at a single blow.

After the grammar, we went on to writing. That day, M. Hamel had made fresh copies for us, written in a beautiful round hand: *France*, *Alsace*, *France*, *Alsace*. They looked like little flags fluttering everywhere in the classroom, hung from the stand on our desks. You should have seen how everyone got down to work, and what silence there was! The only sound was the scratching of the pens on paper. Once some cockchafers flew in; but nobody took any notice of them, not even the smallest ones who went right on tracing their pot-hooks, as if that was French too. On the floor the pigeons cooed very softly, and I thought to myself: 'Will they make even the pigeons sing in German?'

Whenever I looked up from my writing, I saw M. Hamel motionless in his chair and gazing at the various things around him, as if he wished to fix in his mind forever the whole of his little schoolroom. Imagine it! For forty years he had been there in the same place, with his garden outside and his class in front of him. Only the benches and desks had been worn smooth by use; the walnut trees in the courtyard were taller, and the hop-vine he had planted himself now twined about the windows up to the roof. What a heartbreak it must have been for this poor man to leave all these things, and to hear his sister moving around in the room above, packing their trunks! For they had to leave the country for ever the next day.

All the same, he had the courage to hear every lesson to the very end. After the writing, we had a lesson in history, and then the tiny ones chanted their *ba, be, bi, bo, bu*. There at the back of the room, old Hauser put on his spectacles and holding his primer in both hands, spelled the letters with them. You could see that he was trying, too; his voice trembled with emotion; it was so funny to hear him that we wanted to laugh and cry at the same time. Ah, how well I remember it, that last lesson!

All at once, the church-clock struck twelve. Then the Angelus. At the same moment, the trumpets of the Prussians, returning from their drill, sounded under our windows. M. Hamel stood up, very pale, in his chair. Never had he seemed so tall to me.

'My friends,' he said, 'my friends, I – I – ' But something choked him. He could not go on.

Then he turned to the blackboard, took a piece of chalk, and, pressing on it with all his might, he wrote as large as he could:

Vive la France!

Then he stopped, leaned his head against the wall, and, without a word, made a gesture to us with his hand:

'School is over . . . you may go.'

[Translated by J. R. Reid]

The range of feelings experienced by Franz is the main feature of this story that shows how a boy becomes aware of adult issues – the hopes, dashed aspirations and traumas of change that affect a community which appears to have a quiet and orderly atmosphere.

It may be a useful exercise to trace the number of feelings and reactions indicated by the author. This shows how a story that does not appear to be intense in an exaggerated way can convey a great many emotional tones.

The feelings of Franz

1 Fear of being reprimanded for being late

2 Concern and worry about his ignorance of participles
3 Desire for escape to the outlying countryside
4 Resistance to this temptation
5 Awareness that he would be in trouble for being late
6 Consciousness of being ridiculed
7 Anticipation that everything would be normal
8 Embarrassment about being late
9 Surprise about the teacher's clothes and the villagers' presence
10 Wonder and mystery about the sadness
11 Shock about the announcement
12 Bitter regret about his past idleness and truancy
13 Sudden interest in lessons that had previously been repellent
14 Sorrow for the teacher
15 Forgetting of the bad times
16 Shared appreciation for the schoolmaster
17 Confusion and shame about not being able to answer
18 Response to the teacher's lyrical words
19 Amazement about his understanding when he concentrated
20 Appreciation of aspects of the French language
21 Impressed by the silence and commitment of the class
22 Realisation of what the edict meant to Monsieur Hamel
23 Understanding of the dramatic change confronting the teacher
24 Praise for this courage and tenacity over the years
25 Clarity of the memory
26 Mixed feelings of humour and sadness

Although this story focuses on Franz, many of his sensations are obviously shared by the adults who, as former pupils, have returned to their school to witness this last lesson. We, as readers, are party to the scene and are capable of the same experiences as the characters in the story.

18 Descriptive writing

18.1 The requirements

Joseph Conrad was a famous author in the English language. However, by the age of 15 – the age when many people nowadays are taking their first public examinations – he spoke Polish and French, but knew no English. He mastered this during his later teens and twenties to become, during his thirties, a serious writer who had achieved expertise and renown. It is heartening to realise that standards such as this can be attained by 'late starters'.

Once Conrad commented about writing in general, and descriptive writing in particular. He said that its only purpose was, 'to make you hear, to make you feel, and above all to make you see'. That is an observation that is worth learning by heart.

Hearing, feeling and seeing are part of the sensory range that we, as humans, are able to enjoy. Add to these the functions of taste and smell and the five senses are listed.

We have the ability to experience these sensations and to recall them. For most of us our strongest powers of recall involve sight and hearing because these are the areas on which we are most dependent.

So our memories are stocked full of images and sensations from the past. These can be brought out of our 'memory banks' by conscious decisions, spontaneous reactions and by fortunate as well as unfortunate circumstances. Powerful forces, both conscious and subconscious, exist within us. It is a requirement of descriptive writing that we harness them.

Words have powerful forces connected with them as well. Their meanings, when known by many fellow-users of a language, link people by referring specifically to matters of shared knowledge and experience. So the written word can, in a great number of ways, link and 'bond' people, enabling them to share ideas, views and sensations.

The writer can, therefore, transfer thoughts directly from his mind to the minds of his readers. Obviously this is done by all writers – from children learning in nursery schools to professional exponents of the art – and in all the range of writing styles. Yet it is particularly evident in descriptive writing where views and sensations have to be stimulated in readers' minds.

The function of description is either to act as a background for a piece of narrative – an account or story – or it can stand by itself and convey any of the five senses – sight, hearing, touch, smell and taste.

When houses are bought and sold, solicitors undertake what they call 'conveyancing' – they transfer the ownership of a property from one party to another. In much the same way writers have to transfer or convey ideas, views and sensations. Descriptive powers reveal this clearly.

18.2   An approach

Where does one start? There are so many things in life that can be described. Objects exist by the trillion; people by the billion; views are infinitely available. So the obvious place to begin is with ourselves. We have to make the choices, for it is, essentially, the conveyancing of our experiences that makes up descriptive composition. Of course we can describe things that we have never directly experienced (dragons, Outer Mongolia, hang-gliding, for example), but everything that we write about relates to aspects of life that we know something about.

There are three golden rules:

1 *Be selective*
2 *Be specific*
3 *Be symbolic*

1   When you are confronted by the infinite choice of subjects, objects and angles from which to view them, *be selective*. Do not try to include too many features, for the reader will become confused, overwhelmed or 'glassy-eyed'. It is a good idea while planning a piece of descriptive writing to use what could be called a 'window-frame' technique. Try to see, in your mind's eye, the variety of objects or the extent of the view on which you wish to focus as through you are looking through a frame. There is no need to refer to this in the actual piece of writing, but it will give you a definite grouping of the features that you have in mind and the technique can be 'constructively restrictive'.

2   Just remember that there are over half-a-million words in the English language and, although many of them are forgotten, it does mean that every object has a variety of names connected with it. Every person has a name and the Ordnance Survey large-scale maps reveal that even the smallest settlements and fields can be named precisely. Consequently there is every opportunity to *be specific* and to name names. Obviously there are many occasions when collective nouns and generic names avoid the use of excessive individual references, but being able to pinpoint effectively gives writing an authentic and detailed touch. It gives the impression that the writer is in command and that he is not being led by ideas and produced to a certain formula. The style immediately becomes more spontaneous and avoids the problems of stale or hackneyed material.

Look at the two passages given below.

It was hot again at last as I climbed away from the valley and its gentle sloping green and rosy squares and elmy hedges, up between high, loose banks, of elder and briar. High as it was, the large coppice on the left far up had a chiff-chaff singing in it, like a clock rapidly ticking. A parallel, deep-worn, green track mounted the hill, close on my right, and there was a small square ruin covered with ivy above it among the pine trees. It was not the last building. A hundred feet up, in a slight dip, I came to a farm-house, Tilbury Farm. Both sides of the road were lined by mossy banks and ash and beech trees, and deep below, southward on the right hand, I saw through the trees the grey mass of Cothelstone Manor House, beside its lake, and twelve miles off in the same direction the Wellington obelisk on the Black Down Hills.

It was a beautiful morning, and so I decided to go for a walk. The sun was shining brightly as I walked along the country lanes. The trees and hedgerows were beautifully green, and the air was pleasantly warm. Birds sang in the trees, and in the fields the cows looked happy and contented. Soon I saw a little brook sparkling in the bright sunsine. The scent of many flowers was wafted to me on a gentle breeze which had just sprung up. I noticed a small farm nestling in a hollow surrounded by green fields. Away in the distance lay lay the hills.

The first was written by Edward Thomas, a famous poet and writer of English prose who was killed during the First World War; the second by a child in school. They are both grammatically sound and deal with rural scenes. The difference is that the author of the first passage specifies exactly what he saw and heard, while the child writes according to a formula that applied to the juvenile treatment of 'walks in the countryside'.

3   One of the dangers of descriptive writing involves being excessive. This can be either in matters of intensity when, for example, feelings run too high and the so-called 'purple passage' of exaggerated, vibrant prose is used. Or it can be in matters relating to extensiveness when the 'picture-frame' contains too many features. A way of avoiding this is to *be symbolic*. This involves thinking of an image which will act as symbol that can be associated with the ideas to be conveyed, without having to explain or depict with too many words.

Imagine that you are describing a scene on the coast and that you want to suggest that the sea is powerful, has been destructive, but that it provides pleasure and livelihood. Linked to these sea-ward forces you wish to indicate that there are strong movements from the land-ward side that are man-made and not natural. A series of symbolic images could be built into your composition. These need not be explained, but would suggest exactly what you mean to the discriminating reader.

Image: a church on the cliff-top, with part of the church-yard eroded
Suggestion: the dangers that have threatened and occurred over centuries

Image: children playing on the beach
Suggestion: innocence and lack of awareness

Image: derelict fisherman's cottage
Suggestion: a way of life that has passed

Image: the gates of an industrial port and a container-lorry
Suggestion: the resourcefulness of companies needing to do business

Image: numerous holiday-chalets on a hillside close to the bay
Suggestion: the imposition of a different type of holiday 'culture'

Your description will deal essentially with the outward and visible signs of the place and yet it will, by implication, be concerned with inward and invisible conditions.

There are four other aspects of this suggested approach that could be considered: points of interest; time and space; sensory appeal; mood and atmosphere.

1 Always establish a point of interest in your composition, keep it in mind, and, when appropriate, make a reference to it. This will remind your reader of your topic and give a sense of unity.
2 Ensure that you refer, perhaps only in passing, to the time of day, season of the year and to the historical dimension. It is as well in any descriptive piece of writing to give, again perhaps only in the briefest form, something of the geographical context – the country, county, terrain or landscape.
3 Sensory appeals give a sense of liveliness. Visual images include features of colour, shape, size and distance. Sounds proliferate in the quietest of scenes, if only we can listen effectively. Sensations of touch (or movement), smell and taste are constantly experienced and 'banked' within our memories. All of them are materials for the writer to rely upon in order to convey a fuller impression on the subject.
4 Moods are felt by people; atmosphere is evident in places. The way in which we look at a scene is partly determined by how we are feeling and influenced by the place. It is in order to introduce tones of happiness, depression, awe, indifference or fear, etc., if the subject merits insight into the author's mood as well as observations on the place itself. It can be more effective for the author to be a neutral and detached observer who is aware of the atmosphere of a setting, house, factory, town or city, for example. Then he can suggest the impressions of delight, dereliction, squalor, endeavour, ghostliness, buoyancy, isolation or distinctiveness, etc., connected directly with the place rather than with his own condition. This balance between the personal mood and the atmosphere of place, of course, depends upon context, required effect and intention of the author.

The summary of this particular section is a matter of repetition. Just bear in mind the words of Joseph Conrad:

'to make you hear, to make you feel, above all, to make you see.'

— **Activity 18.1** —

Read the following passage. It is the opening of the second chapter of
F. Scott Fitzgerald's *The Great Gatsby*.

About half-way between West Egg and New York the
motor road hastily joins the railroad and runs beside it
for a quarter of a mile, so as to shrink away from a certain
desolate area of land. This is a valley of ashes – a fantastic
farm where ashes grow like wheat into ridges and hills and
grotesque gardens; where ashes take the forms of houses
and chimneys and rising smoke and, finally, with a transcen-
dent effort, of ash-grey men, who move dimly and already
crumbling through the powdery air. Occasionally a line of
grey cars crawls along an invisible track, gives out a ghastly
creak, and comes to rest, and immediately the ash-grey men
swarm up with leaden spades and stir up an impenetrable
cloud, which screens their obscure operations from your
sight.

But above the grey land and the spasms of bleak dust
which drift endlessly over it, you perceive, after a moment,
the eyes of Doctor T. J. Eckleburg. The eyes of Doctor T. J.
Eckleburg are blue and gigantic – their retinas are one yard
high. They look out of no face, but, instead, from a pair of
enormous yellow spectacles which pass over a non-existent
nose. Evidently some wild wag of an oculist set them there
to fatten his practice in the borough of Queens, and then
sank down himself into eternal blindness, or forget them and
moved away. But his eyes, dimmed a little by many paintless
days, under sun and rain, brood on over the solemn dump-
ing ground.

The valley of ashes is bounded on one side by a small foul
river, and, when the drawbridge is up to let barges through,
the passengers on waiting trains can stare at the dismal scene
for as long as half an hour. There is always a halt there of at
least a minute, and it was because of this that I first met Tom
Buchanan's mistress.

Now re-read the recommendations in the earlier part of this section
and see how they apply to the way in which this part of *The Great
Gatsby* is constructed.

'Be selective'   The 'window-frame technique' is particularly applicable here because the view is depicted from inside a passenger train

that stops by this gigantic rubbish-tip just outside New York City.

'Be specific' the disposal-tip, landfill site, call it what you will, contains much material and the activities of the workers and their mechanical devices. However, the author chooses to focus on the brooding presence of a vast pair of glasses and eyes that are shown on a faded and forgotten advertising hoarding or billboard for an optician in a nearby suburb. They, perhaps, specify the need to be ever-observant or remind us of the novelist's all-seeing eye.

'Be symbolic' The scene is meant to be vivid. It suggests other associations that are somewhat sinister. There is a strong element of the 'fantastic' or imaginary; a sense of the 'grotesque'; a macabre touch of death with 'the valley of ashes'. The dismal situation is compelling – partly because of the large dimensions and bleached colours and partly because the railway signalling system compels all trains to stop by the drawbridge for at least a minute.

Check the features – time, space, senses, colours, mood, atmosphere – in order to see how this passage has not occurred by chance, but by the application of certain key descriptive elements.

19 Impressionistic writing

19.1 The requirements

Experiences and pressures upon us produce impressions within. Most of these are sensations that produce either mild pleasure or certain irritations, but there are occasions when we are deeply affected, moved, changed, paralysed or suffer traumatically. Luckily most experiences do not do permanent damage to us. Yet our minds are influenced by everything that occurs to us for our mental powers are having to deal continuously with the 'day-to-day' and 'all-through-the-night' actions around us.

So much of what we experience comes from our being in a passive role. We are observers, standing on the fringes of life, watching either directly from a distance or indirectly through a television. Yet when we are called upon to write about the impressions that we have received from a particular stimulus we are being requested to do something active.

The act of writing is a means of communication in which we are trying to impress someone. 'Impress' may be meant in the sense of creating a favourable reaction (e.g. a letter of application), but it is more likely to involve gaining the attention of another person (a friend) or a group of people (readers of a newsletter, article or book). The point is that we convert ideas that have occurred to us into words of explanation that will, perhaps, have a similar effect upon others. Through writing we are expected to convert the passive into the active.

The requirement of 'impressionistic writing' is to be able to deal successfully, using the medium of words, with the basic human feelings that involve (a) perception (the way in which we as individuals sense things in general and see things in particular), and (b) response (how our emotions cope with these experiences).

There are broadly two ways in which you can become involved with this kind of writing. One is when the examiners or coursework moderators require you to write *in general* about your experiences connected with, say, travel, holidaying, family, friends, influences, unusual circumstances, etc. It will be obvious from the way in which the question is phrased that your treatment of the subject is not to be primarily descriptive, narrative or argumentative. They want to know how you perceive and respond to the subject that has been set, but only if it is applicable to something that you have experienced. That is why choices are given in lists of compositions. You cannot write effectively about a subject that you have not been aware of, enjoyed or suffered from in the past.

The other type of examination question is of a much more *specific* nature. You will be required to perceive and respond to a photograph, line-drawing or extract from a poem. The actual instructions may be quite vague – 'What are your thoughts and feelings on this topic?' or they may be fairly tight in their demands – 'Devise a story based upon this photograph' or 'Describe the impact being made on the people featured in this cartoon.' In all these instances there is no 'right' or 'wrong' answer, but your judgement and skill will be noted in being able to respond in an imaginative and sympathetic way.

(a) General

The requirements that are involved with the general demands concern your thoughts and feelings, with the ways in which your mind works. The term 'stream of consciousness' was applied to the ways in which some writers attempted to convey the flow of impressions by a series of expressions. Sometimes this was meaningful to readers; sometimes mysterious. The fact is that our brains work in such a variety of ways that it is difficult to capture precisely the powerful, fast and inexplicable patterns of thought that 'come to mind'.

Just think for a moment – and that, after all, is a demand with a fair number of implications and complications – of the ways in which your mind works. Consider the feelings that often affect you – the emotions that can be triggered most easily; the thought-patterns that keep returning; the words that arouse you; the well-known routes that your memories take; the verbal short-cuts that you use; people, places and things that have influenced you; fantasies about the future; regrets of the past; fears; sensations involved in just being where you are at the present moment; the quality of the life that you are living. Some of these things do not bear thinking about; others present fine opportunities for day-dreaming.

The point is that we are capable of thinking and also capable of thinking about our own thoughts. This is where impressionistic writing has its sources.

(b) Specific

The requirements of the questions that involve you in story-making or descriptive writing when confronted by a picture or drawing and the demands imposed by an extract from a poem also need special handling. In these cases you have to focus upon a series of disciplines that involve narrative skill, visual and imaginative abilities, and spontaneous response to literary stimulation.

Two attributes in particular are needed: inventiveness, in that you can see the potential for a response that will be appreciated, and a well-stocked mind that is not short of material to use.

Remember that you can be your own best examiner in this matter by realising that, as far as this type of exercise is concerned, dullness disqualifies. If you are one of those individuals who does not enjoy playing with ideas and letting them drift around in your mind, then impressionistic writing is not for you. There are many people who feel much more comfortable with known, tested and basically factual information that does not involve much emotional awareness. The aspects of writing that appeal to them will be more in the categories of the directed, discursive, narrative and descriptive. So know yourself!

19.2   An approach

Although grammatical structure and spelling – the formalities of language – have to be observed, the style of your approach in impressionistic writing depends upon individuality. If you can produce the ideas, then many features of the writing will look after themselves.

However, do remember how the paragraph structure in general and the topic in particular (see Chapter 4) can give your ideas an impact. So it is as well to plan the composition and to let your mind do the wandering and focusing in the initial stages of the exercise.

The best way here is probably to return to Chapter 3 and to consider the ways and means of 'brainstorming'. It is so important to give your mind plenty of scope to absorb, play with, turn over and re-connect the various parts of the stimulus that it has been given. There have to be both destructive and comic tendencies as well as constructive and serious moves in this business. Bringing to the surface the variety of impressions that exist within the subconsious takes time, practice and a certain condition of mind. Recall the advice – dullness disqualifies. Do not waste your time if you find the task beyond you.

19.3   Illustrated material – photographs, drawings, cartoons

Take the stimulus material that you have been given and put it in front of you. Take a clean sheet of paper and place it alongside. In the middle of the top of the new sheet write down the title of the assignment that you have been given. Note carefully what it requires and box it within a series of lines so that it will be highlighted.

In the centre of the sheet, made to be displayed within a triangle (see Figure 19.1) list the words that are to act as 'trigger' devices. The purpose of these words is to enable you to create a frame of ideas (as in Figure 19.2) that will give you a variety of interesting 'angles'.

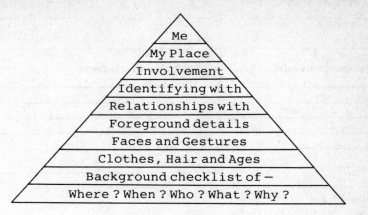

Figure 19.1

Please note the following:

'Me, My place, Involvement, Identifying with, Relationships with' are ways of trying to get you into the picture fairly quickly. Even if the requirement is for you to be fairly objective, try in your mind's eye to be there yourself.

'Foreground details' are to make you look closely at certain features, especially at the 'Faces and gestures', where expressions convey a great deal.

'Clothes and hair' are the two main outward and visible signs of differences between people of different 'Ages'.

'The Five *W*s' act as a checklist to ensure that you note aspects of place, time, people, possible happenings and probable reasons.

19.4   Poetry as stimulus material

Take a clean sheet of paper and transfer to the top of it the complete poetic extract that you have been given. The short time spent on copying will be well-rewarded for you will be absorbing the material as you write. It will also mean that everything – the poetry and your reactions will be noted on the single sheet of paper.

Bear in mind that you are not being asked to analyse the poetry, give meanings to it, engage in logical deduction or accurate assessments. You are being asked to respond to the powers of suggestion by referring to your thoughts and feelings. 'Right' and 'wrong' answers are irrelevant; interesting 'angles' and an engaging reaction are required.

Draw a diagram beneath your copy of the poems that looks something like Figure 19.2.

Read   It is vitally important to study the words of the extract in a variety of ways. After you have read to understand what is there, try to see and

	Read
Evocative words	*Thoughts and patterns*
Insight	

Figure 19.2

hear the words in, perhaps, unconventional ways. Re-read it at different speeds. Imagine that you are a child at school reading it ponderously and then as an actor on a radio programme. Make believe that you have constructed the complete poetic extract not in handwriting, but in neon tubing, with letters six feet in height, as used in display advertising. Which words or phrases would you like to have flashing on and off to attract attention?

Evocative words   Note in the narrower column the words to which you feel attracted because they remind you of something or evoke within you sensations that are worth recording.

Thoughts and patterns   Write down in the wider column the thoughts that are 'triggered' by the evocative words and search for a pattern that may provide you with a definite 'insight'. This then is your main response and will certainly appear in your conclusion.

If you are asked to provide a story or description based upon the poetry, undertake this approach noted immediately above. Then take the material that you have 'sifted' into the Insight section and place it in the centre of another sheet of paper. Using the 'brain-storming' techniques, work out a frame of ideas that reflects the need of description or story-telling.

The balance between being spontaneous and systematic is an important one. There has to be a spring of ideas, several streams of thoughts and a carefully constructed series of channels so that effective communication can take place.

___ **Activities 19.1** ___

The photographs in Figures 19.3, 19.4, 19.5 and 19.6 depict people working and playing. Danger, strenuous efforts, intense concentration and relaxation are featured – and are not necessarily related to the expected activity. In one case, work seems decidedly more leisurely than play.

Figure 19.3

Figure 19.4

Figure 19.5

Figure 19.6

Here is some stimulus material related to the different photo-graphs:

Figure 19.3   'That Steeple . . . and My Sensations'

Figure 19.4   'The Loneliness of the Long Distance Runner'

Figure 19.5   'Practice Makes Perfect'

Figure 19.6   'Retirement Day – after 40 years in the Brewery'

You can approach these activities with either yourself as the subject or with the person in the picture as the narrator. There are few rules, but try to devise a full range of ideas and a plan by re-reading section 19.3 'Illustrated material' before you start writing.

Activities 19.2

Try this exercise involving poetry as the stimulus material. An extract from Raymond Souster's *Flight of the Roller-coaster* should provide enough to 'kick-start' your imagination.

First copy the passage as it appears and concentrate, as you are reproducing the words, on the sensations, memories, mental pictures and dream-like qualities of fantasy that are woven into these lines.

Underneath your copy draw the diagram found in section 19.4 'Poetry as stimulus material'. Then note the words that you find to be particularly evocative. In the wider column put down your thoughts and any patterns that are aroused by these words that you have chosen. Finally, in this note-making session, try to produce one or two ideas that suggest an 'insight' that the poet wishes to arouse within you.

Flight of the Roller-coaster

Once more around should do it, the man confided . . .

And sure enough, when the roller-coaster reached the peak
Of the giant curve above me, screech of its wheels
Almost drowned by the shriller cries of the riders –

Instead of the dip and plunge with its landslide of screams
It rose in the air like a movieland magic carpet, some
                                           wonderful bird.

Activities 19.3

Study this well-known opening chapter. It was written by H. G. Wells in 1910 as the start of his humorous novel, *The History of Mr Polly*. It is not meant to be taken seriously, but it is about a serious subject – our inability, on occasions, to see the causes of our sufferings. Mr Polly 'lacked introspection' and blamed everything upon people, places and things around him.

This is a piece of impressionistic writing for it tries to relate the sensations, problems and mysteries of life without being too precise about their causes and implications. Mr Polly is depicted as being a small world (a microcosm) in himself where there are struggles, conflicts and wars. Everything to him is out of proportion. He knows how he feels, but he understands little.

Read the passage and then note how there are two impressions running side by side – the effects of discomfort and the causes of them. Here is a man irritated by things going wrong, annoyed by his wife, work and situation in life, and perplexed that he re-discovered that very afternoon that life was 'beastly'. The reason for this is that indigestion was caused by a large hastily eaten and somewhat heavy lunch. The demands of appetite can baffle the intellect.

'Hole!' said Mr Polly, and then for a change, and with greatly increased emphasis: '*Ole!*' He paused, and then broke out with one of his private and peculiar idioms. 'Oh! *Beastly* Silly Wheeze of a hole!'

He was sitting on a stile between two threadbare-looking fields, and suffering acutely from indigestion.

He suffered from indigestion now nearly every afternoon in his life, but as he lacked introspection he projected the associated discomfort upon the world. Every afternoon he discovered afresh that life as a whole, and every aspect of life that presented itself, was 'beastly'. And this afternoon, lured by the delusive blueness of a sky that was blue because the March wind was in the east, he had come out in the hope of snatching something of the joyousness of spring. The mysterious alchemy of mind and body refused, however, to permit any joyousness in the spring.

He had had a little difficulty in finding his cap before he came out. He wanted his cap – the new golf cap – and Mrs Polly must needs fish out his old soft brown felt hat. ''Ere's your 'at,' she said, in a tone of insincere encouragement.

He had been routing among the piled newspapers under the kitchen dresser, and had turned quite hopefully and had taken the thing. He put it on. But it didn't feel right. Nothing felt right. He put a trembling hand upon the crown and pressed it on his head, and tried it askew to the right, and then askew to the left.

Then the full sense of the offered indignity came home to him. The hat masked the upper sinister quarter of his face, and he spoke with a wrathful eye regarding his wife from under the brim. In a voice thick with fury he said, 'I s'pose you'd like me to wear that silly Mud Pie for ever, eh? I tell you I won't. I'm sick of it. I'm pretty near sick of everything, comes to that . . . Hat!'

He clutched it with quivering fingers, 'Hat!' he repeated. Then he flung it to the ground, and kicked it with extraordinary fury across the kitchen. It flew up against the door and dropped to the ground with its ribbon band half off.

'Shan't go out!' he said, and sticking his hands into his

jacket pockets, discovered the missing cap in the right one.

There was nothing for it but to go straight upstairs without a word, and out, slamming the shop door hard.

'Beauty!' said Mrs Polly at last to a tremendous silence, picking up and dusting the rejected headdress, 'Tantrums,' she added. 'I 'aven't patience.' And moving with the slow reluctance of a deeply offended women, she began to pile together the simple apparatus of their recent meal, for transportation to the scullery sink.

The repast she had prepared for him did not seem to her to justify his ingratitude. There had been the cold pork from Sunday, and some nice cold potatoes, and Rashdall's Mixed Pickles, of which he was inordinately fond. He had eaten three gherkins, two onions, a small cauliflower head, and several capers with every appearance of appetite, and indeed with avidity; and then there had been cold suet pudding to follow, with treacle, and then a nice bit of cheese. It was the pale, hard sort of cheese he liked; red cheese he declared was indigestible. He had also had three big slices of greyish baker's bread, and had drunk the best part of a jugful of beer. ... But there seems to be no pleasing some people.

'Tantrums!' said Mrs Polly at the sink, struggling with the mustard on his plate, and expressing the only solution of the problem that occurred to her.

And Mr Polly sat on the stile and hated the whole scheme of life – which was at once excessive and inadequate of him. He hated Foxbourne, he hated Foxbourne High Street, he hated his shop and his wife and neighbours – every blessed neighbour – and with indescribable bitterness he hated himself.

'Why did I ever get in this silly Hole?' he said. 'Why did I ever?'

He sat on the stile and looked with eyes that seemed blurred with impalpable flaws at a world in which even the spring buds were wilted, the sunlight metallic, and the shadows mixed with blue-black ink.

To the moralist I know he might have served as a figure of sinful discontent, but that is because it is the habit of moralists to ignore material circumstances – if, indeed, one may speak of a recent meal as a circumstance – seeing that Mr Polly was circum. Drink, indeed, our teachers will criticize nowadays both as regards quantity and quality, but neither church not state nor school will raise a warning finger between a man and his hunger and his wife's catering. So on nearly every day in his life Mr Polly fell into a violent rage and hatred against the outer world in the afternoon, and never suspected that it was this inner world to which I am with such masterly delicacy alluding, that was thus reflecting its sinister disorder upon the things without. It is a pity that some human beings are not more transparent. If Mr Polly, for example, had been transparent, or even passably translucent, then perhaps he might have realized, from the Laocoon struggle he would have glimpsed, that indeed he was not so much a human being as a civil war.

Wonderful things must have been going on inside Mr Polly. Oh! wonderful things. It must have been like a badly managed industrial city during a period of depression; agitators, acts of violence, strikes, the forces of law and order doing their best, rushings to and fro, upheavals, the *Marseillaise*, tumbrils, the rumble and the thunder of the tumbrils . . .

I do not know why the east wind aggravates life to unhealthy people. It made Mr Polly's teeth seem loose in his head, and his skin feel like a misfit, and his hair a dry stringy exasperation. . . .

Why cannot doctors give us an antidote to the east wind?

'Never have the sense to get your hair cut till it's too long,' said Mr Polly, catching sight of his shadow, 'you blighted, desgenerated Paintbrush! Ugh!' and he flattened down the projecting tails with an urgent hand.

20 Dramatic writing

20.1   The requirements

In Chapter 18 emphasis was laid on the remarks made by Joseph Conrad about being able 'to make you feel . . . hear . . . and . . . above all, to make you see'. The intention was to draw your attention to the requirements for descriptive composition. When the need is for dramatic writing, then it may be best to change the word order so that the stress comes on 'above all, to make you hear'.

Although we go to the theatre to see plays and can regard drama as a spectacle, when it comes to writing for examination and course-work purposes it is best to think of the exercise as being primarily an aural experience. We have to convert what we hear – either in real-life conversations or in the imaginary ones that we can invent in our minds – into words that sound authentic.

So the task involves the astute awareness of how people speak to one another and the ability to capture their speech rhythms with the right combination of our own words. In short, it is not easy. With time, it can be perfected.

Professional dramatists have an intuitive skill that captures the essence of human verbal intercourse. However, it is not always straightforward to perceive this when reading their scripts. Their words may not come alive in our minds when we read or even study them. The test of their success may come when actors speak the lines and give the intended vocal emphasis or tone.

Consequently, there is a twofold challenge in this area. It requires special skills to be able to write and to be able to read the elements of drama. Be warned. Do not embark upon questions or projects involving dramatic writing without first testing your abilities.

20.2   An approach

Take a fourfold approach:

1 Mental preparation
2 Physical work
3 Checking
4 Testing

In order to undertake *mental preparation* make sure that you have the desire to succeed. Enthusiasm is vital. Then, all being well, use pen and paper, a small audio-recorder, and your own highly sophisticated 'listening-in' system, the ear! When you are in public places, shopping centres or on buses or trains, eavesdrop discreetly into conversations. Record them either physically on paper and tape or mentally by retaining as much as you can. The entire transcripts of conversations are, of course, not needed, but snippets, excerpts, phrases or conversational interjections can give you many ideas and much pleasure.

Physical work is necessary when you get home or are in the library. The former is much to be preferred as a 'workshop' for this activity because it is often necessary to re-enact the actual conversation, mannerisms and movements of the speakers in order to revive in your mind the record of the talk before it is 're-created' through the written word. You will have to become a temporary member of the acting profession in order to fulfil this part of the exercise and so physical work is needed. Hence the preference for privacy or, at least, the opportunity for being discreet. Then endeavour to act the part of the person whose words you are creating, in the case of fiction, or remembering, in the case of documentary. As you 'perform', write. As you re-enact, amend. Your writing will be 'in rough' and subject to many changes. Drafts need not be neat. Eventually the final draft will emerge and you are ready to check it, but do take a break first. It can be a sound idea to leave a day between the final draft and the checking, so that you transfer your personal role from that of the actor to producer.

The *checking* that is necessary can take a fairly specific and systematic approach. Write down the letters *D–R–A–M–A–T–I–C* on a separate sheet of paper. Then list the key words, bearing in kind the questions that should, to some extent or another, be answered by the quality of your script. These key words are:

Diction	How authentic-sounding are the speech rhythms?
Relationships	Do the characters respond to one another rather than give 'set-piece' speeches?
Audience	Would a group of listeners be able to appreciate the conversations that you have created?
Mood	Do your characters have their own personalities and feelings within the context of your text?
Action	Does anything happen, even if only in the cut and thrust of conversation?
Tension	Does the subject-matter suggest that it is worth arousing human emotions over these issues?
Irony	Are there any hidden meanings or conversational insights that suggest that one or more of the parties involved is/are aware that appearance and reality are not always the same?
Change	Are any of the conversations effective in changing the ways

in which the personalities involved sense the world around them or the feelings within them?

Finally comes the worst part, *testing*, when the words, ideas, speech constructions and reactions of your characters are investigated by others. This normally makes one feel very self-conscious. If you can bring yourself to allow others to read your script, either as part of a play-reading or a role-playing session, then you will have achieved much. If they enjoy it and your dramatic writing comes alive, you will have attained more than most people ever do.

The examiner or reader of your course-work will probably be impressed because, if you have overcome the problems of allowing your work to be tested by others, your future work will have that indefinable ring of confidence about it.

21 The art of reading

21.1 The state of the art

Many people read for pleasure. Surveys have shown that half the adult population of the United Kingdom is in the middle of reading a book. The 1990 book sales were valued at £2114 million and a record 63,980 titles were published. As a popular activity, however, reading has probably, and understandably, declined during the past fifty years. There is an irony in this decline for, as noted, more books are being published than ever before and more leisure-time is generally available. However, the main factors in this change involve the increasing claims on people's time by other visual stimuli – particularly television and videos on the one hand and direct observation promoted by more widespread travel on the other.

More people have to read more because of the demands of their work. It has been estimated that American executives have to spend between 25 and 75 per cent of their time just reading. This includes reading memos and reports, general and personal correspondence, business and trade publications, advertising and related materials. The employees in some companies are expected to have to spend up to two hours a day reading. This does not take into account those who wish to improve their career prospects by taking professional qualifications.

Yet there is a paradox. More money has been spent on education than ever before by governments and individuals. There would, however, appear to be less proficiency and lower standards of reading skills among those who are being taught. The fast-changing social patterns of the twentieth century have, of course, influenced this aspect of life.

The changes in the production methods of print, publications and books have been of enormous significance. It seems hard to believe that for the greater part of the past 2000 years handwriting was the only way in which to reproduce lettering on the page. The invention of the printing press was an astonishing revolution, but it was not until the introduction of the steam-powered printing press in the early nineteenth century that the costs of production became low enough to allow a mass market to develop.

The development of this large market for printed goods was stimulated further towards the end of the nineteenth century with the first of the national Education Acts. Production methods and the style of graphic display improved so much by the middle of the twentieth century that standard as well as specialist books became much more attractive and relatively cheap. Then came the revolutions in paperback production and now there are technical methods whereby machines can read and reproduce type-face with only the mimium of human assistance.

These changes mean that the supply and distribution of books and magazines will become increasingly sophisticated in that more minority tastes will be identified and satisfied. It will mean an increase in the sheer volume of material that is printed. The choices that will confront us in the twenty-first century will be astonishingly varied.

The two areas that should be relatively free of 'machine-interference', even in the years to come, involve choice and writing. The mechanical and technical advances have occurred in order to satisfy the demands of the 'reading market'. What happens in that market-place is determined by ordinary individuals such as ourselves. It is worth recalling that point about 'minority tastes' being satisfied and the responses that are possible to satisfy relatively small areas of demand. So in many ways 'choice' will be protected in the future.

Machines do not read for pleasure! They are a means to an end and the products that they are transferring, in increasingly sophisticated ways, are words. These patterns of words have to be created by human beings in order to inform and stimulate human audiences. That is their purpose. So despite the many changes that have occurred and those that are waiting to happen, writers choose, or are employed, to try to get in touch with readers. Generally speaking, the more readers that a writer can command the better. By the same token, the more material that a reader can successfully command the better.

21.2 The problems

There are, broadly speaking, three main problems confronting us. They all involve coping.

The first is to cope with the feelings of being overwhelmed by the demands on us to perform well in a society and in places of work that require us to use technical skills. The art of reading, with its advanced levels of awareness, begins with the basic techniques of being able to master the meanings of words with ever-increasing speed. There is much to do and it is inevitable that our feelings of confidence will be tested.

The second area of difficulty involves finding time and the opportunity to get things done. The pressures that are on people to become qualified, find work, travel to it, earn money, bring up families, shop, holiday . . . and watch television are considerable. How is it possible to use effectively the 15,000 days allotted to us during the average working-life?

The third problem concerns the speed with which we read. The average person manages 200–250 words per minute, although experts tell us that 700 words per minute is the rate to which most adults should aspire, for that is well within the normal potential of people.

21.3   The solutions

The answers to these problems are to be found by assessing three features of reading – *quality*, *quantity* and *scope*.

The standards which we set for ourselves, or which are imposed upon us, partly determine the levels of attainment which we achieve. In the case of reading standards these directly affect the *quality* of our lives. This is because the activity of purposeful reading can provide one or more of the following: knowledge; understanding; imaginative awareness; mental absorption; rapport; pleasure, and personal development. The acceptance of this vital contribution of the activity to our well-being is the first step towards self-improvement. If you want to do something, you usually find time to do it.

The complexities of organising time do require some carefully prepared solutions. Much advice is to be found in any bookshop on the shelves displaying the textbooks and manuals relating to business matters. *Getting Things Done – The ABC of Time Management* by Edwin C. Bliss (Future Publications) gives simple, straightforward and off-beat techniques of saving time and some suggestions about spending it successfully.

We are obviously advocating that time is well-spent on reading and that this activity comes into your personal category of 'prime time'. Once that element of PPT (personal prime time) is established in your regular daily routines, you will guard it against the intruding forces that wish to steal it from you.

The secrets are to have systematic devices to incorporate your cherished activities (the PPTs) into your life-style and to be aware of the notion of 'in-filling'. Although we may live fairly active lives, and sometimes feel that they are incredibly busy, with a little ingenuity you can work into the odd minutes the time and occasion to read.

The actual requirements for reading – the hand-held book, the book-mark and, perhaps, the reading-glasses in pocket or bag – are not too difficult to organise. It can be undertaken at a moment's notice. The gaps in our routines, the breaks between tasks, waiting and travelling time, the last moments of the day can be utilised and used for 'in-filling' with reading. Even if you find only 20 out of the 960 or so minutes available each day, then you have made a good start.

The American writer, Henry David Thoreau, in his book, *Walden*, suggested that the most important thing a person could do was to 'affect the quality of the day'. To be able to use our own influence to improve the world immediately around us, partly in order to create pleasures for ourselves, is an art to be cultivated. Effective reading will assist this process.

The *quantity* which we can absorb when reading depends upon our intentions as well as our abilities. There is reading material (such as catalogues) to be skimmed through; there is print (such as newspapers and magazines) to be dipped into; there are books (such as light novels, thrillers, romances) to be read quickly; there are textbooks (manuals, examination texts) to be studied, and there are literary masterpieces (classical novels, the standard works of great authors) to be contemplated slowly. The significance of the reading material before us and its relevance to our needs will be factors in determining how fast we read. This should be a matter of personal choice.

Alas, our abilities as readers can be hindered by stagnant skills. The difference between the high literacy rates achieved in Western Europe and North America and the relatively low standards of adult reading can be explained by the fact that quite a number of people do not continue to practise the skills learnt in school. Too many adults read like children.

Faster reading can help comprehension as the essential ideas and complete picture (the '*gestalt*' mentioned in Chapter 12) are more easily gained. Fewer eye movements (and a slow reader may take as many as twenty eye movements for each printed line) hinder progress when two or three movements across the page are enough to comprehend the information contained on the line.

There are basically five ways to encourage safe acceleration in the reading process:

1 *Preview your material*   Check the 'signposts' – the titles, subheadings, captions, topics mentioned in the first sentence of the paragraphs – in order to determine which reading speed is required.
2 *Avoid moving your lips*   Under no circumstances should you move your lips as you read to yourself. This encourages what is called 'subvocalisation' – listening to your own words within your mind. It retains childish tendencies and has an inhibiting effect on good speed.
3 *Do not look back*   'I've started, so I'll finish!' is the catchphrase of a general-knowledge quizmaster on television. His stated intention is applicable to speed-reading for it is best, once you have started, to keep moving on. It is tempting to look again at some of the ideas that you do not understand, but these can be re-viewed later.
4 *Pick out the main points*   Try to discover the one idea (the topic) that is important in each paragragph.
5 *Select and store*   As you are reading make a mental note of the facts or insights that appeal or are important to you and get into the habit of trying to store them in your memory ready for future use.

Books are available on this subject of effective reading in shops and libraries. Courses are offered through many colleges and companies. Take advantage of them if you feel that they will help.

Finally, the *scope* for reading material is vast. Every day billions of words are published and the technical expertise with which these are put together is remarkably advanced. We are confronted with a considerable choice and it is up to us to exercise this choice, bearing in mind that, in the long term, it is to our own advantage to read material that promotes the first three qualities listed above – knowledge, understanding and imaginative awareness.

Think of the following four sources for material that will be of benefit to you: newsagents; bookshops; libraries and work-places.

The so-called 'broadsheets' (*The Times*, *Daily Telegraph*, *The Guardian*, the *Independent* and *The Financial Times*) are among the finest newspapers published anywhere in the world and are available in newsagents throughout the United Kingdom and parts of Europe on every weekday of the year. *The Sunday Times*, *The Observer*, the *Sunday Telegraph* and the *Independent on Sunday* take their place on the newsagents' shelves on the appropriate day of the week. Incidentally, there is an even wider choice for readers in Scotland. In addition to the above 'English' newspapers are the quality daily journals that are produced in the capital, Edinburgh, and the largest city, Glasgow – *The Scotsman* and *The Herald*. The weekly, *Scotland on Sunday*, can be added to this impressive list. Here is quality journalism readily and inexpensively available.

Once a week a whole range of magazines appears in order to satisfy the needs and encourage the interests of all sorts and conditions of people. Enthusiasms, specialities, hobbies, leisure and sporting interests are catered for. Fine styles of English prose are to be enjoyed in the *Spectator* and *The Economist*. News of books and reading matter itself is to be found in *The Times Literary Supplement* and the *Literary Review*. The latter offers a mailing-service through a reputable bookseller. Once a month the shelves are restocked with yet another range of journals.

All large towns and most small ones have bookshops. Some are associated with national retailers like W. H. Smith; others, like Waterstones and Dillons, deal solely in books. Many books are sold through independent booksellers and these shops retain individual and much-admired features of the trade. Browsing is encouraged.

The network of public libraries throughout Britain has been established for many years and their stocks, many of which are out of sight in book-stacks, are huge. They encourage reading in many different ways – from delivery services in rural areas to arranging talks by well-known authors in the larger city libraries. Many a well-qualified person has started his or her quest for knowledge in these institutions that are as much a part of our heritage as the books they display and loan.

When specialist reading material is required, your school, college or workplace should be investigated. It is, after all, in the interests of management that the 'workforce' should be 'students' in one form or another. Effective study produces good results.

Never hesitate to improve your techniques of literacy, for a flourishing of the art of reading will be a by-product. It is easy to underestimate your abilities and to neglect the training that started in the early stages of schooling.

Recall the words of Edmund Burke, 'Nobody made a greater mistake than he who did nothing because he could only do a little.'

Think of the opportunities for personal growth that are suggested by Sir William Watson's words, inscribed above the State Library in Sacramento, the state capital of California. They come from his sonnet entitled, 'Shakespeare':

'Into the Highlands of the Mind Let Me Go.'

 **Answers**

Chapter 5

Test 5.1

Main	Subordinate (or dependent)
1 He was driving the car	that I nearly bought
2 This generator provides the electricity	that supplies the village
3 the train pulled away	just as I reached the station
4 the audience began to leave	before the film ended
5 The whistle blew	as he scored the winning goal
6 I hope	you understand main and subordinate clauses
7 What I said at the meeting	was reported in the papers next day
8 The answer to your question is	that the economy of the country needs more and more investment

Test 5.2

1 . . . people// . . . buy// . . . houses// . . . life.
2 . . . poll// . . . declared// . . . midnight.
3 . . . mistake// . . . returned// . . . them//. . . . airport.

Chapter 6

Test 6.1

	1	2
Noun	person / sentence / mind	man / sentence / behaviour
Pronoun	who	who / he
Adjective	A / a / strong	The / every / strange
Verb	analyses / has	analysed / read / showed
Adverb		

Preposition		
Conjuction		
Interjection		
Noun	3 newspapers / sentences / examples	4 words
Pronoun	that	you / you
Adjective	most / good	the
Verb	are / are	should / stop / look / listen
Adverb	there	occasionally
Preposition	In	to / around
Conjunction		and
Interjection		Oh!

Chapter 8

Test 8.1

largely is the first entry on page 639; *last* is the last entry on the same page.

Test 8.2

1 . . . I decided to take advantage of the opportunity
2 . . . Jones admitted defeat
3 . . . looking after his own advantage
4 . . . . evades responsibility by passing it to someone else
5 . . . persuaded them to take part in the scheme

Test 8.3

1 superficial;   2 complex;   3 flexible;   4 optional;   5 fakes.

Test 8.4

1 fatal;   2 honour;   3 prologue;   4 ameliorate;   5 forthwith.

Chapter 10

Test 10.1

1 *P*; 2 *I*; 3 *P*; 4 *I*; 5 *I*.

Test 10.2

1 Narrative; 2 Descriptive; 3 Descriptive, but could contain narrative and dramatic elements; 4 Discursive; 5 Discursive, but could contain descriptive with narrative and/or discursive elements; 6 Conversational; Impressionistic; 8 Impressionistic.

Chapter 11

Test 11.1

1 Comma omitted at end of salutation.
2 First line of letter in wrong place.
3 Comma omitted at end of salutation. First line of body of letter not indented.
4 *Dear* should begin with capital *D*. Comma omitted at end of salutation.

Test 11.2

1 Capital *S*.
2 Full stop after signature, Spelling mistake.
3 Comma omitted after *sincerely*.
4 Capital *F*. Full stop inserted after signature.
5 Comma omitted after *faithfully*.
6 Capital *E*. Comma omitted after *ever*.

Chapter 13

Test 13.1

Gist of passage: Not until slow-motion pictures were invented, late in the nineteenth century, could artists represent galloping horses realistically.
Main points.
1 Legs of galloping horse move too quickly for human eyesight to identify separate movements

2 Before invention of slow-motion films artists used one of two conventions:
   either (a) with front legs in air;
   or   with front legs stretched forwards and rear legs stretched backwards.
3 (a) Horses do stand on hind legs, but not when running;
   (b) Legs stretched looked speedy, but obviously untrue to nature.
4 Slow-motion films enabled artists to study horse's leg movements and to represent them accurately.
   Note. The original passage contains 220 words. The examiner's word limit for the summary will dictate how much of the detail in the plan you will use. A 50-word limit is likely. That would entail telescoping points 2 and 3 of the plan.

Test 13.2

The chief opposition spokesman for education said that he had listened to the minister's speech with care but that he had found nothing new or constructive in its proposals. Indeed, he regarded that speech as a flagrant betrayal of the election promises made by the minister's party. Far from spending more on education, the minister proposed to hold expenditure at the level of the current year. In a time of raising prices that was tantamount to reducing the money spent on education, and he accused the minister of weakening the service that it was his duty to strengthen.

HUGH BAIRD COLLEGE

LIBRARY